Testwise

Understanding Educational Assessment

Volume 1

Nora Vivian Odendahl

ROWMAN & LITTLEFIELD EDUCATION

A division of
ROWMAN & LITTLEFIELD PUBLISHERS, INC.
Lanham • New York • Toronto • Plymouth, UK

Published by Rowman & Littlefield Education
A division of Rowman & Littlefield Publishers, Inc.
A wholly owned subsidiary of The Rowman & Littlefield Publishing Group, Inc.
4501 Forbes Boulevard, Suite 200, Lanham, Maryland 20706
http://www.rowmaneducation.com

Estover Road, Plymouth PL6 7PY, United Kingdom

British Library Cataloguing in Publication Information Available

Library of Congress Cataloging-in-Publication Data

Odendahl, Nora Vivian.
  Testwise : understanding educational assessment, Volume 1 / Nora Vivian Odendahl.
      p. cm.
  Includes bibliographical references and index.
  ISBN 978-1-61048-011-6 (cloth : alk. paper) — ISBN 978-1-61048-012-3 (pbk. : alk.
paper) — ISBN 978-1-61048-013-0 (electronic)
  1. Educational tests and measurements. I. Title.
  LB3051.O34 2010
  371.26—dc22   2010041389

Printed in the United States of America

Contents

PRINCIPLES

Prologue

To understand the ways in which our nation assesses learning is to understand something about ourselves. Why?

Tests and other forms of *assessment* influence what we are taught and what we remember.* They can affect our patterns of behavior and our self-perceptions. They even play a role in shaping the social, political, and economic landscape that we inhabit. At the same time, they can exist only with public consent, however tacit.

Yet the mechanisms of this force in our lives often remain a mystery.

To begin with, what does assessment mean? An umbrella term, it includes but is not limited to the formal tests or quantitative measurement with which this book is primarily concerned. It is "any systematic method of obtaining information . . . used to draw inferences about characteristics of people, objects, or programs" (American Educational Research Association [AERA], American Psychological Association [APA], & National Council on Measurement in Education [NCME], 1999, p. 172). Thus, in education, assessment can span diverse procedures for eliciting evidence of students' skills and knowledge, from nationwide examinations to teachers' informal methods for finding out what their students have learned and are able to do.

The purposes of educational assessment may be to diagnose, classify, select, place, predict, monitor, or change. Assessment may focus on the achievement or instructional needs of individuals, or it may provide data about groups categorized by classroom, school, state, nation, gender, ethnicity, language, disability, family income level, and so on. In turn, decision

---

*See the Glossary for definitions of specialized terms. The first mention of each such term is in italics.

makers at different levels use this information for crafting policies and influencing individual destinies.

Being assessed is an everyday experience; anyone who has gone to school has taken countless quizzes, course exams, and *standardized tests* with *multiple-choice* and essay questions. Moreover, the news media regularly cover controversies about using test scores either to hold teachers and schools accountable or to make decisions about students' grade-to-grade promotion, high school diplomas, or college and graduate admissions.

Yet such everyday familiarity does not necessarily bring insight. Often the only question debated is whether there is "too much" testing in schools.

Perhaps the realm of testing seems too forbidding to enter—a maze of complexities, situated in a minefield of controversies. No wonder, because although testing is a routine of education, students and the public hear little about what it means and how it works. Even policy makers who make decisions about testing may perceive it as beyond their ken, an arcane discipline requiring a specialized language (Madaus, 1993). Members of the assessment profession themselves can have difficulty communicating across their silos of subspecialties.

Testwise: Understanding Educational Assessment is intended to help improve this situation by lifting the curtain to explain principles and practices, issues and challenges, and inevitable trade-offs. The literature on testing is rich but often abstruse, and I hope to make this wisdom more accessible. The goal is to help readers think, talk, and make decisions about assessment in educational settings.

One way to demystify testing might be to turn directly to its technical aspects and explain such terms as *validity* and *reliability*. But before taking that step, we can start by picking up a familiar toolset, the six questions that journalists ask. The table on page ix, "Asking Journalistic Questions About Educational Tests," outlines possible types of queries.

These questions are, in fact, ones that we will pursue in greater depth (and I will suggest further resources to be found in articles, books, and websites). As the list shows, understanding any given test involves many activities.

Volume 1 of *Testwise* is concerned with two fundamental areas:

—*Considering historical and social contexts.* Every test is a creature of its time and place. Tracing the evolution of educational testing reveals the different ways in which people have defined and tried to make "good" tests. Important issues recur and have no easy resolutions, but recognizing historical precedents and parallels to today's challenges may help in finding better answers.

Underlying this history are also deeper philosophical implications, which matter as much as the technical quality of testing. How a nation assesses learning both reflects and perpetuates certain cultural values. What do our tests teach students about such values as scientific inquiry and objectivity, or societal opportunity and justice?

Asking Journalistic Questions About Educational Tests

Who?

- Who created the test? Who chose the test? Who is giving the test? Who is scoring the test? Who is using the scores to make decisions?
- Who are the students taking the test, in terms of their backgrounds and characteristics? What does each student believe about his or her ability to succeed?

Where?

- Under what physical conditions is the test administered?
- In what kind of cultural and societal context does the testing take place?

When?

- At what point in the student's intellectual development does the testing occur? What opportunities has the student had to learn the tested material?
- On what date did the testing occur? What else was happening at that time?

What?

- What knowledge and skills is the test intended to measure? Are these the same ones that the test actually measures?
- What changes are made to accommodate students with special needs?
- What other efforts are made to treat all students fairly and equitably?
- What do the test scores really mean? What *don't* the scores tell us?
- What are both the intended effects and the actual consequences of the test?

Why?

- Why is the test being given? Why use a test rather than some other means?
- If scores are reported as numbers, why? If reported as performance categories, why? Why do individual students or certain groups of students perform in particular ways on the test? How does one investigate the different possible explanations?

How?

- How does the test measure knowledge and skills (e.g., using multiple-choice or open-ended questions)?
- How is the test scored—by a computer application or by a person? What rules are used for assigning scores?
- How consistent would a student's scores be if the student were to take a different version of the same test? If the student were to take the test on a different occasion?
- How will the scores be used in making educational decisions about students, curricula, schools, etc.? What other information should also be considered?
- How well do the testing procedures, and the ways in which scores are interpreted and used, meet professional standards?
- How much does the test cost in terms of time, money, and other resources? Do the benefits outweigh the costs?

—*Understanding assessment principles.* Although influenced by public opinion, educators' views, and governmental policies, educational testing has limited external regulation. It does, however, possess its own body of theory and guidelines.

The most important theoretical principle is validity, which includes but goes beyond matters of sound test construction. The *validation* process requires making a comprehensive, logical, and well-supported argument about how a particular test's scores should be understood and used. Validation includes scrutinizing the assessment procedures for relevance, accuracy, consistency, usefulness, accessibility, and *fairness.*

Nevertheless, even the highest-quality testing elicits only samples of student performance, not complete information—and test scores are only ways of interpreting these samples, not absolute truths.

Building on these and other concepts explored in the first volume, Volume 2 of *Testwise* takes a closer look at:

—*Applying principle to practice.* Abstract principles have to be translated into real tests for real students; test designers have to decide which skills and knowledge to assess and how to assess them. "How" decisions include question format: *selected-response* tasks, in which the student selects from among answers that are provided on the test; or *constructed-response* tasks, in which the student generates a product or performance. Each approach entails its own rules and conventions as well as its own advantages and disadvantages for particular purposes.

Classroom assessment is related to externally imposed testing but also has differences. Here, teachers' goals include adapting instruction appropriately and helping students develop the ability to evaluate their own learning processes and their own work products. Skills in self-monitoring are useful beyond school, and a society that understands basic principles of assessment—as a form of reasoning from evidence—may make better decisions about testing (and other matters).

—*Thinking about tomorrow.* While heeding the lessons of the past, our approaches to assessment of learning should also probe new ideas, experiment, innovate, anticipate the future, and look beyond the borders of our own country. As we go forward, new forms of technology and research findings in different disciplines will shape the investigation of skills, knowledge, and other attributes relevant to academic achievement.

The two volumes of *Testwise* are intended to make the reader just that, by offering a guide to critical thinking about educational assessment. I hope that this approach will be helpful to anyone concerned about the ways in which we define and demonstrate learning.

Chapter One

The Origins of Educational Measurement: A Quest to Quantify

Units in which to measure the changes wrought by education are essential to an adequate science of education.

—Edward L. Thorndike, 1910 (p. 8)

With the emergence of educational measurement as a discipline came daunting challenges, thorny issues, and heated debates, some of which were specific to their era but many of which still resonate today. Yet if there is one unifying theme for the founding of the field in the late nineteenth and early twentieth centuries, it is the attempt to use scientific methods to capture and quantify what seems ineffable: knowledge and intellectual skills.

Bringing the concept of scientific measurement into education and psychology was a paradigm shift from the centuries-long tradition of qualitative assessment. Different lines of inquiry led to this same turning point. One focused on uncovering what Edward L. Thorndike (1874–1949) called "the changes wrought by education"; the other on investigating mental capacities as biological phenomena. How these two approaches originally arose and eventually influenced each other is the subject of this chapter.

BEFORE 1900: QUALITATIVE ASSESSMENT IN EDUCATION; MEASUREMENT IN THE SCIENCES

The First Two Millennia of Evaluating Learning

Although the earliest known program for systematically assessing learning was actually an employment test, it foreshadowed many later developments in educational testing. In 210 B.C.E., under the Han dynasty, the Chinese government introduced competitive civil service examinations that assessed both scholarship and military skills. This program, which continued with many changes over time until 1905, is especially noteworthy for having pioneered the practice of using tests for sociopolitical goals. The tests helped broaden eligibility for government posts, limit the power of the hereditary aristocracy, and inculcate values that reinforced the existing political structures (Elman, 1991).

At the same time, the program illustrated many recurrent challenges in testing. For example, cheating and gaming the system were common and went beyond such obvious strategies as smuggling answers into the test administration or hiring substitutes to take the exam. By 681 C.E., it became clear that some examinees were using memorized essays. To elicit original responses displaying the examinees' actual knowledge of history and philosophy, the examiners added another section in which examinees had to compose poetry on these subjects, but again, some examinees adapted by relying on memorized poetic conventions (Suen & Yu, 2006).

Another perennial issue arose during the Sung Dynasty (960–1279), when examiners tried to assess more than simple recall of classic literary works. Instead, they asked examinees to demonstrate analytic skills by discussing particular issues in these texts. But examiners ultimately abandoned this experiment in measuring higher-order reasoning and thinking because government officials worried that the scoring of examinees' responses would be too subjective. Even today, similar concerns about subjectivity affect decisions about question formats and scoring procedures (Madaus & O'Dwyer, 1999).

In medieval Europe, where opportunities for education were scarce, systematic assessment procedures were also rare. However, theological examinations at the University of Paris and the University of Bologna began in the late twelfth century. They took the form of oral disputations conducted in Latin, often in front of an audience, and covering knowledge of specified texts. Even though written tests were introduced in the 1500s when paper became more widely available and Chinese influence reached westward, the oral *viva voce* ("by or with the living voice") expanded to encompass a larger range of disciplines and predominated in European universities until the Enlightenment (Madaus & Kellaghan, 1993).[1]

For centuries, an examinee's performance in the *viva voce* was described qualitatively or simply classified as pass versus fail. In the mid-1700s, the University of Cambridge broke with tradition, by instituting written sections for the "Mathematical Tripos" exam and ranking the examinees. Ranking was further facilitated in the 1790s when a mathematics professor, William Farish (1759–1837), began assigning numerical scores to students for their performance (Madaus & O'Dwyer, 1999).

Farish's innovation would have far-reaching implications for policy and society. Numerical scores could be accumulated, aggregated, and then "classified, averaged, and normed. They could be used to describe and compare groups or institutions, and to fix individuals, groups, and institutions in statistical distributions" (Madaus & Kellaghan, 1993, under "Brief History of Testing," ¶ 4).

In the Nineteenth Century, New Purposes for Assessing Learning

Until the 1840s, educational assessment in both Europe and the United States typically focused on individual achievement and was still conducted orally in elementary and secondary schools. American practices began to depart from European ones in 1845 when Horace Mann (1796–1859), a lawyer and advocate for universal public education, introduced changes in the format and purpose of school testing.

As secretary of the board of education for the state of Massachusetts, Mann criticized the Boston public schools' use of individual oral examinations and urged replacing them with written examinations that had prescribed timing for each question. He argued that written tests would allow teachers to pose more questions; give students a better opportunity to display their knowledge; be more impartial; and offer fairer comparisons of student achievement across classrooms and schools (although, in fact, teachers chose students to be tested) (Witte, Trachsel, & Walters, 1986).

To emphasize the modernity, convenience, and objectivity of the written exams, Mann compared them to another technology that had just emerged: photography. His tests captured "a sort of Daguerreotype likeness, as it were, of the state and condition of the pupils' minds" that could be "taken and carried away, for general inspection" (1845, p. 334, quoted in Witte et al., 1986, p. 19).

Mann's program also pioneered the use of tests for judging the performance of someone other than the actual examinee. Because government officials viewed the scores as measures of schools' effectiveness, the tests served to make teachers and principals accountable to these officials. Such *accountability testing* became common enough by the 1870s that the head of the National Education Association felt the need to warn against the practice (Resnick, 1982).

In the mid-1890s, a physician interested in children's development, Dr. Joseph Rice (1857–1934), helped introduce statistical methods into the scrutiny of curricula and teaching methods. Rice's best-known work involved giving a standardized spelling test to elementary school students and comparing the scores with the amount of classroom time that students spent on spelling.

The results were striking. After testing 30,000 students, Rice determined that those who spent about fifteen minutes per day on spelling performed as well as those who worked on spelling for an hour a day (Pulliam, 1991). These findings would subsequently influence how spelling was taught. Thus Rice set a precedent for using evidence gained from assessment to inform instruction.

As is now apparent, Mann's and Rice's innovations were in keeping with the spirit of their age. They reflected the trend of industrial capitalism toward achieving greater standardization, precision, and efficiency (Madaus & Kellaghan, 1993).

Measuring the Mind with Tools From the Natural Sciences

Despite differences in purpose and method, the historical examples mentioned so far were all concerned with investigating knowledge and academic skills that examinees could presumably acquire through study. However, during the nineteenth century some researchers sought to extend the natural and physical sciences by measuring intellectual attributes as biological phenomena—thereby equating the mind with the brain.

One seed of this approach was planted in the early 1800s, when Johann Friedrich Herbart (1776–1841) proposed that mathematics could be used in psychology. Comparing investigation of the mind to that of the physical universe, Herbart (n.d./1877) argued that because mental phenomena such as perception or emotion could exist in greater or lesser degrees, they could be observed and quantified just as physical phenomena could. In fact, such measurement might reveal the underlying principles of the mind. This perspective helped promote psychology's evolution from a philosophical and conceptual discipline to an experimental and quantitative one, with the first psychological laboratory established by Wilhelm Wundt (1832–1920) in 1879 (Hatfield, 2007).

Also emerging in the early-to-mid-nineteenth century was a biological-medical field called *craniometry* that focused on measurement of human skulls. Many craniometrists took the very literal view that the larger the skull, the keener the mind that had once occupied it.*

As Stephen Jay Gould (1941–2002) describes in *The Mismeasure of Man* (1981), these craniometrists included physicians Samuel Morton (1791–1851) and Pierre Paul Broca (1824–1880), who at times selectively chose and

---

*Today, neuroscientists do not use skull measurements to measure brains; they use magnetic resonance imaging (MRI) to obtain much more accurate information about the size and shape of brains in living humans, including specialized brain areas and structures associated with different aspects of cognitive functioning.

manipulated data of skull measurements in order to claim that white males were more intelligent than women and than men of other races. But even where their skull measurements were precise and accurate, the inferences the craniometrists drew were without warrant. Offering no evidence about their subjects' actual ability to perform intellectual tasks, and ignoring the fact that modern humans have smaller brains than those of whales, elephants, dolphins, or Neanderthals, the craniometrists nonetheless asserted a strict correspondence between intelligence and size of the physical brain.

In Gould's view, craniometry served as a precursor for much of early intelligence testing, relying on flawed assumptions about biological determinism and about intelligence as a single quantity.* In fact, the founder of modern intelligence testing, Alfred Binet (1857–1911), began his investigations in 1898 by trying to continue Broca's work on correlating brain size and intellect. Unsuccessful, Binet would turn to a different method of mental measurement after 1900 (as discussed in the next section).

Yet the biological approach to measuring the mind yielded some concepts and methods still used today. The chief contributors were Francis Galton (1822–1911) and one of his students, Karl Pearson (1857–1936), both working in England. They shared an interest in using quantitative techniques to classify observations of traits and investigate human development systematically. For example, in depicting differences among children, they employed *distribution* curves showing the patterns of age, height, and (presumed) intelligence across a given group or population.

Such techniques revolutionized the natural and social sciences. A few decades later, describing the brand-new field of educational measurement, Ayres (1918) praised Galton for creating "the statistical methods necessary for the quantitative study of material which seemed at the outset entirely qualitative and not at all numerical in nature" (p. 11).[2]

However, Galton also introduced the term "eugenics" in 1883, while advocating that the human species be modified through selective breeding. Both he and Pearson promoted beliefs in hierarchical racial differences. Thus, some of the seminal contributions to quantitative measurement in the social sciences, such as the use of percentiles, the computation of *correlations*, and the concept of statistical significance, were originally associated with sociopolitical agendas that would later be discredited and repudiated (Resnick, 1982).

Elsewhere, in the United States, James Cattell (1860–1944), who had studied with Wundt in Germany and briefly worked with Galton in England,

---

*Gould (1981) defines biological determinism as the view that "shared behavioral norms, and the social and economic differences between human groups—primarily races, classes, and sexes—arise from inherited, inborn distinctions and that society, in this sense, is an accurate reflection of biology" (p. 20).

decided to focus on measuring individual differences in psychological and physical attributes within an educational setting. Cattell (1890) explained his larger purpose:

> Psychology cannot attain the certainty and exactness of the physical sciences, unless it rests on a foundation of experiment and measurement. A step in this direction could be made by applying a series of mental tests and measurements to a large number of individuals. (p. 373)

Accordingly, Cattell tried to apply Galton's theory that intelligence was a matter of "neurological efficiency" by using "psychophysical" tests of reaction times, sensory perceptions, and memory to predict future performance of incoming students at Columbia University. But one of Cattell's own graduate students, Clark Wissler (1870–1947), found that individuals' scores across tests did not show a consistent pattern, nor did they appear to be predictive of a student's subsequent course grades (Plucker, 2003).

Even though these particular attempts were not successful, Cattell's and Wissler's methods for designing mental tests and analyzing test results laid the foundations for the field of *psychometrics* (quantitative measurement of psychological attributes). Moreover, in 1892 Cattell helped establish the American Psychological Association, the same professional organization that sets today's standards for psychological testing.

INTELLIGENCE TESTING IN
THE EARLY TWENTIETH CENTURY

Intelligence Testing in Schools Prior to World War I

Moving away from the venerable tradition of evaluating what students had learned, many psychologists and educators in the United States began to focus on measuring general intellectual capabilities. Two events of 1904 contributed to this trend, even though they both occurred on the other side of the Atlantic Ocean.

First, French educational officials asked Binet, a lawyer turned psychologist, to find a way to identify students who were struggling and might need special attention. Using tasks intended to require the kinds of everyday knowledge and reasoning that he had observed in children over the years, Binet created an assessment to diagnose learning impairments.

Binet assigned age levels to the tasks—the more difficult the task, the higher the age level. He calculated a child's "mental age" by identifying the age level of the most difficult tasks that the child could perform correctly, then subtracting the child's actual age. The concept of an *intelligence quotient* or IQ arose later, when, in accordance with the recommendation of German psychologist Wilhelm Stern (1871–1938), the scoring method was adjusted to divide mental age by chronological age (Gould, 1981).

The second significant event in 1904 was when a British student of Wundt's, Charles Spearman (1863–1945), published an experimental study that used only 123 subjects but was grandly titled "'General Intelligence' Objectively Determined and Measured." Rejecting Binet's "practical" method of using problem-solving or reasoning tasks, Spearman followed Galton and Cattell's psychophysical approach by administering tests of sensory discrimination to some schoolchildren. He also gauged "school cleverness" and "common sense" via the students' grades and via interviews with teachers and the students themselves (Spearman, 1904, pp. 241–42, 250–51).[3]

To identify relationships among these sets of data or "factors," Spearman invented the mathematical technique of *factor analysis*. However, Spearman (or at least, his followers) then made the "invalid inference" that positive correlations in performance across tests and other types of measures had a single, unambiguous cause: a person's fixed amount of intelligence (Gould, 1981, pp. 250–57). Spearman's naming of this correlation as "the general factor" or "*g*," implying a "Universal Unity of the Intellective Function," furthered the idea of intelligence as a unitary entity (1904, p. 273).[4]

Although the distinctions have been blurred over time, Spearman's assumptions and conclusions differed fundamentally from those of Binet, who believed that intellectual development occurred at varying rates and could be influenced by environment. Binet did not view IQ as innate intelligence or as a means of ranking all students; instead, Binet viewed his mental-age *scale* as merely a means to identify children who needed more help. Not only did Binet worry that low scores would become self-fulfilling, but he also favored a personalized, individual approach over mass testing (Plucker, 2003; Gould, 1981; Brown, 1992).

Nevertheless, the idea of measuring students' intelligence was rapidly embraced in the United States. Not only were birthrates and immigration rates surging at the beginning of the twentieth century, but also many students were failing schools' existing tests. During the Progressive era of 1900–1917, reformers thought that the best way to improve schools' efficiency would be to separate students of apparently different levels of ability into different educational tracks (Resnick, 1982). However, even those schools that did try to track pupils had no systematic means of classifying them. And administrators did not trust teachers to improve the situation, because most teachers of this era had little formal training and were seldom valued as professionals (Brown, 1992).

Intelligence testing seemed to offer a solution. Influential followers of Galton in the United States argued that grouping students according to "scientifically" measured mental ability would help teachers conduct classes more effectively and be kinder to pupils who might be frustrated by overly challenging curricula (Bracey, 1995).

One such follower, psychologist Lewis Terman (1877–1956) of Stanford University, would become a key figure in intelligence testing. Having conducted experimental testing on California schoolchildren from 1911 to 1915, he published an English-language revision of Binet's test, the Stanford-Binet test, in 1916. He claimed that his examination—lasting less than an hour—could "contribute more to a real understanding of the case than anything else that could be done" to diagnose and classify students according to "native ability" (1916, ¶ 6).

Terman's revision used Stern's IQ-ratio calculation and provided standardized materials and administration procedures. It also included so-called "norms," statistical tables for comparing a student to the rest of the population. However, the norms supposed to represent typical performance had been obtained by testing only 1,000 students from nearby middle-class schools (Chapman, 1988).

At the time of the First World War, Terman and one of his graduate students, Virgil E. Dickson (1885–1963), were testing public school students in Oakland, California, as part of the effort to classify and track students. In addition to using the Stanford-Binet, Dickson was trying out measures that Terman was helping to develop for the U.S. Army.

The Army Mental Tests in World War I

The relatively late entry of the United States into the war meant that military forces had to be mobilized as quickly as possible, and placing the approximately 1.7 million men recruited by the Army in 1917–1918 into appropriate positions was a formidable challenge. Robert Yerkes (1876–1956), then president of the American Psychological Association, gathered a group of psychologists, including Terman, to develop a test for this purpose. Terman advocated using a paper-and-pencil version of the Stanford-Binet test, which Arthur Otis (1886–1954) had revised to permit group administration rather than the established practice of individual, personalized administration (Chapman, 1988).

From the two-week session devoted to adapting Otis's version emerged the "Alpha" and "Beta" tests. The text-based Alpha, which focused on comprehension, reasoning, and memory, was intended for recruits who could read and write English; the Beta, which relied on "concrete materials" such as pictures and diagrams, was intended for "foreigners and illiterates" (Terman, 1918, pp. 179–80). To guard against "coaching," the psychologists created several different test "'forms,' each differing entirely in substance from every other 'form,' yet all exactly equal in difficulty and alike psychologically" (pp. 178–79).

Scores for "intelligence" were reported as letter grades and also translated into mental ages based on the Stanford-Binet student norms. For comparison, the testing also included college students, prisoners, manual laborers, and even several hundred female prostitutes (Yoakum & Yerkes, 1920).

Yet looking at Alpha *test forms* reproduced in Yoakum and Yerkes's 1920 account (now available online), one finds many questions that seem irrelevant to any military duties and that, while purporting to measure intelligence, would instead measure cultural experience and knowledge of trivia. Such questions included: the products endorsed by certain celebrities, the locations of Ivy League schools and auto manufacturers, the names of card games and fabrics, and the total number of Henry VIII's wives.

As Gould (1981) describes, no less important to the outcome of the project was the effect of very nonstandardized, even chaotic testing conditions (despite Terman's admonition that "the greatest care must be taken to keep conditions uniform" in accordance with the "Examiner's Guide"). These problems included rooms so noisy that recruits—some of whom had never before taken a test—could not hear the instructions; drastically inadequate time limits; reassignment of men who could not read or speak English to the Alpha tests simply because the waiting lines for the Beta tests were too long; and many other serious violations of protocol.

Then, in interpreting the test results, Yerkes observed that low education levels and ill health were associated with poor performance on the tests—but he failed to consider that adverse environments, rather than hereditary intelligence, might have affected the scores. He also failed to draw the obvious inference from the fact that scores for soldiers who were immigrants rose with each year of residence in the United States (Gould, 1981). Instead, Yerkes concluded that the average mental age of adult recruits was as low as thirteen (although conscientious objectors did earn higher scores, as Yoakum and Yerkes grudgingly noted). One might wonder how these same Americans could ever have helped win the war.

Such a chain of dubious test construction, irregular testing conditions, and flawed score interpretation vividly illustrates the kinds of weak links that can undermine the intended meaning of test results—and shows why standardizing procedures is such a priority in large-scale testing. The fact that a score of zero was the score most frequently attained on six of the eight Alpha test forms speaks for itself (Gould, 1981, p. 214). Even so, the public perception that the Army Mental Tests had been successful in sorting recruits served to bolster the case for similar use of intelligence testing in schools.

Equally important, as it would turn out, was the tests' use of question formats that Frederick J. Kelly (1880–1959) had introduced in 1914 as a way to make reading tests easier to score, less time-consuming, and more precise (Kelly, 1916). These new *objective* formats included multiple-choice and short-answer *items* (test questions).

Adopting Kelly's approach, the Army Mental Tests featured items "ingeniously arranged so that practically all could be answered without writing, by merely drawing a line, crossing out or checking. By the use of scoring stencils the personal equation was entirely eliminated from the grading of papers" (Terman, 1918, p. 178). Using the new formats in a large-scale program showcased their potential for improving efficiency while reducing cost and subjectivity in scoring.

Intelligence Testing in Schools After World War I

As mentioned above, by time of World War I, many public schools in the United States already divided students into different educational and vocational tracks. The prewar movement toward using intelligence tests for this purpose gathered strength from 1919 to 1923. Introducing the "National Intelligence Tests" and "Terman Group Tests," Terman found a ready market in school districts that had just established new bureaus of research and measurement (Resnick, 1982). According to Brown (1992), "By 1925 the entire public educational system of the United States had been reorganized around the principles of mental measurement, and the psychological profession had produced more than seventy-five tests of general mental ability" (p. 4).

Terman maintained that sorting children into the appropriate tracks was actually a means of promoting equal opportunity. It was "as 'unjustifiable and dangerous for the educator to prescribe the same educational treatment for all as it would be for a physician to prescribe the same medical treatment for all'" (Terman, 1924, quoted in Giordano, 2005, p. 81).

Brown (1992) suggests that by using just such analogies and metaphorical language—borrowed from the respected disciplines of medicine and engineering—the early twentieth-century psychologists were able to introduce their methods and philosophy into educational systems. They cast themselves as physicians able to diagnose both mental deficiencies and unrecognized talent. This approach was all the more persuasive because it depicted intelligence testing as a continuation of the medical inspections and public health initiatives widely conducted in schools of the era. Thus, when critics such as journalist Walter Lippmann (1889–1974) began to question the fairness and efficacy of using intelligence tests for educational tracking, the psychologists as quasi-engineers and quasi-physicians already had the advantage.

These postwar intelligence tests were pivotal in the history of twentieth-century American education, as "the basis for new programs, curriculum changes, ability grouping, and a host of other educational alternatives" (Pulliam, 1991, pp. 140–41). The intertwining of psychology and pedagogy now encompassed many levels, from concepts to experiments. Measurement approaches used in psychological testing would significantly influence those used in education.

ACHIEVEMENT TESTING IN
THE EARLY TWENTIETH CENTURY

Achievement Testing in Schools

At the same time, educational achievement testing was also flourishing, as is evident in Monroe's 1918 catalog of over 100 standardized tests for subjects ranging from arithmetic to music to physics. A contemporary observer of schools remarked: "The air is filled with tests and talk of tests" (Bliss, 1922, quoted in Giordano, 2005, p. 92).

The new multiple-choice and short-answer formats, permitting the administration of greater numbers of questions in a given time period, hastened the spread of achievement testing as well as of intelligence testing. Objective-style tests were advocated as solutions to subjective grading, divergent curricula, a need for academic standards, and the hours teachers spent creating and scoring their own examinations (Giordano, 2005). By the early 1920s, among test publishers, "the boast was made that 'most of the tests [on] the market, unless measuring handwriting, do not call for written answers'" (Pressey & Pressey, 1922, p. 186, quoted in Clarke, Madaus, Horn, & Ramos, 2000, p. 162).

Yet those handwriting tests were quite important at the time. Before the rise of intelligence testing, handwriting tests were believed to reveal students' characteristics and considered the "closest to a general ability test likely to predict success in school and later life" (Resnick, 1982, p. 181). For example, Thompson's 1911 book on handwriting cites research supporting the idea that "for a large number of cases accuracy in handwriting tends to vary directly with school intelligence" (p. 115). At the same time, though, Thompson explains how handwriting skills can be taught and improved with practice.

From the perspective of measurement, even more significant was the approach to evaluating handwriting that was introduced by E. L. Thorndike, who had been a student of Cattell's and who was involved in both intelligence testing and achievement testing.

As Thompson (1911) recounted, in 1910 Thorndike convened a panel of "competent judges" to rank-order 1,000 samples of student handwriting. Based on the distinct levels of quality that the judges discerned, he developed a fourteen-point scale for scoring handwriting in terms of legibility, beauty, and general merit. The "Thorndike Scale" provided grade-appropriate exemplars corresponding to the values on the scale, so that a teacher could decide which exemplar his or her student's handwriting sample most closely resembled. While acknowledging that different teachers using this tool might not always agree on the score, Thompson considered Thorndike's approach useful for making uniform comparisons, tracing improvement, and setting standards in the classroom and in the hiring process.

Thorndike had an even more ambitious agenda. Like other psychologists of his day, Thorndike invoked biology and physics as models, and he believed that inherited capacities (multifaceted rather than unitary) played some role in achievement. However, much of his work focused on investigating the effects of "training"—in particular, measuring the effects of different instructional methods:

> At least three-fourths of the problems of educational practice are problems whose solution depends upon the *amount* of some change in boys and girls. Of two [instructional] methods, which gives the *greater* skill? . . . Units in which to measure the changes wrought by education are essential to an adequate science of education. (Thorndike, 1910, p. 8)

Echoing Herbart's ideas of a century earlier, Thorndike (1918) posited that the effects of instruction were real and could be quantified, because "Whatever exists at all exists in some amount." These effects were revealed in "educational products" (such as students' speech, writing, answers to math problems, etc.), which could be measured "with some precision" and the results "conveniently recorded and used" (p. 16).[5]

Hence the importance of measurement scales with equal units, analogous to rulers, thermometers, or weight scales. Ayres (1918) believed that the Thorndike Scale, "based on the equal difference theorem formulated by Cattell, marked the real beginning of the scientific measure of educational products" (p. 12). Although more cautious about using the term "scientific," Monroe, DeVoss, and Kelly (1924) praised handwriting scales for banishing "the old false standards represented by perfect specimens" and replacing them with attainable standards of achievement (p. 200). A plethora of scales for handwriting and other subjects emerged in the 1910s and 1920s, eventually setting the stage for prescribed achievement criteria in the form of *performance standards*.

Despite (or perhaps because of) the growth in achievement testing over the first three decades of the twentieth century, criticism was by no means uncommon. Opponents argued that selected-response and short-answer questions restricted assessment to factual information and thus led to curricular emphasis on superficial memorization. The new measurement bureaus for schools had to make the case that testing was worth the costs and the loss of time for instruction (Giordano, 2005). Still, the concept of standardized testing with uniform tasks, conditions, and scoring had taken root in an era excited about the possibilities of a new science of education.

Standardized Tests for College Admissions Purposes

Whereas schools turned to tests to help solve instructional needs, colleges turned to tests to help solve selection needs. Although only a small percentage of U.S. high school students went on to college in 1900, many colleges still had to screen applicants and held their own admissions exams for this purpose. To address the inefficiency, expense, and lack of uniformity in this process, in 1899 the East Coast Association of Colleges and Secondary Schools formed a "College Entrance Examination Board" to oversee common examinations for participating institutions.

From this beginning, as Valentine (1987) recounts, would evolve the admissions and placement tests offered by today's College Board. Not only did the original Board seek to improve coordination in the college-admissions process, but also the members wanted to raise the level of high school instruction so that students would be better prepared for college. In keeping with then-current approaches to achievement testing, the Board began by identifying nine academic subjects to be covered and then created *essay tests* that required the students to write responses to test questions. (This initial approach would later be called the "Old Plan.")

Essay testing meant that teachers from colleges and secondary schools had to gather together and develop protocols for evaluating the essays (see Elliot, 2005, for a history of the scoring up to World War II). Interactions among instructors at the scoring sessions, as well as the content of the exams, helped establish common standards for high school courses (Valentine, 1987).*

---

*In fact, McConn (1936) described the years 1890-1915 as "the Age of Standards," when the focus was on "prescribed subject matter" and "some more or less definitely envisaged degree of attainment" (p. 447). According to McConn, "To set Standards, and enforce Standards, and raise Standards, and raise them ever more, was nearly the whole duty of teachers and principals and presidents." (Sound familiar?)

However, with rapid growth and diversification of high schools after 1900, the centralized control of curriculum exerted by the Board's exams came under attack. Teachers who founded the National Council of Teachers of English in 1911 sought to reassert localized control (Lunsford, 1986). Critics charged that the tests "created a gate beyond which racial minorities, immigrants, and poor persons could not pass" because they required subjects not offered in all schools, such as classical languages (Giordano, 2005, p. 83).

Given the problems with using subject-specific entrance exams, by the 1920s many colleges were turning to the U.S. Army Alpha tests or other intelligence tests. Seeking an alternative that would measure general academic skills, the Board commissioned Princeton University professor Carl C. Brigham (1890–1943) to oversee the creation of a new "scholastic aptitude" test using selected-response and short-answer questions. This "New Plan" test was administered experimentally for the first time in 1926, and a separately developed test for admission to medical school followed shortly thereafter.[6]

In contrast to the Old Plan subject-area essay tests, the New Plan test avoided disagreements between teachers about scores, was more efficient and economical, appeared to be a better predictor of college grades, and caused less controversy because it did not dictate curricular standards (Valentine, 1987). The Old Plan and New Plan tests coexisted until World War II, but subsequently the essay tests became the multiple-choice SAT Subject Tests™. Large-scale essay readings conducted under the aegis of the College Board revived only in 1955, with the advent of the Advanced Placement (AP®) program.[7]

Distant and obscure as this early history of admissions testing might now seem, it exemplifies classic, enduring issues—debates unlikely to be resolved once and for all. Technical considerations include the merits of using essay tasks versus multiple-choice tasks and of measuring general academic skills versus subject-specific proficiencies. (Advocating a return to subject-specific college admissions testing, Atkinson and Geiser believe that the premises of the curriculum-based Old Plan tests "may have been sounder than anyone realized at the time" [2009, p. 2].) Policy questions are how testing affects educational opportunity and drives curricula and instruction, and whether control over curricula and tests should be localized or centralized. These themes would persist as the twentieth century unfolded.

Chapter I: Key Points

- Along with the first large-scale testing program, in ancient China, emerged such perennial issues as security, subjective scoring, and use for sociopolitical purposes. In the West, most testing done in schools and universities was oral, with results described qualitatively.
- During the 1800s, the adoption of written formats and numerical scoring set the stage for quantitative, standardized approaches to measuring students' knowledge and intellectual skills, as well as the use of student test data to hold teachers and schools accountable.
- At the same time, researchers who believed that intelligence could be observed via physical features and sensory manifestations introduced statistical methods for mental measurement that emulated methods used in the natural and physical sciences.
- To these quantitative measurement techniques was added the 1914 innovation of selected-response and short-answer question formats. Intended to make testing more objective and efficient, they facilitated the rapid growth of testing in the early 1900s.
- Testing in schools couched its claims in the language of science and medicine. Intelligence testing was used to sort students into academic and vocational tracks according to their supposedly innate capacities. Achievement testing focused instead on ranking and rating students' academic performance and "educational products."
- From 1900 onward, standardized testing for college admissions purposes became customary. The early history of the College Board program exemplified recurrent challenges and debates regarding the format, content, scoring, and consequences of educational tests.

NOTES

1. Like the Chinese exams, these too may have inspired test-preparation materials and possibly cheating. An anonymous text written by a faculty member at the University of Paris between 1230 and 1240 appears to be a "*vade mecum* for students, listing the questions most frequently asked during oral examinations and giving succinct answers to them" (Madaus & O'Dwyer, 1999, p. 691).

Moreover, according to Delandshere (2001), some of these oral examinations were "formalities" because they were undertaken only when the student's teacher was sure that the student could succeed. Yet other oral disputations did not just reiterate the student's acquired knowledge but actually served as a means of discussing and developing new lines of thought.

2. Ayers (1918) emphasized the pivotal nature of Galton's work thus:

Progress in the scientific study of education was not possible until people could be brought to realize that human behavior was susceptible of quantitative study, and until they had statistical methods with which to carry on their investigation. Both of these were contributed in large measure by Sir Francis Galton. As early as 1875 he published scientific studies of the traits of twins, of number-form, of color-blindness, and of the efficacy of prayer.

Out of his work came much of experimental and educational psychology, and indirectly, educational measurements. (pp. 10–11)

3. Even today, researchers continue to explore the extent to which certain kinds of sensory discrimination may correlate with cognitive abilities. An example is a study by Meyer, Hagmann-von Arx, Lemola, and Grob (2010), whose results seem to support Spearman's hypothesis that general intelligence and general sensory discrimination are strongly related.

4. However, Spearman later insisted that *g* was not intelligence itself, but a statistical entity derived from intelligence tests. Deary, Lawn, and Bartholomew (2008) call attention to the transcript of a 1931 meeting, in which Spearman emphasized that success in life needed psychological qualities beyond intellectual ones. Spearman also emphasized that there were numerous specific mental abilities and insisted that *g* was only a general factor, not identical with intelligence.

5. E. L. Thorndike (1918) explained his philosophy of educational measurement in his "Credo":

> Whatever exists at all exists in some amount. To know it thoroughly involves knowing its quantity as well as its quality. Education is concerned with changes in human beings; a change is a difference between two conditions; each of these conditions is known to us only by the products produced by it—things made, words spoken, acts performed, and the like. To measure any of these products means to define its amount in some way so that competent persons will know how large it is, better than they would without measurement. To measure a product well means so to define its amount that competent persons will know how large it is, with some precision, and that this knowledge may be conveniently recorded and used. This is the general *Credo* of those who, in the last decade, have been busy trying to extend and improve measurements of educational products. (p. 16)

The chapter is well worth reading and is available online (see References), as is the chapter by Ayers.

6. For a description of the 1926 version, with sample questions, see Lawrence, Rigol, Van Essen, and Jackson (2003). Their report also traces and explains the many changes in the test materials over the decades since then. The name, too, has changed; it is now officially "SAT®."

Soon after the 1926 New Plan test came the 1928 "Scholastic Aptitude Test for Medical Students," intended to help predict success in medical school and thereby lower the high attrition rate. E. L. Thorndike criticized this ancestor of the Medical College Admission Test (MCAT®) for overemphasizing memorization, and subsequent changes in the test would reflect evolving definitions of the knowledge and skills needed for medical education (McGaghie, 2002).

7. This program's intention to shape high school curricula would be explicit and far reaching, because each test specified curricular goals. Unlike the Old Plan tests, however, the AP tests would be optional and college applicants would take only one or a few, rather than a complete set across the curriculum.

SELECTED READINGS

Brown, J. (1992). *The definition of a profession: The authority of metaphor in the history of intelligence testing, 1890–1930.* Princeton, NJ: Princeton University Press.

Chapman, P. D. (1988). *Schools as sorters: Lewis M. Terman, applied psychology, and the intelligence testing movement, 1890–1930.* New York: New York University Press.

Giordano, G. (2005). *How testing came to dominate American schools: The history of educational assessment.* New York: Peter Lang Publishing, Inc.

Spearman, C. (1904). "General intelligence" objectively determined and measured. *American Journal of Psychology 15*, 201–93.

Suen, H. K., & Yu, L. (2006). Chronic consequences of high-stakes testing? Lessons from the Chinese civil service exam. *Comparative Education Review, 50*(1), 46–65.

Thorndike, E. L. (1918). The nature, purposes, and general methods of measurements of educational products. In G. M. Whipple (Ed.), *The seventeenth yearbook of the National Society for the Study of Education: The measurement of educational products* (Part 2, pp. 16–24). Bloomington, IL: Public School Publishing Company.

Chapter Two

In the Modern Era:
A Tool for Classroom and Society

When social planning, as it relates to education, becomes more forthright and deliberate, the role of measurement assumes greater importance in the process.

—Walter W. Cook, 1951 (p. 4)

If early educational measurement unabashedly aspired to the condition and status of natural science—to depict mental attributes as objectively and precisely as biology depicts physical attributes—then its modern counterpart has made equally ambitious claims of utility. Many people view testing primarily as a technology for improving instruction, promoting learning, reforming education, and facilitating social progress.

Testing has, of course, always been used to serve practical goals, but the explicit use of testing for policy purposes is a more recent phenomenon. In particular, it was encouraged by the behaviorist psychological theories introduced in the 1930s, positing that desired behaviors, including the acquisition of skills and knowledge, can be strengthened by feedback and reinforcement. Then, during World War II, policy makers turned to testing to further both military and political agendas.

Since the era of Civil Rights and Sputnik, spurred by the view that deficiencies in education cause economic and societal woes, policy makers have deployed testing in an array of efforts to improve schools and student achievement. However, because reform policies relying on educational testing have had many unintended consequences over the years, each new initiative using testing as a strategy must start by grappling with the legacies of previous attempts.

TECHNICAL DEVELOPMENTS
THAT PROMOTED MASS TESTING

A prerequisite for using testing to achieve large goals is the capability to test large numbers of students. Several types of technical innovations paved the way.

The first was expediting of scoring processes. After World War I, the new item formats allowed clerks to score tests by hand with answer keys or templates, but scoring still required significant commitments of time, labor, and money. Seeking a solution, science teacher Reynold B. Johnson (1906–1998) unveiled a prototype in 1934 for the "IBM805 Test Scoring Machine."

Produced from 1938 until 1963, this machine used electrical contacts to register pencil marks as correct or incorrect answers (International Business Machines, n.d.; see the Web page for a photo). Its successor used a beam of light instead, and was invented in 1955 by Everet F. Lindquist (1901–1978) to process answer sheets from his Iowa Tests of Basic Skills (ITBS®). Today, computer-integrated optical scanners are still used to score paper-and-pencil answer sheets (Clarke et al., 2000).

A second factor was the growth of educational measurement as a discipline. University programs in educational psychology and measurement expanded. Reference works and textbooks proliferated, most notably the 1951 first edition of *Educational Measurement*, edited by Lindquist, and the 1954–1955 documents that were the precursors of today's official *Standards for Educational and Psychological Testing*.

Last, mathematical and statistical methods relevant to testing, such as ways of calculating test-score reliability, continued to evolve. (See chapter 6 for more about reliability, which means consistency of measurement.) Some of the methods, including sampling techniques, were specifically aimed at gathering and analyzing information on large numbers of examinees (Clarke et al., 2000).

All these innovations made educational testing "more manageable, standardized, easily administered, objective, reliable, comparable, and inexpensive as the numbers of examinees increased"—and made it "the technology of choice for policymakers" (Madaus, 1993, p. 20). But equally important were new ideas about teaching and learning that emerged in the 1930s.

THE RISE OF TYLER AND DECLINE OF TERMAN

Basing Assessment on Educational Objectives

In contrast to Terman and other proponents of biological and educational determinism stood Ralph Tyler (1902–1992). "I've never met a child who couldn't learn," he once said (Stanford University, 1994, ¶ 29). This belief in students' potential resonates throughout the work of Tyler. Along with Lindquist, he helped steer educational assessment away from early models (as a ritual of reproducing memorized facts or a means of sorting students into tracks) toward a more modern model, based on such concepts as educational objectives and cognitive development.

During the early 1930s, Tyler was trying to help faculty members at Ohio State University who were concerned about students' high failure rates in required courses. He suggested to them that

> "The typical so called achievement test is simply a test of what students remember about things that appear in their textbooks, and . . . you are not just teaching them to memorize." This conclusion led us to talk about what the instructors' objectives were, that is, what they really hoped their students would be learning. And then they said that a test should provide evidence of whether students were learning those things or not. (Tyler, quoted in Nowakowski, 1981, question 14)

By seeking a different approach, Tyler was challenging the prevalent attitudes about achievement testing at the time, as championed by Ben D. Wood (1894–1986). Wood believed that testing could be limited to matters of factual knowledge, because he assumed that students who possessed this knowledge also had the thinking skills to apply it as needed. In contrast, Tyler argued that "if higher-order cognitive skills were the objectives of instruction they had to be measured directly" and that educators should define the objectives of instruction in terms of behavior as well as knowledge (Madaus & Stufflebeam, 1989, p. xii; Clarke et al., 2000).

For example, in a college biology course, students should be able to show "skill in getting information from appropriate sources." If presented with a given experiment, students ought to be able to "propose hypotheses which would constitute reasonable inferences" from the details of the experiment (Tyler, 1934/1989, p. 22).

Tyler's 1934 *Constructing Achievement Tests* laid out methods for test development still recognizable today. Tyler emphasized defining curricular goals in terms of skills and knowledge that students can demonstrate. Then, the tasks on a test must sample these behaviors with sufficient breadth and depth to permit larger inferences about students' progress toward meeting the goals (Shepard, 1993). The question formats (selected-response, constructed-response, oral, carrying out a physical procedure, etc.) should not be chosen on the basis of efficiency but instead optimally designed to "give evidence of the progress students are making" (Tyler, 1934/1989, p. 26).

Tyler also created the field of educational evaluation. His *Basic Principles of Curriculum and Instruction* (1949/1969) urges that schools seek to define their educational purposes; consider what learning experiences best serve these purposes; and, using assessment information, evaluate how well the purposes are met.

One outgrowth of Tyler's ideas was a project that measurement professionals undertook in 1948, hoping eventually to produce a large bank of test items and tasks that universities could share. A former research assistant of Tyler's, Benjamin Bloom (1913–1999), led the committee.

Creating a theoretical framework of educational objectives would, the committee believed, provide a basis for systematic test development. Like a biological classification scheme dividing species into kingdoms, the resulting "taxonomy" divided the objectives of education into the cognitive domain of knowledge and mental skills, the affective domain of attitudes and emotions, and the psychomotor domain of manual or physical skills.

In 1956 Bloom, Englehart, Furst, Hill, and Krathwohl published the first volume of the taxonomy, focused on the cognitive domain. It posited a hierarchy of intellectual skills or behaviors according to increasing abstraction and difficulty. From low to high:

- Knowledge (acquiring information, such as facts, methods, ideas, and theories)
- Comprehension (understanding and drawing logical inferences from information)
- Application (using abstract ideas, rules, or methods in specific situations)
- Analysis (deconstructing something into constituent parts and understanding their relationships)
- Synthesis (combining information and ideas to produce something new)
- Evaluation (using systematic criteria to make judgments about quality) (pp. 201–7)[1]

For decades, *Bloom's taxonomy* informed the frameworks of many educational tests, and it is still used in various programs. It facilitated the "measurement-driven instruction" of the 1950s–1970s, in which testing was intended to ensure that students mastered a curricular unit before moving on to the next (Haertel & Herman, 2005). Although other taxonomies and revisions to Bloom's taxonomy have been proposed, its crucial emphasis on higher cognitive skills has served to encourage testing of what Lindquist (1951) called the "ultimate objectives" of education, rather than simply the "immediate objectives" of acquiring information.

Theories About Intelligence Evolve

While Tyler reshaped achievement testing, Terman's campaign to reorganize schools around intelligence testing was not entirely successful. Not only did intelligence testing offer little to meet everyday needs for measuring students' progress, but also it came under attack from the perspectives of theory and of societal consequences.

In fact, even when the Galton-Spearman-Terman model of a unitary, stable intelligence was emerging, it was not universally endorsed. E. L. Thorndike, for example, was more concerned with abilities in practical, specialized areas such as handwriting, and his own test of intelligence investigated different aspects (von Mayrhauser, 1992). Following this line of thinking, Louis L. Thurstone (1887–1955) proposed in 1938 that the capacity for learning involved different factors and called for using separate tests. Thus, any comprehensive assessment of intellectual attributes should result in multiple scores for different "primary mental abilities" rather than a single IQ score (Schwarz, 1971).

Some followers of Spearman later retreated from the theory of biologically determined general intelligence. David Wechsler (1896–1981), who had worked with Thorndike and Yerkes on the U.S. Army Alpha tests and then studied with Spearman and Pearson, came to believe that environment and personality played a role in shaping intelligence, defined as the ability to reason and to act effectively (Plucker, 2003). Wechsler's own intelligence tests had separate scores for "verbal" and "performance" dimensions in addition to an overall score.

Subsequent theorists explicitly posited separate categories of mental abilities. In his 1983 *Frames of Mind: The Theory of Multiple Intelligences*, Howard Gardner described different, independent "intelligences," each of which was dynamic:

> a set of skills enabling the individual to resolve genuine problems of difficulties that he or she encounters and, when appropriate, to create an effective product— and . . . the potential for finding or creating problems, thereby laying the groundwork for the acquisition of new knowledge. (pp. 60–61)

Even when Robert J. Sternberg challenged Gardner by citing the pervasive positive correlations observed on different ability tests, Sternberg (1988) did not revert to a unitary theory. Instead, he proposed a "triarchic theory" of human intelligence as the "purposeful adaptation to and selection and shaping of real-world environments relevant to one's life," so that the ways in which such abilities are manifested differ according to cultural context (pp. 72–73, 76). The analytic, practical, and creative mental-management abilities that constitute intelligence could be improved through continuous learning.

In recent years, psychologists have widely adopted the so-called Cattell-Horn-Carroll (CHC) theory of cognitive abilities. This approach deemphasizes *a priori* theory in favor of an open-ended project: empirical research that applies factor analysis to psychometric data and integrates these results with other research findings. The goal of the project is to map the mind as a taxonomy of demonstrated relationships among broad and narrow intellectual abilities (McGrew, 2005 and 2009).

Intelligence Testing Loses Its Influence on Education

Apart from the theorists' deconstruction of a unitary intelligence, the other line of opposition to intelligence testing focused on cultural *bias* and misuse of scores. A notable example of both was Brigham's 1923 *A Study of American Intelligence*, which argued that Yerkes's data showed different levels of intellectual ability among ethnic groups. Legislators used this book to support passing the 1924 Immigration Restriction Act barring many European refugees from entering the United States—with devastating consequences. Brigham himself would later recant; in 1930 he published a formal retraction repudiating theories of hereditary, "native" intelligence (Gould, 1981; Lemann, 1999).

With the advent of the Civil Rights era in the 1950s, intelligence tests came under legal scrutiny. Successful challenges to the use of intelligence tests for placement into remedial or special-education programs included *Hobson v. Hansen* (1967), *Diana v. California State Board of Education* (1970), and *Larry P. v. Riles* (1972). Courts ruled that the tests were biased either because they were administered in a language that the students had not mastered (*Diana*) or because the norming sample did not represent the students taking the test (*Hobson*). The subsequent 1979 ruling on *Larry P.* also decreed that "the evidence indicated that IQ tests could not give a simple number corresponding to an innate trait called intelligence" (Hollander, 1982, pp. 210–11).[2]

For these reasons, in contrast to what Terman envisioned, intelligence testing is not at the center of today's educational system. As Binet originally intended, such tests are still often used to identify learning disabilities, via a "discrepancy model" method that compares a student's IQ scores with indicators of academic achievement (high IQ scores vs. low achievement might suggest a disability). However, critics charge that this strategy is not cost-effective, does not permit early diagnosis, and may incorrectly place students into special education classes (Walser, 2007).[3]

Many schools are instead exploring a prevention-oriented approach called "response to intervention" (RTI). Schools begin early to screen all students for those who may be at risk, and monitoring continues in order to identify a student's specific learning issue when it arises. As needed, students receive intensive, targeted instruction. The school and teachers closely observe a student's performance to see if it improves under an initial intervention; if not, additional interventions are tried. (See National Center on Response to Intervention, 2010.)[4]

Moreover, many state educational systems stress that intelligence-test scores should not be the sole basis for placing students in "gifted" programs. In fact, a study by Duckworth and Seligman (2005) found that students' levels of self-discipline predicted academic achievement (in terms of GPA) better than IQ scores.

One coda to the reign of intelligence testing can be seen in research conducted by Carol S. Dweck. She has investigated the effects of believing that intelligence is a fixed capacity, as opposed to believing that intelligence can grow through effort and learning. Experimental results indicate that—at least for younger students—holding the latter view may promote better academic performance, because believing in malleable intelligence seems to foster students' motivation and resilience, whereas believing in fixed intelligence can cause students to lose confidence and enjoyment when they make mistakes or struggle with a difficult task (Dweck, 2007).[5]

Indeed, the very language of assessment has changed from the early days of intelligence testing, with school testing now aimed at acquired "proficiency" rather than innate "ability" (Bock, 1997). Achievement testing regained its place as the central form of assessment in education, albeit in new incarnations. Tyler's influence would prove more lasting than Terman's; one might say that a doctrine of free will prevailed over that of predestination.

MID-CENTURY: TESTING AND OPPORTUNITY

World War II

Just as in the 1910s, in the 1940s testing again figured in the course and aftermath of a war. But this time, the new Army General Classification Test, which included tasks on vocabulary, mathematical reasoning, and block counting, was explicitly described as measuring only capacity for military duties—and not measuring intelligence, education, or leadership (Craf, 1943). Recruits who obtained high scores could apply for officer's training or other specialty training, and by the end of the Second World War, 12 million soldiers had taken this test.

Concerned about the possibility of postwar mass unemployment, political upheaval, or another depression, President Franklin D. Roosevelt and Congress sought to reintegrate the returning soldiers into society. One strategy was to provide veterans with educational opportunities, as specified in the 1944 Servicemen's Readjustment Act, now called the GI Bill of Rights. The 1944 Act included financial support for veterans to attend college. Yet this assistance was not sufficient by itself, because an estimated 10 million veterans lacked high school diplomas (Quinn, 2002).

Therefore, as early as 1942, the U.S. Navy had commissioned an alternative high school graduation credential, the "Test of General Educational Development" (GED), whose development was overseen by Tyler and Lindquist. This primarily multiple-choice test was successful in the sense that almost all the veterans who took it passed—perhaps in part because the required passing score was set quite low and the test itself concentrated more on general reading, writing, and math skills than on knowledge about specific subjects.* Later accepted for civilian use, the GED would be revised over time in response to criticisms that it was too easy and required too little study of actual high school subjects (Quinn, 2002). Over 17 million Americans have earned GEDs.

As Roosevelt and other lawmakers had hoped, rather than crowding the job market, millions of ex-soldiers took advantage of the GED program and the financial assistance for college. At the peak, in 1947, about half of all students entering college were veterans.

In contrast to the few, mainly wealthy students who had gone to college before the war, the masses of new college graduates "raised expectations throughout the country, and their skilled labor contributed to a burgeoning and literate technological middle class. There was no going back to the old America dominated by agriculture and by life in small towns" (Greenberg, n.d., under "A Flood of Veterans," ¶ 3). Attending college became a far more common way of achieving economic and social mobility.

Postwar

With a vastly larger pool of applicants to evaluate, after the war many colleges began adopting the test that had previously been used by a few Eastern schools: the College Board's New Plan test, forerunner of today's SAT®.

The person responsible for this development was Henry Chauncey (1905–2002), who as an assistant dean at Harvard University during the 1930s had used the multiple-choice New Plan test to identify scholarship students and broaden the undergraduate body beyond the prep-school elite. Chauncey was commissioned in 1943 by the U.S. military to help in the process of officer selection. By successfully administering an adapted SAT in a single day to 300,000 people across the country, Chauncey showed that it would be logistically feasible to give the SAT to high school students nationwide (Brewster, 2004). He became the first president of Educational Testing Service, which

---

*Lindquist (1951) argued that this approach better reflected the types of learning provided by military experience and provided "more direct measures of the ultimate outcomes of a general education than could be secured through any available subject examinations" (p. 132). The debate about skills vs. subject knowledge recalls a similar debate in the Old Plan and New Plan exams of the early 1900s.

had been founded by former Harvard president James Conant (1893–1978) to consolidate testing organizations in the United States.

In 1959, a new organization founded by Lindquist, American College Testing, Inc. (now ACT, Inc.), would offer a different college-admissions test intended to focus more on mastery of subject areas than on general verbal and quantitative skills. (In practice, though, the absence of a national curriculum meant that the ACT® came to resemble the SAT, enough so that most colleges accept scores from either test.) The 1940s–1950s also saw the inception of admissions testing for entry into graduate school, business school, and law school.

However, on the same ground of opportunity, criticisms of these and other educational tests increased as societal issues of race and ethnicity drew attention during the Civil Rights era. Opponents argued that the content and administration of tests were biased against minorities and that adverse societal effects of testing should be the overriding consideration (Giordano, 2005).

From a different perspective, though, the results of testing could also be used in arguing for progressive agendas. Advocates for disadvantaged children "pointed to glaring disparities in standardized test performance between their constituents and middle-class children to support their case for increased aid" (Madaus & Kellaghan, 1993, under "Brief History of Testing," ¶ 9). Thus, test scores could be seen either as a reflection or as an agent of an educational system that denied opportunity.

One other development relevant to opportunity occurred at mid-century, when testing programs began to address the needs of students with disabilities—for example, by offering a Braille version of a test, reading the test aloud, or providing an amanuensis for students physically unable to write their own answers. Since then, testing *accommodations* have been mandated by federal statutes such as Sections 309 and 504 of the Rehabilitation Act of 1973, the Individuals with Disabilities Education Act (IDEA) of 1975, and the Americans with Disabilities Act (ADA) of 1990 (Phelps, 2006; Adams, 2000). (See chapter 7 for more about issues of accessibility.)

EDUCATIONAL REFORM AND ACCOUNTABILITY

New Attention to Educational Quality

In the 1960s, both the Civil Rights movement and fears of lagging scientific progress raised public concern about the quality of education. Two research programs aimed at investigating school efficacy and student achievement— or lack thereof—would affect testing in the longer term.

One of these projects was the federal government's National Assessment of Educational Progress (NAEP), which calls itself "the nation's report card."

The program originated in a 1963 suggestion by the then-U.S. Commissioner of Education that it might be desirable to conduct "a 'census' on the knowledge and skills of American students" in order to inform policy (Bracey, 1995, p. 100). Ralph Tyler was appointed by the Carnegie Foundation in 1964 to head the program, which first administered tests to a sampling of students nationwide in 1969 and whose governing board, procedures, and appropriations are established in federal law (20 United States Civil Code, Sections 9621–9624).

Although it has not retained all the features Tyler originally envisioned, such as collaborative tasks, today's NAEP program administers biennial tests to a representative sampling of students from every state at three grade levels. The purposes are "to compare student achievement in states and other jurisdictions and to track changes in achievement of fourth-, eighth-, and twelfth-graders over time in mathematics, reading, writing, science, and other content domains" (Institute of Education Sciences, 2008b, under "What are the goals of the NAEP program?" ¶ 1).

State, school, and individual student participation is voluntary and carries no consequences for students, teachers, or schools—but federal funding for state educational systems is contingent on states' participating in the fourth- and eighth-grade tests. (See Yeager, 2007, for more about NAEP.)

The other influential research project of the 1960s was the 1966 Equality of Educational Opportunity Survey, whose methods of investigation included the use of standardized tests. The project's findings focused national attention on debate of the effectiveness of public education and ushered in new ways of evaluating students, teachers, and schools (Airasian & Abrams, 2002).

Instead of "evaluating the inputs or resources devoted to education [e.g., school facilities, pedagogical strategies, instructional materials]," the new outcomes-based assessments focused on "measuring the outputs or results—operationalized by student performance on available multiple-choice tests" (Clarke et al., 2000, p. 164). In the 1970s and 1980s, states measured educational outcomes by administering basic skills tests to high school students as a condition of graduation. Policy makers believed that so-called minimum competency testing would spur school systems to serve those students who most needed help (Airasian & Abrams, 2002).*

Reform and Accountability

In addition to the introduction of minimum competency testing, other events and trends starting in the 1970s would lead to today's emphasis on educa-

---

*These minimum competency exams were the forebears of basic skills high school exit exams, which in turn have been supplanted to some extent by subject-specific, end-of-course examinations. For more on the implications of this trend, including costs and logistical challenges, see Zabala, Minnichi, McMurrer, and Briggs (2008).

tional standards and attempts to use assessment for educational reform. One emerging trend was the application of ideas from the world of commerce to education.

Calls to adopt business models were not entirely new; in the early 1900s, schools were urged to follow Frederick Taylor's model of business management to maximize efficiency (Linn, 2001). But in his 1970 *Every Kid a Winner: Accountability in Education*, Leon Lessinger invoked a "business and management paradigm whereby a person is held responsible for performing according to terms previously agreed upon" (Pulliam, 1991, p. 216). As consumers dissatisfied with the quality of education for which they were paying, the public responded to this idea.

Connecting business and education was, and is, not merely an analogy. The public increasingly perceived a very direct causal relationship between the educational system and the condition of U.S. businesses. In 1983, when a weak U.S. economy contrasted sharply with other countries' strong economies, the National Commission on Educational Excellence issued *A Nation at Risk*. It sounded a high-decibel alarm:

> The educational foundations of our society are presently being eroded by a rising tide of mediocrity that threatens our very future as a Nation and a people. . . . If an unfriendly foreign power had attempted to impose on America the mediocre educational performance that exists today, we might well have viewed it as an act of war. (National Commission on Educational Excellence, 1983, under "A Nation at Risk," ¶ 2 & 3)

Among the report's many recommendations for change, including the adoption of "more rigorous and measurable standards," was systematic testing of students via standardized tests of achievement at each major transition point in education, especially at the end of high school.

Public support was strong enough that by 1992, forty-two states required tests of the type described above. As Madaus and Kellaghan (1993) sardonically note, the rationale for expanding testing had a certain circularity, in that the public and policy makers perceived testing as a "prescription to cure the ills of American education, which [had] been described in terms of test performance in the first place" (under "Current Evolution of Tests," ¶ 1).

At the same time, the minimum-competency approach was evolving into a more comprehensive approach, in the form of *standards-based assessment*. This approach involves specifying academic *content standards* (essentially, educational objectives); using these standards to design curricula and tests; and then describing student performance in terms of prescribed proficiency levels (so-called performance standards).

In contrast to the minimum competency tests, which concentrated on high school outcomes, the standards-based assessments spanned multiple grade levels and usually included subject-area tests. Hoping to spur educational reform and make U.S. businesses more competitive internationally, policy makers began to demand that most or all students meet the standards and began to hold teachers and school administrators accountable for the outcomes (Airasian & Abrams, 2002).

Standards-Based Assessment Across the Nation

At the 1989 Charlottesville Education Summit, President George H. W. Bush and the nation's governors agreed on the concept of national educational objectives, if these could be pursued without undermining state and district control of education. The resulting 1994 legislation, called Goals 2000: Educate America Act, provided funding to help states develop their own educational standards and standards-based assessments, and states embarked on this process.

However, by 1999, when Goals 2000 was up for reauthorization, its requirements for accountability and stipulations for specific expenditures had already been weakened. It was not renewed, in part because of fears that it would lead to the establishment of a national curriculum and thereby strengthen the role of the federal government in setting educational agendas and policies (Superfine, 2005).

Increased testing during the 1970s and 1980s had met with a commensurate increase in criticisms. Many of these concerns were articulated in a 1990 report whose title embodied the tension between enforcing accountability and promoting opportunity: *From Gatekeeper to Gateway: Transforming Testing in America.* Created by a panel of educators, scholars, and policy makers, this document echoes the emphasis of *A Nation at Risk* on the interdependency of educational and economic goals.

Yet the authors of *From Gatekeeper to Gateway* took a more mixed view of testing as a means of achieving those goals. While some testing had been "a positive force for numerous individuals and institutions . . . [c]urrent testing is over-relied upon, lacks adequate public accountability, sometimes leads to unfairness in the allocation of opportunities, and too often undermines vital social policies" (National Commission on Testing and Public Policy, 1990, p. ix).

Moreover, from a pedagogical standpoint, scholars of education such as Lorrie A. Shepard (1989) expressed concern about ways in which large-scale standardized testing could limit the breadth and depth of material covered. Committee negotiations over test content could have a "homogenizing effect," and the use of multiple-choice formats and short reading passages constrict the range of skills assessed (p. 5). Shepard and others warned that attaching serious consequences to the tests might cause teachers to narrow their instruction by focusing on the basic skills to be covered in these tests.

Despite such concerns, and despite the fact that Goals 2000 had not been renewed, federal policy makers would nonetheless continue to look to testing as a means of bringing about educational reform. However, because the Constitution of the United States did not explicitly establish federal control over education, the federal government cannot simply order states to participate in a national test or adopt national standards.

Instead, the federal government can exert the power of the purse. A special initiative such as the Race to the Top (RTTT) competition is the exception; more typically, federal leverage comes through Title 1 grants that provide extensive funding for remedial programs and for disadvantaged students. Obtaining such funding has led states to comply with the provisions of the 1965 Elementary and Secondary Education Act, which was renewed in subsequent years and then substantively expanded in the 2001–2002 No Child Left Behind Act (NCLB).

NCLB defined accountability primarily in terms of test results for reading and mathematics. Not only did states have to participate in NAEP, but they also had to institute their own tests based on explicit standards for proficiency—then find ways to bring all students up to a "proficient" level. In turn, "individual schools [had to] meet state 'adequate yearly progress' targets toward this goal (based on a formula spelled out in the law) for both their student populations as a whole and for certain demographic subgroups" (Editorial Projects in Education, 2007, under "Academic Progress," ¶ 1).

Over time these mandates, with sanctions for schools failing to meet the targets, appear to have had mixed consequences, some unforeseen and unintended. Thus, among the legacies of NCLB was a rethinking of accountability, including such heavy reliance on testing. The concern is that "educational practice in the United States is dominated by a drive to raise scores on large-scale assessments," (Koretz, 2009, p. 4).

However, research suggests that under NCLB math skills at the elementary level improved, especially for low-income and minority students (Dee & Jacob, 2010). Most important, by requiring that achievement data be reported by ethnicity, gender, disability status, income, etc., NCLB brought attention to different groups' needs.

ISSUES AND TRENDS

Apart from the ongoing debate over using testing as a means for educational reform, recent issues include addressing dissatisfaction with states' K–12 testing programs and with the perceived effects of selected-response tests on learning. Another challenge is to integrate new theories and research findings about learning into assessment. These areas of interest are introduced below and are further explored, along with others, in volume 2.

Questioning Recent Practices

Among many other things, NCLB raised questions about what standards-based assessment means in a country without national standards. As critics pointed out, NCLB required states to ensure that K–12 students were on track to achieving proficiency in reading, math, and eventually other subjects, but the states were free to create their own tests and define their own standards of proficiency.

Such latitude meant that unlike NAEP scores, NCLB test scores could not be compared across states. For example, comparing the percentages of fourth-grade students achieving NCLB "proficiency" in math across different states was meaningless, because the material tested, the difficulty of the tests, and/or the criteria for proficient performance could differ from one state to the next. Only by mapping state proficiency standards onto NAEP standards could any comparisons be made, albeit with many caveats about dissimilar tests. (For the methods and results, which remain controversial among experts, see Bandiera de Mello, Blankenship, & McLaughlin, 2009.)

This problem has led to renewed interest in establishing national academic standards and tests based on those standards, as exemplified in the Common Core State Standards Initiative (CCSSI; see www.corestandards.org) and Linda Darling-Hammond's 2010 description of goals for a new era of assessment.

A second set of issues has to do with how test formats affect both instruction and measurement. The late 1980s brought calls for using portfolios and open-ended, constructed-response tasks, including more realistic types of *performance assessment*. Occasionally invoking the venerable tradition of oral disputation, educators and theorists such as Grant Wiggins (1989), Shepard (1989), and Lunsford (1986) urged designing assessments "to more closely resemble real learning tasks," "to require more complex and challenging mental processes from students," and to acknowledge the possibility of different approaches and answers (Shepard, pp. 6–7). (A related call was, and is, for more reliance on non-test information, such as teachers' comments, student projects and exhibitions, school inspections, data about attendance and graduation, etc.)

However, constructed-response tests and portfolios have enormous logistical and budgetary implications and raise concerns about subjective scoring affecting the quality of information obtained. In fact, many states avoided or discontinued such assessments because of time and cost (see U.S. Government Accountability Office, 2009). Recent efforts often focus on using computer technology to enhance selected-response testing, via more imaginative tasks and more nuanced scoring methods; or to make constructed-response assessments more feasible, via logistical capabilities and automated scoring (see U.S. Department of Education, 2009, for a discussion of possibilities and challenges).

Innovations in Assessment

A third focus of interest is classroom assessment, as opposed to testing used for selection or accountability purposes. Here, testing can have a function even apart from providing information: frequent testing appears to be more effective than review alone in helping students retain knowledge over time (Roediger & Karpicke, 2006).

Other classroom assessment may be *diagnostic*, intended to ascertain a student's strengths and weaknesses (e.g., in reading skills) so that appropriate types of instruction can be identified and planned. It may also be *formative*: "activities undertaken by teachers—and by their students in assessing themselves—that provide information to be used as feedback to modify teaching and learning activities" (Black & Wiliam, 1998, p. 140). According to Wiliam (2000), the "defining feature of a formative assessment is that *the information fed back to the learner must be used by the learner in improving performance*" (p. 118).

In assessment for learning, as opposed to of learning, the teacher observes, poses various questions and tasks, and uses the results to adapt instruction appropriately. Students may participate by evaluating their own learning as well. Often the approach will be qualitative in nature (e.g., comments or other written texts, checklists, *rubrics*, graphic organizers) rather than quantitative (scores or grades). Some theorists envision these contextualized approaches, together with constructed-response and performance test formats, as a means of transforming assessment from a psychometric model to one that they believe would better reflect research on cognition and learning (Gipps, 1994; Shepard, 2000; Moss, Pullin, Gee, & Haertel, 2005).

A fourth area of exploration focuses on implementing findings from such research. In particular, Ferrara (2006) suggests, the publication of *Knowing What Students Know: The Science and Design of Educational Assessment* in 2001 was the "event that integrated cognitive psychology, learning theory and research, and the practice of educational achievement testing" (p. 2).

The authors of *Knowing What Students Know* contrast recent cognitive theories with earlier behaviorist theories, which posited knowledge as relatively static. Depicting knowledge as conditional, fluid, and dynamic, cognitive theories explore

> how people develop structures of knowledge, including the concepts associated with a subject matter discipline (or domain of knowledge) and procedures for reasoning and solving problems. . . . In cognitive theory, knowing means more than the accumulation of factual information and routine procedures; it means being able to integrate knowledge, skills, and procedures in ways that are useful for interpreting situations and solving problems. (National Research Council [NRC], 2001, p. 62)

Thus, testing would focus less exclusively on acquired knowledge and more on intellectual processes necessary to developing expertise in some area. Tests

and tasks would "reveal information about thinking patterns, reasoning strategies, and growth in understanding over time" (NRC, 2001, pp. 4, 62–63). Rather
than covering discrete topics, tests would be designed around conceptual frameworks or major ideas within a discipline; for example, in science, the idea that
matter is composed of particles in the form of atoms and molecules. They might
also be designed around "proficiencies and processes" such as those at the heart
of the Common Core State Standards for Mathematics (CCSSI, 2010b, pp. 6–8).

Such views have informed the proposal of *learning progressions* (LPs) as
an empirical alternative to traditional content standards, which are more aspirational in nature. A concern is that traditional content standards, organized
horizontally by grade level, may become superficial and disconnected.

In contrast, as Heritage (2008) explains, LPs take a vertical perspective, looking at how expertise and understanding within a discipline actually develop over
time. (Thus, for example, students would understand the meaning and implications of atomic theory at increasingly sophisticated levels.) Rather than represent potentially subjective or politicized goals, LP models are to be based on
evidence and research. (For more detail and many other examples, see the 2005
NRC report on K–12 science assessment; as well as Heritage, 2008; Corcoran,
Mosher, & Rogat, 2009; and Bertenthal, Pellegrino, Huff, & Wilbur, 2009.) The
challenge then becomes how to evaluate learning when using an LP framework.

Nowhere are the concerns and innovations discussed thus far more clearly
illustrated than in two RTTT proposals for new K-12 assessment systems.
Groups of states banded together as consortia to submit these proposals, and the
winners of federal RTTT money in 2010 were the Partnership for Assessment
of Readiness for College and Careers (PARCC) and the SMARTER Balanced
Assessment Consortium (SBAC).

Despite some differences, both the PARCC (2010) and SBAC (2010) proposals reveal similar themes. One theme is comprehensive alignment and integra-
tion, resulting in more comparable test data across states. State consortia would
use their shared Common Core Standards or learning progressions to drive curricula, instruction, and shared tests. Then, different levels of assessment would
be aligned within the system: from day-to-day formative classroom assessment,
to periodic/interim assessment, to end-of-course *summative assessment*.

Reviving the quest to go beyond traditional selected-response tests, the two
proposals envision not only incorporating new item types that better simulate
real-life tasks, but also constructed-response tasks, research projects, class
presentations, problem-solving scenarios, etc. The proposals rely heavily on
computer and Internet technology, including a significant amount of automated scoring, to overcome the logistical problems and costs that bedeviled
previous such attempts.

Even beyond the aspirations of the PARCC and SBAC proposals, there is
one more possibility to consider. How might advances in neuroscience affect
assessment of learning? New insights have already arisen from observing

both patterns of brain activation and structural changes in the brain, such as those famously exhibited by London cabbies possessing "the knowledge" of the city's complex street map.

As an example of applying neuroscience to assessment, one study extended Dweck's research by measuring electrical activity in the brains of subjects who took a test of general knowledge. The subjects were told which questions they missed; given the answers to all questions; and then retested on the questions they missed. Compared to subjects who expressed a belief in malleable intelligence, those who believed in fixed intelligence not only did worse on the retest but also, while taking it, showed activation of a different brain area and less activity related to memory (Mangels, Butterfield, Lamb, Good, & Dweck, 2006, p. 75). Another study found that intensive remedial instruction for children with reading problems improved reading performance and caused lasting increases in activation of the relevant cortical areas (Meyler, Keller, Cherkassky, Gabrieli, & Just, 2008).

Contemplating such research suggests a host of new issues for evaluating learning, even a futuristic vision of exams with students lining up for brain scans instead of marking answer-sheet bubbles or tapping on computer keys. However, if there is any lesson in past attempts to measure the workings of the mind as biological phenomena, it is to treat apparent advances with humility and caution—and avoid Craniometry 2.0.

In each new approach, then, recurrent motifs appear. Next we will look more closely at three central themes: science, technology, and power.

Chapter II: Key Points

- In the United States, technical advances in test format and scoring as well as in the disciplines of psychometrics and statistics helped facilitate the rise of mass testing and its use as a technology to achieve both educational and societal goals.
- Intelligence testing in schools eventually came under attack both for its theoretical bases and social consequences. The behaviorist approach introduced in the 1930s created a new model, focused on measuring students' progress toward specified educational goals and providing feedback to aid learning and instruction.
- With World War II came an emphasis on testing as a technology for promoting opportunity, first for returning veterans and later for broader demographic groups applying to college. Yet debate about whether testing serves more as "gateway or gatekeeper" would grow and remain central in educational policy.
- Concern about the quality of public education and about the effects of apparently lagging student achievement on economic prosperity has led to government-mandated testing programs intended to enforce accountability and achieve educational reform.
- Current assessment issues include: benefits and drawbacks of standards-based accountability testing, effects on instruction of different test formats, innovations made possible by computers, the role of formative assessment in learning, and how to incorporate new insights from cognitive psychology, pedagogical theory, and neuroscience.

NOTES

1. One can discern the ancestry of Bloom's taxonomy in the list of goals that Tyler (1934/1989) described for a zoology course. It started with "a fund of information about animal activities and structures" and ended with "an ability to express effectively ideas relating to zoology." It also included the ability to propose and test hypotheses (p. 39).

2. In *Hobson v. Hansen* (1967), the court cited IQ tests' reliance on Caucasian, middle-class norming samples in ruling that the tests were culturally biased and should not be used for tracking students (ERIC Clearinghouse on Tests, Measurement, and Evaluation, 1985, under "Ability Tracking," ¶ 2).

In *Diana v. California State Board of Education* (1970), the state had to cease relying solely on IQ tests administered in English to identify nonnative speakers as intellectually handicapped (Hollander, 1982).

In the 1972 decision on *Larry P. v. Riles*, the court ruled against the use of IQ tests to place students in special-education programs because the court found that the "racial differences in test scores were due to cultural bias in the tests" (ERIC Clearinghouse on Tests, Measurement, and Evaluation, 1985, under "Special Education Placement," ¶ 3).

3. An example of intelligence tests intended primarily to help diagnose learning difficulties is the Kaufmann Assessment Battery for Children (K-ABC), developed by Alan and Nadeen Kaufmann in 1983.

However, a report from a presidential commission highlights a statement by a scholar in the field that "there is no compelling reason to continue to use IQ tests in the identification of learning disabilities" and that eliminating costly IQ tests would help shift the focus to providing needed services (Vaughn, quoted in President's Commission on Excellence in Special Education, 2002, p. 22).

4. Response to Intervention is a complex and fast-evolving field. It also has its critics, who are concerned that the strategy may be a means to limit the number of students in special education; that the process may put too much of a burden of proof on teachers; and that the prescribed "evidence-based" interventions may not necessarily be effective. For more on this subject, consult relevant articles in *Education Week* and the materials at these websites: the National Center on Response to Intervention (http://www.rti4success.org), the RTI Action Network (http://www.rtinetwork.org), and the National Research Center on Learning Disabilities (http://www.nrcld.org).

5. At the same time, as Glenn (2010) reports, some subsequent research has suggested that for older students, the relationship between beliefs about intelligence and academic performance may be less clear because of other complicating factors. Simply believing in malleable intelligence is not a magic bullet.

SELECTED READINGS

Corcoran, T., Mosher, F. A., & Rogat, A. (2009, May). *Learning progressions in science: An evidence-based approach to reform*. Philadelphia, PA: Consortium for Policy Research in Education.

Lissitz, R. W., & Shafer, W. D. (2002). *Assessment in educational reform: Both means and end.* Boston: Allyn and Bacon.

National Research Council (NRC). (2001). *Knowing what students know: The science and design of educational assessment.* Committee on the Foundations of Assessment. J. Pellegrino, N. Chudowsky, & R. Glaser (Eds.). Board on Testing and Assessment, Center for Education. Division of Behavioral and Social Sciences and Education. Washington, DC: National Academy Press.

Partnership for Assessment of Readiness for College and Careers (PARCC). (2010, June 23). *Application for the Race to the Top comprehensive assessment systems competition.* Retrieved September 8, 2010, from http://www.fldoe.org/parcc/

Shepard, L. A. (2000). The role of assessment in a learning culture. *Educational Researcher, 29*(7), 4–14.

SMARTER Balanced Assessment Consortium (SBAC). (2010, June 23). *Race to the Top assessment program application for new grants.* Retrieved September 8, 2010, from http://www.k12.wa.us/SMARTER/RTTTApplication.aspx.

Tyler, R. W. (1934/1989). Constructing achievement tests. In G. F. Madaus & D. L. Shufflebeam (Eds.), *Educational evaluation: Classic works of Ralph W. Tyler*, pp. 17–91. Boston: Kluwer Academic Publishers.

Chapter Three

Educational Assessment
and National Values

I'm an American. I was born to be tested.

> —Anonymous graduate-school applicant,
> quoted by F. Allan Hanson, 2000 (p. 67)

In the preceding chapters, we have seen how both scientific and technological aims have driven the history of assessment in the United States. These aims correspond to what Lee J. Cronbach (1916–2001) identified as the two essential uses of tests: to describe and to make decisions (1971). Such a duality also implies two ways of evaluating the worth and success of testing.

If the goal of testing is description and discovery—to observe and analyze what students have learned, how they think, or what they can do—then the criteria are those of science. We ask, "Is it accurate?" and "Is it true?"

However, if the goal of testing is to make decisions, solve a practical problem, or advance a policy agenda, then the criteria are those of technology. We ask not only "How well does it work?" but also "How well does it serve society?"

Answers to these questions lie beyond the testing procedures themselves, in the society that creates them and that defines truth and utility. In this chapter we will explore how testing is inseparable from its cultural context: our nation's value system, ideals, and intellectual currents. Thus the ways in which our educational system assesses learning reveal something about us.

SCIENCE

A key concept of the eighteenth-century Enlightenment was empiricism, which posits that humans acquire knowledge primarily through the senses, by examining evidence and data (as opposed to constructing knowledge via abstract reasoning). As Eva L. Baker (2001) emphasizes, this and other Enlightenment ideas have influenced not just the political structure of the United States but also the trajectory of education and assessment. We tend to believe that the observable ways in which students perform on tests show us how their minds are working.

The era in which empirical methods came to dominate the sciences and psychology coincided with the emergence of educational measurement as a discipline. After World War I, "logical empiricism" (also known as logical positivism) became influential. Logical empiricists believed that scientific inquiry involved evaluating a given theory or hypothesis against evidence derived from observation or experimentation. They assumed that natural phenomena are governed by coherent laws, and new theories must be logically consistent with established theories. Focusing solely on theory and evidence, logical empiricists were unconcerned with the social dimensions of scientific activity (Messick, 1989; Longino, 2006).

Logical empiricism and Quine's more pragmatic idea of theory as a "complex web of belief," subject to revision through new evidence, played a role in shaping mid-century ideas about how one could know what students have learned. A theoretical framework, such as one about the nature of reading skills, would allow psychometricians to collect evidence about examinees and objectively measure their proficiency.

As Berlak (1992a) points out, the idea of "objective measurement" assumes consensus can be reached about the framework and about what constitutes suitable evidence: "For example, a standardized reading test purportedly indicates a person's ability to read in the real world, not just in the testing situation, and 'ability to read,' it is assumed, has a more or less universally understood and accepted meaning" (p. 13). Using impersonal, mechanically scored tests, with students' performance reported in terms of numbers, has only served to further the notion that objective, neutral observation is possible (Porter, 1996).

Yet from the 1950s onward, some thinkers began to reexamine the empirical, quantitative principles on which science and educational measurement have long been based—that is, the very standards by which we judge accuracy and truth. Since then, we have become more aware that "science" itself is a matter of time and place. We must wrestle with such questions as: Is scientific objectivity possible or even desirable? Can mental attributes be quantified? Should they be quantified? How do observation and measurement affect, not just reflect, the person being observed?

Questioning the Idea of Scientific Objectivity

The first of those questions was raised by philosopher Karl Popper (1902–1994), who proposed that strictly objective observation of facts is not possible.

Because all observations are "theory laden," they are inevitably influenced by one's initial hypotheses and "are as much a function of purely subjective factors (interests, expectations, wishes, etc.) as they are a function of what is objectively real" (Thornton, 2006, Section 4, ¶ 1).

Thus, if an educational test is based on a theoretical framework or hypothesis about proficiency in some academic area, the emphasis would be on how the theory influences the observations in particular directions.

As a modest example, two different end-of-course tests for a class in U.S. history could embody different models of proficiency by privileging either recall or critical analysis of the material. A test that used essay tasks would imply that proficiency includes the ability to organize and communicate relevant facts and ideas coherently. Even setting a passing score would imply a theory about what constitutes "adequate" mastery of the material. Thus, the kinds of evidence collected and the interpretations of that evidence—the test scores—would all depend on a particular theoretical framework.

Postmodern thinkers took Popper's insight about the limits of objectivity much further by emphasizing the extent to which science and knowledge are socially and culturally determined and therefore relativistic rather than absolute. Moreover, although the philosopher of science Thomas Kuhn (1922–1996) did not claim that science was essentially a sociopolitical enterprise, he did open the door to this line of thought by rejecting logical empiricism and emphasizing the importance of perception.

Kuhn argued that science does not advance in a linear manner through discovery of additional laws about natural phenomena that are logically consistent with the known laws. Instead, science unfolds by means of occasional "revolutions." Scientists create an entirely new framework of assumptions, values, methods, and language when the existing one no longer provides satisfactory explanations of phenomena (Bird, 2008).

Such challenges to empiricism and the postmodern emphasis on the cultural dimensions of science led to recognizing that

> [e]ducational assessment needs to be seen as a social, as much as a scientific, activity and hence one that is deeply embued with the bias and subjectivity inherent in any human interaction. . . . We need too to recognize assessment as a social product, in which the values and traditions of particular cultures and the interests of specific groups within them combine to produce particular definitions of quality or merit. (Broadfoot, 2000, pp. xi, xii)

From this perspective, Berlak (1992b) views assessment less as a traditional scientific methodology than as a particular way of talking about or describing what students have learned and can do. Among other things, using tests whose results are expressed quantitatively leads to talking about achievement in terms of numbers, whereas using tests that describe performance in terms of characteristics and traits leads to talking about achievement qualitatively.

Such thinking clearly had an effect on testing trends from the 1980s onward. A current—even a torrent—of dissatisfaction with objective-style measurement spurred interest in allowing students to construct their own responses and in reporting scores as verbally expressed performance labels or proficiency levels.

Scientific Realism and the Legacy of Relativism

However, with another swing of the pendulum came a retreat from relativism back toward the characteristic empirical stance of the United States. Recent "commonsense realism" views scientific inquiry as a process of using systematic methods to improve both observations and interpretations of those observations. Scientific realists are more optimistic than are relativists about our ability to discover what is really happening and describe it accurately: "Subject to a recognition that scientific methods are fallible and that most scientific knowledge is approximate, we are justified in accepting the most secure findings of scientists at face value" (Boyd, 2002, ¶ 1).

The late-1900s model of "evidence-based medicine," which assumes that claims for the efficacy of a treatment or practice can be empirically supported or refuted, has influenced education as well as other disciplines. (Once again, as in the early twentieth century, medical metaphors offer legitimacy.) Within U.S. educational policy, there has been a shift away from postmodern, qualitative forms of inquiry (interviews, oral histories, collections of artifacts, etc.), toward the use of "scientifically based research," with an emphasis on gathering concrete evidence and conducting systematic experiments, usually including quantitative assessment procedures (St. Pierre, 2006).

This approach is articulated in two publications from the National Research Council: *Scientific Research in Education* (NRC, 2002b) and *Advancing Scientific Research in Education* (NRC, 2004a). The authors of the former report call attention to new possibilities for scientific research, thanks to innovations in observational methods, data analysis, and computer capabilities, and they propose a set of principles for scientific inquiry to be applied to educational research. One can see the concept of empirically based learning progressions as a logical development.[1]

The premise of scientific inquiry in education also underlay the Education Sciences Reform Act of 2002 (Pub. L. No. 107-279), which established the Institute of Education Sciences (IES) within the Department of Education. This legislation defined (too narrowly, according to the authors of the NRC's *Scientific Research in Education* report [2002b]) the "scientifically based" research and educational evaluation that the IES was intended to promote. According to the act, researchers must "apply rigorous, systematic, and objective methodology to obtain reliable and valid knowledge relevant to education activities and programs" (§102, 18 A)—just like that advocated in the early 1900s.[2]

Such research has begun to explore educational programs, policies, and practices, including testing, and has sometimes produced disconcerting results. As in medicine, experimentation is complicated by the fact that the subjects are humans.[3]

Yet even those who approve of renewed emphasis on empirical methods caution that research and assessment need to be balanced with teachers' professional wisdom so that decisions will consider "the local context and culture" of the particular schools affected (Trybus, 2007, p. 8). In fact, argues Newman (2008), conducting multiple experiments on the district level may yield information that is more nuanced, more immediately relevant, and more robust than the results of a single, nationwide study.

Today, then, a scientific approach to educational assessment has a somewhat different meaning than it did in the early twentieth century, with the legacy of relativism curbing overconfidence about objectivity and empirical inquiry. Although the authors of *Knowing What Students Know* (2001) advocate careful and systematic observation, they caution:

> What a student knows and what one observes a student doing are not the same thing. The two can be connected only through a chain of inference, which involves reasoning from what one knows and observes to form explanations, conclusions, or predictions. . . . Assessment users always reason in the presence of uncertainty; as a result, the information produced by an assessment is typically incomplete, inconclusive, and amenable to more than one explanation. (NRC, 2001, p. 42)

The weight of history also falls on attempts to connect new findings in neuroscience with educational practices and assessment of mental attributes. Even such an advocate as Willis (2008), who believes that the physical neuroscience of learning can contribute to effective curricula and teaching strategies, reminds her readers about erroneous "brain-learning myths" of the past. She stresses the need for "hard evidence" supporting such approaches as using neuroimaging for diagnosis of learning problems.

Given the checkered history of objectivity, we seem to recognize today that when we assess learning, it is not a simple matter to decide what is accurate and true. This awareness accounts in part for a vein of public skepticism about tests and the information they produce.

Questioning Quantification of the Mind

A well-known definition of measurement is "the assignment of numerals to objects or events according to rules" (Stevens, 1946, p. 677).[4] Thus the endeavor to measure mental attributes and the effects of education scientifically has meant trying to describe skills and knowledge in terms of numbers assigned by rules. Several measurement models exist for representing psychological phenomena, each of which has different implications about the reality and nature of these phenomena, but all the models rely on statistical methods and mathematics to—in essence—help the mind understand itself.[5]

Nowhere has the quantification of learning processes been pursued more eagerly than in the United States. Baker (2001) places it in the context of "the American belief in the superiority of quantitative over less-standardized information and the complementary view that numbers are inherently more trustworthy" (p. 5). As an example, she cites a California poll in which a majority of parents preferred using standardized tests rather than teachers' evaluations to determine student promotion to the next grade.

The emphasis on numbers and on educational products has made it possible to view achievement as an entity that can be measured to make "presumably objective and unbiased quantitative statements about how little or how much an individual, school, state or local educational authority possesses of this commodity compared to others" (Berlak, 2000, p. 190). Quantitative results are, of course, far more convenient than qualitative ones for the purposes of classification and comparison.

Yet theorists such as Ebel (1961/1996) have questioned the belief that human characteristics such as intellectual skills exist as a quantity to be measured, independent of the measurement procedures. Michell (1999) further asks whether, even "if quantity is present in every situation . . . measurement is required of all the sciences" and, in particular, whether it is appropriate for the field of psychology and mental attributes (p. 3). Quantitative measurements of intellectual attributes can be misleading: for example, when two examinees can earn the same total score by correctly answering different questions within the test, so that the measured attributes may have little overlap.

Most important, argues Michell, if the structural features of mental processes such as learning and understanding are not themselves essentially quantitative in nature, then they cannot be fully represented by numbers. Thus the very notion of psychometrics comes into question.

Pursuing this line of thought, Garrison (2004) criticizes the assumption that "the mind or a purported function of mind is a property capable of gradation. [But] there are many properties that do not permit gradation—such as *Pilsner, feline, wooden,* and *human.* In other words, the psychometric dictum of E. L. Thorndike that if something exists, it must exist in some amount, is false" (p. 65).

From an ethical standpoint, he further charges that even if it seems more justifiable to measure amounts of learning than to measure amounts of intelligence, such quantification is still morally flawed because it focuses on ranking people, thereby designating degrees of human worth.

These questions are important ones to consider as education policy embraces a "data-driven culture." It may serve the quintessential American goal of being more efficient, more productive—but it is necessarily reductive as well. Data reveal some truths and conceal others. In the end, quantification of learning is a convenient fiction.

Recognizing the Observer Effect

Compounding doubts about objectivity and numerical precision is the *observer effect*. The act of observing may cause changes in whatever is being observed: "The very *what* of what is being measured can be affected by the very *how* by which it is measured" (Bracey, 1995, p. 95). A familiar example is when teachers and students significantly adapt their instruction or learning to prepare for a test's anticipated content.

The result of such processes is, says anthropologist F. Allan Hanson (2000), that:

> [i]n a very real sense, tests have invented all of us. They play an important role in determining what opportunities are offered to or withheld from us, they mould the expectations and evaluations that others form of us (and we form of them), and they heavily influence our assessments of our own abilities and worth. Therefore, although testing is usually considered to be a means of measuring qualities that are already present in a person, in actuality tests often *produce* the characteristics they purport to measure. The individual in contemporary society is not so much described by tests as constructed by them. (pp. 67–68)

In fact, from Hanson's perspective, this result is exactly the point of using test scores: they provide a concrete, actionable means of representing something that is complex and ambiguous. In particular, to the extent that testing is used to predict future behavior or accomplishment, it is "an instrument of social efficiency" (pp. 69–70). Retrospective assessment also enhances efficiency, by reframing problems in such a way that social policies presumably could address them. Creating a statistical category of students failing to meet prescribed standards for academic proficiency turns the problem into a matter that society must fix rather than "an unfortunate or reprehensible condition of individual persons" (Porter, 1996, p. 37).

Even the act of taking a test may be affected by what the examinee thinks the observer is trying to observe. For example, when a test is described as measuring innate ability rather than acquired skills, an examinee's performance on the test may be adversely affected by the activation of negative stereotypes about the abilities of a group with which the examinee identifies.

Steele and Aronson (1995) inferred this phenomenon of *stereotype threat* from experiments, including one in which African American students scored lower on a verbal skills test when it was described as measuring innate ability than when it was described as a tool for observing how students solve problems. (See chapter 7 for more on this subject.)

It is not surprising, then, to find resistance against these observer effects, which seem to depersonalize examinees. Americans pride themselves on their individuality as much as on their efficiency and scientific prowess. For example, a billboard posted by a Pennsylvania organization concerned with public schools proclaimed: "Your child is more than a test score."

Over time, the above critiques of empiricism, objectivity, quantification, and observational effects have all become part of the dialogue about educational assessment and part of "a challenge to the very belief in the power of science itself to lead to social progress" (Broadfoot, 2000, p. xi). Adherents of what I call the "postmeasurement" movement, such as Shepard (2000) and Moss et al. (2005), question the adequacy and effects of psychometric approaches to assessing learning, and they call for pursuing qualitative approaches that emphasize social and cultural contexts of learning. They seek to redefine what accurate, truthful information from assessment would mean. A consortium of New York State public schools translated these goals into performance-oriented assessment practices (see Tashlik, 2010).

Whatever side one takes on the debate, it is clear that designing and scoring tests, as well as interpreting and using scores, involve selection, evaluation, and judgment; that numerical data imperfectly represents cognitive processes or attributes; and that testing can shape, rather than just mirror, the intellectual development of students.

Still, perceiving these complexities does not seem to dim the characteristic American confidence, because optimism that defies constraints is part of our national character. Somehow, we can have it all: assessment that is rich, varied, socially situated, supportive of learning—and is a model of empirical rigor.

TECHNOLOGY

In the United States, assessment is not just left to the teachers and scholars investigating the effects of education (as they might prefer). It is also deployed by policy makers and organizations as a technology for achieving that most important of American goals, progress.

Countless testing programs have been conceived to promote individual, institutional, or societal progress according to the notions of the day. When progress is defined as educational opportunity and educational reform, then how well testing works is judged accordingly.

Opportunity for Individuals

"The idea of opportunity for everyone is woven deeply into the fabric of the United States," but, Lemann (1999) suggests, educational opportunity can be construed in different ways, each implying a different type of testing (p. 344). He distinguishes assessment used for competitive selection (as in school tracking or admissions processes) from assessment used for expanding universal access to education (as in the GED program for veterans). In Lemann's view, the former type of assessment emphasizes individual advancement and the latter progress of society as a whole.

However, the picture is more complicated. For example, how well the GED program serves to promote societal progress is a matter of debate. One study suggests that for high school dropouts who earn a GED, as compared to those who do not, the benefits include somewhat higher incomes, better health, and greater political and social involvement (Song & Hsu, 2008). Another study finds that the economic benefits are minimal, that few recipients complete college, and that the availability of the GED as an alternative actually encourages some students to leave high school without graduating (Heckman, Humphries, & Mader, 2010). Should the program be discontinued, or can it be modified to address the perceived problems?

Moreover, from the perspective of a capitalist system, testing intended to promote individual advancement is not the opposite of testing intended to promote societal progress, because individual opportunity is also considered a means of promoting general social mobility and economic progress. As Lemann himself argues, much of the initial motivation for expanding college-admissions testing in the late 1930s and after World War II was to identify those students who would be best able to lead the country and whose success would therefore serve the national interests.

Yet it has been difficult to identify sound measurement approaches that ensure equal outcomes for individuals and groups regardless of background. Fullinwider and Lichtenberg (2004) conclude that "from an equity point of view—one that aims to close the achievement gap between white and affluent students on the one hand and minority and low-income students on the other," most types of measures, including grade point averages, NAEP, and admissions tests, reproduce the same group disparities (pp. 11, 111–12). Even a neurostudy of otherwise normal nine- and ten-year-olds revealed a tendency for children from low socioeconomic backgrounds to have impaired functioning of the prefrontal cortex—the "executive" area of the brain, involved in complex cognition (Kishiyama, Boyce, Jimenez, Perry, & Knight, 2009).

Ways of addressing differential performance on achievement tests may focus on the assessment procedures themselves, or on strategies beyond the testing procedures, including educational interventions and mentoring. (See chapter 7 for more on this subject.)

Despite these problems, testing in the United States—as compared to testing in many other countries—is actually less likely to close off opportunities permanently or to determine an individual's economic fate. This fact in itself speaks to national values. (Could one say that the test of a society is how it tests its students?) Even the states that require students to pass exit exams for a high school diploma offer multiple opportunities for retaking the test and other arrangements for students who do not pass.

Notably, the United States has no federally controlled test for entry into higher education. In fact, for various reasons (sometimes as a matter of their own competitive advantage), hundreds of four-year colleges and most community colleges require no admissions tests. The abundance of institutions of higher learning in itself reflects national priorities.

That relative flexibility contrasts with the situation in such countries as Japan, where, upon leaving junior high school, students take exams that lead to a vocational or academic track, thereby significantly shaping their economic prospects. Then, in contrast to U.S. practices, Japanese students' scores on national entrance examinations are generally used as the sole criterion for university admissions (National Institute on Student Achievement, Curriculum, and Assessment, 1998).

Basing access to higher education entirely on test scores is common in other parts of Asia, in Europe, and around the world. For example, the government of South Africa requires twelfth-grade students to take "matric examinations" determining first whether they will graduate and then whether they can attend college. Only the relatively few who do well on the second, more difficult set of tests can attend universities (Wines, 2007).

Yet even in countries exerting such control over access to education, testing still can be an improvement on traditional patronage and nepotism. Rewarding merit is "the dominant agenda of examinations and test agencies around the world who even today continue what is often a heroic struggle to provide equitable and defensible accreditation and selection mechanisms" (Broadfoot, 2000, p. ix).

A poignant historical example of the interlinking of assessment, opportunity, and national values occurred in 1977, when the Chinese government revived the national university entrance examinations that had been discontinued during the Cultural Revolution. For "a whole generation consigned to the countryside, it was the first chance to escape what seemed like a life sentence of tedium and hardship" (Lague, 2008, p. 4). In that year, fewer than 5 percent of examinees were granted admission to universities, but by 2007 more than half of all examinees were admitted, a dramatic change that reflected changes in Chinese national priorities as well.

Defining opportunity in terms of access to higher education is not, however, the entire story. In the United States, many students enter college insufficiently prepared, a possible factor in dropout rates. According to one report, more than a third of all college students take remedial courses— even though most of these students had high school GPAs of at least 3.0 (Strong American Schools, 2008, pp. 5, 9).

An example of an attempt to address this situation is the California Early Assessment Program (EAP), which offers voluntary testing to identify eleventh-grade students needing intervention in order to develop the skills necessary for entering college. More important, it provides additional preparation for those students and training for their teachers. So far, it appears that a student's participating in EAP reduces the probability of needing remedial courses in college and costs both the state and the student less than college-level remediation would (Howell, Kurlaender, & Grodsky, 2009).

Thus the relationship of testing to individual opportunity and social mobility remains potentially promising, if often ambiguous in practice. However, one of the best ways that governments and societies can demonstrate good intentions is by providing students with the resources they need before they take tests that will affect their futures.

Opportunity and Educational Reform

From any perspective, improving the quality of public education is fundamentally a matter of improving opportunity. In recent decades, such a goal is the explicit purpose of standards-based *accountability assessment*, whether it involves holding students themselves accountable (as in high school exit exams) or holding teachers and schools accountable for the students' performance.

Advocates see this kind of testing as offering the potential for aligning learning and instruction, providing incentives for changing ineffective practices, and identifying student needs (Darling-Hammond, 2006).[6] Some advocates even point to the research demonstrating malleability of the brain and potential for neuronal growth as support for the position that expecting all students to meet prescribed academic standards is reasonable and fair (Wang, Beckett, & Brown, 2006, p. 312).

Furthermore, from a purely pragmatic standpoint, standards-based accountability assessment can provide legal leverage. In the past couple of decades, plaintiffs challenging state governments have won most of the cases having to do with "adequacy claims"; that is, that if the state sets academic standards, then schools must have the resources to provide an education enabling students to meet those standards. Such cases have led states to define what constitutes an "adequate" education, with funding outcomes based on estimates of what meeting these criteria would cost in a given district (Rebell, 2008). Groups such as students with learning disabilities can obtain more resources by these means.

At the same time, there are also serious arguments against accountability testing, especially when the purpose is to hold teachers and schools accountable. From a technical standpoint, group test scores contain multiple sources of error and unreliability that can affect their meaning (Kane, 2010). When the tests results have little effect on the students themselves, the results may be less accurate. The available psychometric methods for identifying the contribution of teachers and schools to student achievement are limited and hotly debated (see chapter 8). And, as vividly illustrated in the problems that beset New York State's tests, the pressures of accountability can lead to practices that undermine the value and credibility of the test information (see Medina, 2010).

In addition to pointing out "issues related to intellectual freedom, student diversity, local autonomy, and teacher empowerment," opponents criticize the types of tests used, a disproportionate focus on lower-performing students, and the ultimate efficacy of the approach, especially when many of the underlying problems may be beyond the reach of the educational system (Wang et al., 2006, pp. 312–13; Pulliam, 1991; Baker, 2007; Resnick, 2006). Out-of-school factors such as ill health compounded by lack of medical care, nutritional deprivation, family stresses, and dangerous neighborhoods lie unaddressed when the focus is placed on school accountability (Berliner, 2009).

Within the educational system itself, shifting the blame for any lack of progress to the schools, teachers, or students themselves can be a way of avoiding more costly reforms. But relying on testing alone for reform only exacerbates the problem of struggling students' having unequal access to qualified teachers (Haertel & Herman, 2005; Darling-Hammond, 2006).

To negotiate these divergent perspectives, educators and assessment experts have suggested approaches intended to make accountability feasible while avoiding some negative consequences. These include using multiple, rather than single, measures of achievement (including such data as retention and graduation rates, as well as subsequent performance in college); focusing on "opportunity to learn" instead of, or in addition to, outcomes (i.e., assessing whether conditions in each classroom promote opportunity for all students to learn); implementing a greater amount of performance and formative assessment; utilizing technology for learning and assessment; and limiting the number of standards to be assessed (Baker, 2007).

Any relationship between testing and reform is complex and conditional. Testing by itself cannot accomplish change, but it can play a role. For example, in reading the case studies of exemplary high schools compiled by Ferguson, Hackman, Hanna, and Ballantine (2010), one finds that a well-regarded state accountability test, college admissions tests, and AP programs served in various ways to motivate and monitor the schools' own initiatives for improving instruction and learning.

In the end, policies that involve accountability testing have a burden of proof. First, as W. James Popham (2007) argues, any tests used in the process of evaluating teachers or schools must be demonstrated to be "instructionally sensitive"—that is, there must be a meaningful relationship between test scores and effectiveness of instruction. Second, any claims about the effects of such policies need to be investigated empirically rather than left as matters of belief.

POWER

Whether used in selection processes, accountability, or other ways that affect lives, the technology of assessment exercises power. More subtle are the ways in which testing may be employed to reinforce societal values and to define knowledge. Here the question is how well these uses of testing serve to benefit society.

Reinforcing Societal Values

Much of the thinking about how assessment reinforces values and norms is indebted to historian and philosopher Michel Foucault (1926–1984). Foucault described assessment—educational, medical, or other—as a mechanism of control. An institution wields power by observing what an examinee does, then evaluating the examinee according to prescribed norms or standards, and ultimately forcing the examinee to adopt a course of study or treatment (Gutting, 2003, under 3.3, ¶ 2–4).

Comparing the power of testing to that of atomic energy, Bloom (1968) voiced a similar view:

> To control the matriculation system of a country is to control its educational system, to develop tests which are widely used for selection and prediction purposes is to determine which human qualities are prized and which are neglected, to develop instruments which are used to classify and describe human beings is to alter human beings and to affect a person's view of himself. (pp. 1–2)

Some may see manifestation of this power as helpful in promoting desired social goals, such as literacy, scientific progress, and artistic achievement. Others may see it as a more insidious form of social control, as testing inculcates norms and standards into examinees so that they become the means by which one judges oneself: "Grades in school, scores on standardized examinations, and the bottom line on an accounting sheet cannot work effectively unless their validity, or at least reasonableness, is accepted by the people whose accomplishments or worth they purport to measure" (Porter, 1996, p. 45).

Thus, assessment is not simply a top-down form of control wielded by those who make or use tests. Instead, by subscribing to its implied values, those who are subject to assessment become assessors themselves. This phenomenon could be seen as the ultimate coercion—or as an opportunity for bottom-up empowerment.

Defining and Controlling Knowledge

In addition to instilling social norms and shaping personal identity, tests (just like textbooks and curricular standards) can serve to define and control knowledge. According to Delandshere (2001), this process can be traced back to the replacement of oral disputations by written exams that began to narrow the range of knowledge tested and make it more static and monolithic, even before the era of multiple-choice tests. Insofar as the test-development process requires that dissenters defer to the majority opinion, and the tests then require that examinees respond in certain ways, an assessment will enshrine "mandated knowledge that requires compliance" (p. 128).

It is clear that creating a test (or standards on which the test is based) does mean privileging certain skills and knowledge, sometimes certain political views. This latter point was dramatically illustrated in the controversy over conservative officials' reshaping of Texas standards for social studies (see Stutz, 2010). Another example can be seen in a test publisher's cautious guideline, reflecting political debates taking place at state levels: "The topic of evolution, with associated topics of natural selection, fossils, geologic ages . . . dinosaurs, and similarities between people and primates, should not appear in K–12 testing unless required by specific content standards" (ETS, 2009a, pp. 42–43).

Yet natural selection is an apt metaphor, even if Frederiksen and Collins (1990) actually had organizational theory in mind when they asserted that educational systems adapt themselves to the characteristics of the tests used within them. Some critics of current-day tests believe that testing actually impedes progress, insofar as it may shape brain development by privileging traditional capacities such as analysis and procedure and deemphasizing innovation and collaboration (Rae-Dupree, 2008). Hillocks (2002) charges that writing tests with decontextualized essay topics and scoring criteria reinforce the teaching of "vacuous" thinking and formulaic composition.

On the other hand, tests may preserve knowledge essential to cultural literacy and curricula that some students and teachers value; for example, an AP test in advanced Latin literature helped support otherwise endangered courses until it was discontinued (Brinley, 2009). Recent emphasis on assessing computer and Internet skills, even testing them as part of high school graduation requirements, has enhanced the academic status of these new competencies.

In these and other ways, tests may well teach students what is considered important, accurate, or correct. Then, just as in the biological realm, the traits associated with success are the ones that are perpetuated, in this case certain types of knowledge and skills. Again, the power of testing may be a good or a bad thing—depending.

The Implications of Power

Insofar as the assessment enterprise is an exercise of power, supported by the explicit or tacit consent of society, it is akin to a political process. With that process come analogous responsibilities. Most people would probably agree that elected officials should uphold the Constitution and other laws, heed the lessons of the past, serve the best interests of their constituents, be held accountable for their actions, and aspire to promote the ideals of our nation—honesty, opportunity, fairness, progress. And all of these goals they must accomplish within budgetary and time constraints. The same could be said for the makers and users of educational tests.

When we hold up the mirror of our nation's assessment practices, we want to see our democracy reflected there. In a democracy, openness and information about the legislative process are key to promoting goals outlined above. So too should testing be as transparent as possible, with intelligible information

---

Chapter III: Key Points

- The rise of educational testing in the United States and traditional criteria for accuracy and truth of test results reflected the idea that assessment of student learning is a form of scientific measurement. They also reflected the influence of logical empiricism, which assumed that testing a theory about a phenomenon against actual observations would allow one to confirm or refute the theory and reach objective conclusions about the phenomenon.
- In the latter part of the 1900s, skepticism arose about the possibility of objective, neutral observation. Postmodern, relativist thinkers called attention to the cultural bases of scientific methods, theories, and knowledge. They questioned the appropriateness of quantifying mental attributes and pointed out the existence of an "observer effect" such that the act of testing changes the examinee. Testing thus changes what is being measured.
- Recently, there has been a movement back toward a realist stance that acknowledges the influence of culture and subjectivity but essentially accepts traditional scientific methodology. Still, there are many experts who call for more qualitative, contextual kinds of assessment—that are nonetheless acceptable from the standpoint of empirical scrutiny.
- How to employ testing as a tool for progress is a matter of debate. Can testing promote equitable selection processes and individual opportunity; can it help bring about educational reform? Claims about efficacy should be investigated empirically.
- Testing is a technology that can also be used to reinforce societal values and norms, shape personal identity, and both define and control knowledge. Thus, it is about who we are and who we want to be. Wielding such power, the makers and users of tests have obligations to examinees and to society and should make testing programs as transparent as possible.

---

made available to the public. It is, perhaps, significant that the United States has pioneered the use of professional guidelines for testing, with detailed specifications for the data and documentation that testing programs should provide.

But like the political process, the assessment process might benefit from more active participation by stakeholders. As we will see in the next chapter, such collaboration—even if it involves contention—could build on diverse types of influence and insight that different constituencies already possess.

NOTES

1. These principles (NRC, 2002a, pp. 3–5) are:

   - Pose significant questions that can be investigated empirically.
   - Link research to relevant theory.
   - Use methods that permit direct investigation of the question.
   - Provide a coherent and explicit chain of reasoning.
   - Replicate and generalize across studies.
   - Disclose research to encourage professional scrutiny and critique.

In fact, this approach also describes validation research for tests (see chapter 5).

2. Some connections between the early twentieth and early twenty-first century are striking. The 2002 ESRA emphasizes: conducting "random-assignment experiments," using methods that provide reliable data, being cautious about inferring causal relationships, and "ensuring that studies and methods are presented in sufficient detail and clarity to allow for replication" (§102, 18 B).

The same kinds of principles are used in a 1918 proposal by George Melcher to bring "empiricism and science" to the measurement of achievement via a "control experiment." He describes a careful protocol for studying the effectiveness of an instructional method or other factor and offers similar cautions about making inferences as well as advice about keeping records and repeating the experiment (pp. 139, 141–42).

3. However, there has been concern over null results: when studies indicate that a particular instructional method, type of intervention, school policy, etc., has little or no discernible effect. Such outcomes have led to questions about the value of empirical studies, but Gersten (2009) reaffirms their worth. On the one hand, because the criteria for demonstrating efficacy have become more stringent, any positive findings are more likely to be correct; on the other hand, it is important to identify and rethink educational strategies that do not actually benefit students.

4. Compare with this definition from Lindquist a few years later (1951): "An educational achievement test may be described as a device or procedure for assigning numerals (measures) to the individuals in a given group indicative of the various degrees to which an educational objective or set of objectives has been realized by those individuals" (p. 142).

5. For comparisons of measurement models in the discipline of psychology, see Borsboom (2005). To put it simply, classical test theory focuses on observed test performance rather than the underlying cause(s) of that performance; latent variable theory (also known as item response theory) comes closer to the scientific-realist stance of asserting that there is an actual psychological attribute underlying test performance; and representational or fundamental measurement theory depicts relationships among empirical observations without assuming anything about the causes. Educational testing commonly employs the first two models, which are discussed in chapter 6; the third model provides insights into issues related to measurement scales.

6. As Haertel and Herman (2005) explain:

> Testing is usually just one part of a more comprehensive reform strategy. For example, assessments might be expected to identify students requiring remedial assistance, focus attention on teachers whose students are doing especially well or poorly, identify schools where additional resources are needed, or draw attention to achievement disparities among demographic groups. (p. 3)

SELECTED READINGS

Baker, E. L. (2001). Testing and assessment: A progress report. *Educational Assessment, 7*(1), 1–12.

Delandshere, G. (2001). Implicit theories, unexamined assumptions and the status quo of educational assessment. *Assessment in Education: Principles, Policy, and Practice, 8*(2), 113–33.

Filer, A. (Ed.). (2000). *Educational assessment and testing: Social practice and social product.* London: Routledge Falmer.

Fullinwider, R. K., and Lichtenberg, J. (2004). *Leveling the playing field: Justice, politics, and college admissions.* Lanham, MD: Rowman & Littlefield Publishers, Inc.

National Research Council (NRC). (2002b). *Scientific research in education.* Committee on Scientific Principles for Education Research. R. J. Shavelson & L. Towne (Eds.). Center for Education. Division of Behavioral and Social Sciences and Education. Washington, DC: National Academy Press.

Stevens, S. S. (1946). On the theory of scales of measurement. *Science, 103*(2684), 677–80.

Wang, L., Beckett, G. H., and Brown, L. (2006). Controversies of standardized assessment in school accountability reform: A critical synthesis of multidisciplinary research evidence. *Applied Measurement in Education, 19*, 305–28.

Chapter Four

Perspectives and Directives

*Educational and psychological testing and assessment involve and sig-
nificantly affect individuals, institutions, and society as a whole. . . . The
interests of the various parties involved in the testing process are usually,
but not always, congruent.*

—AERA et al., 1999 (p. 1)

How should educational tests be designed and used? Is there a set of laws,
rules, or guidelines? And if so, whose code is it and how is it enforced?

In searching for rules, we might first come across some relevant federal
statutes, but these cover only certain aspects of certain types of tests. We
would have to go elsewhere to find a document similar to a U.S. Constitution
for testing: the *Standards for Educational and Psychological Testing* (AERA
et al., 1999).

The *Standards* resembles the Constitution insofar as it articulates generally
accepted principles that practitioners are supposed to interpret and apply to
specific cases. However, in contrast to the Constitution, this set of prescrip-
tive statements dates back only a half century; it is periodically revised and
updated to reflect new developments in psychometrics; and it is not well
known to the public. Even though it is consulted in legal cases involving testing, it does not have the status of law or any legal force in its own right. And
because it focuses mainly on large-scale testing, it cannot address all types of
educational or psychological assessment.

Further, the *Standards* represents the consensus of only one constituency:
members of the measurement profession. Other people with their own views
are affected by educational testing and play various roles in shaping policy
and criteria.

The stakeholders span these four categories:

- **Citizens.** They are the general public, that is, people in their capacity as citizens, whether as students, parents, taxpayers, voters, or advocates for a social or political cause. This group also includes nongovernmental organizations.
- **Educators.** They are members of the educational system: faculty and administrators at the K–12, college, or graduate levels. Educators routinely make or use many types of assessments, but testing is not usually their primary focus.
- **Specialists.** They are professionals in the field of educational assessment. Among this group are university professors in the disciplines of educational psychology and measurement, as well as the psychometricians, statisticians, researchers, test developers, and others who work in the test-publishing industry.
- **Regulators.** This group includes persons and organizations with governmental or legal roles: state and federal departments of education, elected representatives and appointed officials, and members of the judiciary system and legal profession.

Of course, these distinctions are not mutually exclusive. Nonetheless, they help identify different perspectives and bases of authority for framing guidelines, laws, and policies.

CITIZENS

Largest of the groups is the citizen constituency, since it is the entire public affected by the nation's educational system. "Citizens" comprise three subcategories or segments: students, individual citizens, and nongovernmental organizations whose missions have some relationship to education. Here the concern is usually focused not on the quality of tests but on how testing affects students.

The first segment—students who take the tests—is obviously the one most directly affected. It is thus ironic that this group is the least likely to try to influence testing policy or recommend guidelines, but it is not surprising, since students tend to be young, transient, and lacking in financial or organizational resources.

Evidence about student views is fragmentary and sparse, although test developers may collect feedback about tasks being administered experimentally. In research literature, there are a few articles about students' views of a particular test or tests in general (e.g., Triplett & Barksdale, 2005).

Efforts to elicit thoughtful input from students would be worth pursuing, especially if students were to learn more about basic principles of assessment. What do students think are fair ways of evaluating their proficiencies and achievements? My own anecdotal queries suggest that older students value clear expectations, tasks that are realistic or intriguing, and a sense of accomplishment from completing the tasks. (In actual testing, though, examinees are more likely to complete multiple-choice items than to complete constructed-response tasks such as essays.)

The second segment of citizen-stakeholders is the public overall, as parents, taxpayers, and so on. Apart from views that individuals publish, opinion polls offer evidence of public sentiment. The questions about testing tend to be very general, but the answers are important because voters have the power to shape educational policies.

Results from these surveys suggest some dissatisfaction but not outright opposition. For example, the Reality Check survey found that respondents are concerned about "too much testing," followed by "teaching to the test" (Pew Research Center, 2007, under "What's Right—and Wrong—with 'No Child,'" ¶ 3). The 2009 Phi Delta Kappa-Gallup Poll also found mixed views about the effects of NCLB, but two-thirds of respondents favored the use of a national, standardized test given annually to track student progress in grades three to eight (Bushaw & McNee, 2009, p. 12).

The third and last segment of the citizen category is the array of nongovernmental organizations whose civic or social missions have some relationship to educational assessment. They may make general policy statements, provide information about testing, conduct research studies, or lobby legislators. (See, for example, Kober, 2002.)[1]

Views that these groups hold about testing usually reflect the debate about whether accountability testing is effective in promoting better instruction and learning. For example, some advocacy groups are opposed to requiring students to pass tests to advance to the next grade or to graduate from high school. Others, such as the American Diploma Network, see such testing as potentially useful in closing achievement gaps by upholding more rigorous standards.[2]

Views are similarly divided about accountability testing at the school level. The FairTest organization considers it harmful because "demanding that disabled and limited English proficient students reach 'proficiency' on standardized tests sets many schools up for failure" (National Center for Fair and Open Testing, 2008, ¶ 6). Yet, as noted in chapter 3, many organizations representing these same students support universal accountability testing (with appropriate accommodations or alternatives) as a means of directing more attention and resources to students who are struggling.[3]

Of particular interest, since it represents a consensus on testing among otherwise widely disparate groups, is the "Joint Organizational Statement on

'No Child Left Behind' Act" that was submitted to Congress in October 2004 and signed by over 100 different civic, social, and educational organizations. While endorsing the general goals of the 2002 legislation, it called for less reliance on standardized tests as the indicators of student and school progress. Rather than rejecting assessment outright, though, the statement called for improving its quality and the ways in which it is used.

Like so much of the public discourse about testing, this statement suggests (inaccurately) that standardized testing is a monolithic entity. Yet it also suggests the possibility of more constructive discussion, in which the question is not only how much, but also what kind of testing and how it fits into the larger context of education.

Public discourse about testing could benefit from being more like public discourse about education in general, which is not solely about how many hours students spend at school but also about such matters as pedagogical approaches (e.g., in reading or math). An example of useful input can be seen in a study that asked potential employers for their views on how undergraduates' learning should be assessed. Researchers queried business executives about important skills for employees and about the types of tests or evaluations of college students that might provide the most useful information to prospective employers.[4]

Members of the public, educators, and test makers could engage in other such dialogues, but raising the general level of "assessment literacy" is a prerequisite. Thus, Popham (2003) suggests ways for measurement specialists to promote such literacy, with an emphasis on proper uses of educational tests. In fact, the final major recommendation of *Knowing What Students Know* (NRC, 2001) is that specialists develop programs in cooperation with the media to improve public understanding about assessment principles, methods, and applications.

Rather than after the fact, though, could this process start much earlier, with teachers and students talking about the meaning and use of assessment? Classroom practice has already taken up such concepts and techniques as rubrics for evaluating student work, peer review, and self-assessment. Increased awareness about assessment criteria and methods could also help students master more general principles of critical inquiry and reasoning. (See chapter 12 in volume 2 for more on this subject.)

EDUCATORS

The lives of educators—teachers, professors, and school or university administrators—are intertwined with assessment. Educators usually study assessment methods and principles in their training; they take licensing and certification tests; they create assessments for their own students; and they may be significantly affected by accountability or admissions testing. To find educators' views, one can look to individual opinions, survey data, textbooks for educators, and professional organizations. The two recurrent, interrelated themes are exerting control over assessment and using assessment in ways that benefit instruction.

The theme of control is, of course, more politicized and contentious. Not only do educators express their individual opinions about this issue in writing, they also do so in actions. A few teachers have even undergone suspension rather than administer state-mandated tests. Perhaps this approach may recur; in 2010, in England, teachers' unions approved a voluntary boycott of the national tests used to rank schools.[5]

Findings in surveys suggest how educators' views of assessment tend to correspond not only with their control over it but also with the extent to which it provides immediate feedback to aid teaching. When Guskey (2007) asked administrators and teachers to rank sources of evidence about student learning according to relative importance and trustworthiness, both groups ranked internally developed assessments (such as student portfolios or teacher-written tests) higher than externally developed district or state tests. (Still, the respondents rated grades assigned by teachers themselves almost as low as external tests.)

A poll of over 40,000 teachers generally echoed these findings. While deeming state and district tests somewhat important in measuring student achievement, the teachers' overwhelming consensus was that students' classroom participation and performance on classroom tests and assignments were better measures. The teachers viewed student engagement and growth over the academic year as the most accurate measures of their own performance (Scholastic/Gates Foundation, 2010).

Textbooks for teacher training offer another glimpse into educators' perspectives. A study of five widely used introductory textbooks on assessment revealed a focus on guidelines for creating classroom assessments; scoring portfolios of student work; and using classroom assessments to "monitor progress, plan instruction, diagnose strengths and weaknesses, and document accountability" (Campbell & Collins, 2007, pp. 9, 15).

This emphasis is congruent with Guskey's findings about educators' preference for internal sources of information about student learning over external assessments. However, it may not adequately address the reality of teachers' experience. Campbell and Collins (2007) found that the textbooks do not uniformly cover interpretation of data from external assessments, and these researchers suggest instituting core content standards for educators' knowledge about assessment. Indeed, both the PARCC (2010) and SBAC (2010) proposals call for professional development programs to foster teachers' assessment literacy.[6]

The other major source of educators' views is professional and institutional organizations. Among these groups' policy statements and guidelines are common positions on the nature and control of assessment.[7]

With regard to the nature of assessment, a recurrent theme is using other measures in addition to test scores to gauge student progress and achievement. For example, the National Science Teachers Association (2001) recommends using diverse ways to assess science learning, including student-directed experiments, portfolios, group and individual interviews, and scenarios offering real-world problems to solve (under "Declarations," bullet 7). Teachers' unions advocate the use of multiple types of nontest data, from absenteeism to parental involvement to level of coursework, to help gauge school progress (NEA, 2008, ¶ 2 & 3).

Strategies proposed by K–12 educators for gaining a measure of control over externally imposed tests range from working with the existing system to reshaping it more fundamentally. Calls for aligning test content with curricula and learning standards, as well as for ensuring that teachers have input into the test-development process, reflect frustration with externally imposed tests (AFT, 2008a). To facilitate such input or to help choose from among available assessments, the National Council of Teachers of Mathematics (2008) offers tools for evaluating tests, via a detailed, report-generating template.

Some organizations go further and explicitly advocate localized control. For example, the National Council of Teachers of English (2004) urges that schools, teachers, parents, and students have autonomy over or input into assessment, with schools and teachers selecting tests, parents helping to set criteria, and students choosing their own writing topics. Not surprising, perhaps, since this same organization formed in the early 1900s as a means of wresting back control of curriculum from the College Entrance Examination Board.

For obvious reasons, educators at the postsecondary level focus less on the politics of assessment. Instead of having to respond to external mandates, organizations representing higher education are (so far) much freer to propose assessment initiatives. For example, the Voluntary System of Accountability Program explores the use of different tests, primarily skills-oriented measures (see Klein, Liu, & Sconing, 2009). The Association of American Colleges and Universities (2007) is investigating whether outcomes of undergraduate education can be measured by using prescribed criteria to evaluate electronic portfolios of student coursework.

A final theme in the position statements and guidelines from educators' organizations is the practical implications of assessing student learning. For example, the National Science Teachers Association (2001) calls for more time for teachers to create assessments, additional professional development opportunities related to assessment, and sufficient funding for aligning curriculum, instruction, and assessment.

Such pragmatic considerations are as important as theoretical criteria in determining the quality of assessment. Educators provide crucial input because they are the only constituency offering a frontline perspective on student learning, and policy makers should take advantage of this resource.

For the designers and developers of external tests, nothing is more helpful in making realistic, workable assessments than to be able to consult the educators whose students would take the test. Teachers can judge the types of tasks, topics, skills, timing, and formats appropriate for their students, as well as describe the kinds of information and feedback from tests that would further learning goals.

SPECIALISTS AND THEIR
PROFESSIONAL GUIDELINES

Although this group might seem the most homogenous of all the four categories, given its professed allegiance to the *Standards*, any two randomly chosen members might have widely different types of expertise. Some specialists work within schools, policy organizations, professional accreditation organizations, or state departments of education. Others work in academe, in disciplines such as educational psychology, educational measurement and statistics, quantitative research methods, or psychometrics. Still others work in the test-publishing industry, specializing in statistical analysis, research, or development areas.

Bringing these dispersed members of the profession together are such organizations as the National Council on Measurement in Education (NCME), the American Educational Research Association (AERA), the American Psychological Association (APA), the Psychometric Society, the National Association of Test Directors, and the Association of Test Publishers (ATP). Some specialist organizations are university-based institutes, such as the National Center for Research on Evaluation, Standards, and Student Testing; the National Board on Educational Testing and Public Policy; and the National Center on Educational Outcomes. (For a list of professional journals, see "Other Resources" at the end of this book.)

Within the professional sector, a recurrent theme is how assessment theory and practice continually unfold together. As specialists seek to translate conceptual frameworks into practice, the realities of actual testing experiences and empirical findings come back to reshape theory. So too do events beyond the realm of measurement.

Educational Measurement—the Book

Of the countless books that have been written by and for specialists, the four editions of *Educational Measurement* are most notable for showing the state of the art at intervals from the mid-twentieth century onward. Sponsored by the American Council on Education (ACE) and the NCME, these reference works represent a semiofficial body of theory, especially given the editors' pedigrees. Not only did E. F. Lindquist edit the first (1951) version, but also Robert L. Thorndike (1910–1990), son of E. L. Thorndike and himself a specialist in assessment of cognitive abilities, edited the second (1971).

In his preface to the 2006 edition, Robert L. Brennan (who then held the E. F. Lindquist Chair of Measurement and Testing at the University of Iowa) comments that a comparison of the various editions "illustrates both the enduring nature of many measurement topics and the evolving nature of the field" (p. xv). Each edition revisits central topics and introduces new ones; for the specialist, it is well worth owning all of the editions.

Still, the most recent version has some striking differences from the first, and not just in the new focus on computer technology. There is increased emphasis on constructed-response and performance assessment—though the need for more research in these areas is urged just as much in 2006 as it was in 1951 (Lane & Stone, 2006, pp. 423–24). Legal and fairness issues, nowhere to be found in the 1951 edition, now receive extensive coverage. Methods for investigating the validity of test scores reflect comprehensive theoretical frameworks. And there is one other difference: the existence of the *Standards* as the Constitution of educational and psychological assessment.

The *Standards*

In 1955, the AERA and the NCME (then called the NCMUE) issued a small beige pamphlet. Despite the publications' comparative weights and sizes, the thirty-six-page *Technical Recommendations for Achievement Tests* and its successors would prove as influential as its more imposing cousin, *Educational Measurement*. For fifty years, says Harris (2006), successive versions of the *Standards* have served and helped shape "two demanding and sometimes competing entities—the profession of educational and psychological measurement and the industry of test publishing" (p. 43). In other words, the *Standards* is the bridge from the theoreticians to the practitioners.[8]

In creating a companion document for the American Psychological Association's *Technical Recommendations for Psychological Tests and Diagnostic Techniques* (APA, 1954), the committee members who put together the 1955 *Technical Recommendations* recognized the significance of their new venture.

While acknowledging the guidance that textbooks on educational measurement had hitherto provided, they noted that to date there was "no statement by a professional body which could be regarded as a *standard* of approved practice for the guidance of both users and producers of tests" (p. 5).

Intended as a guide for large-scale and published tests, the *Technical Recommendations* articulated usable principles for validity, reliability, test administration, test scoring, and use of test scores. It included some examples of good and bad practices, but recommendations remained general to avoid discouraging innovation. It also specified essential kinds of explanations and information that should accompany a test.

In the next version (APA, AERA, & NCME, 1966) the psychological and educational standards merged, but each decade that the guidelines were updated and augmented, artifacts of the *Technical Recommendations* persisted. The *Standards* series thus resembles a palimpsest of continuity and change in testing.

The six chapters in part 1 of the most recent (1999) *Standards* correspond almost directly to the six original sections in the 1955 version, albeit in a different sequence. And, just as the first pamphlets emphasized the importance of documentation, so too does the 1999 *Standards*, although now such supporting documents are expanded beyond test manuals to include "technical manuals, users' guides, specimen sets, examination kits, directions for test administrators and scorers, or preview materials for test takers" (pp. 4, 64).

At the same time, this palimpsest has undergone some scraping away, and new text has been overlaid on the original substrate. One noticeable change over time has been in the comments that flesh out each standard. In the 1955 and 1966 versions, the comments often included references to actual tests as illustrations of good or bad practice; by the 1974 version, such examples no longer included names, and today, any examples tend to be entirely hypothetical.

A second change has been in the hierarchical categorization of standards. Until 1985, standards were designated as Essential, Very Desirable, and Desirable; in 1985, they were categorized as Primary, Secondary, and Conditional; and in 1999, categorization ceased, because, according to the editors of the 1999 version, it could result in neglect of standards not designated as primary.

The third and most obvious change, though, has been in the expansion in scope and coverage by the *Standards*, now a 194-page book. Material descended from the 1955 *Technical Recommendations* forms only one of the main parts. Part 2 is devoted to fairness and part 3 to the use of testing in psychology, education, employment, credentialing, program evaluation, and public policy. Noteworthy additions include discussion of the societal context of fairness, coverage of issues associated with state assessments, and greater attention to the consequences of testing (Camara & Lane, 2006).

Taken as a whole, then, the *Standards* series mirrors the evolution of psychometric theory and technical innovations in assessment. But the incorporation of fairness and consequences also shows increasing awareness of societal and political factors.

Over time, just as the content has expanded, so too has the group of measurement specialists from whom input has been solicited. The Joint Committee in charge of the 1999 *Standards* circulated three drafts of this book and received almost 8,000 pages of comments. Given the fact that the *Standards* has been revised each decade, it is no surprise that work on another edition started in 2005, with preliminary committees formed at that time. Anyone who wished to submit revisions and comments could do so through the APA website.

Some suggestions for future editions of the *Standards* involve adding information about such matters as designing assessments that are accessible to all students, evaluating the intended and unintended consequences of tests and testing programs, and using technology in assessment (Camara & Lane, 2006, p. 39).

Various experts all urge illustrating the principles articulated in the *Standards* by offering specific examples, either actual or hypothetical—as was done in the early versions. Both Linn (2006) and Koretz (2006) suggest an analogy to using case law, which clarifies the meaning of legal statutes by providing precedents and discussing specific controversies. In fact, going beyond illustrations of discrete standards to provide an annotated example of a complete testing program would also be helpful.

Other Professional Guidelines

Of the other documents worth noting, one is the "Code of Fair Testing Practices," which is available at the APA website and presents excerpts from the *Standards* for a more public audience (Joint Committee on Testing Practices, 2004). Also of interest are the International Test Commission's guidelines (for test adaptation, for test use, and for computer-based and Internet-delivered testing), which were developed by committees representing national organizations around the world and incorporate existing guidelines, such as the *Standards* (International Test Commission [ITC], 2000, 2001, 2005, & 2008).

A possible adjunct to the 1999 *Standards* are articles about *universal design* that, like their counterparts in architecture, offer principles and strategies for making tests more accessible to all students (e.g., Thompson, Johnstone, & Thurlow, 2002; see chapter 7 for more).

In a collaboration between educators and measurement professionals, the Council of Chief State School Officers and the Association of Test Publishers (2010) have derived a set of "best practices" based on states' and test publishers' experience with large-scale testing programs.

Last, the Joint Committee on Standards for Educational Evaluation (an offshoot of committees working on the *Standards*) has produced three books supplementing the *Standards*. One is *The Student Evaluation Standards* (2003), which is concerned with classroom assessment and intended for educators. In contrast to the 1999 *Standards*, it provides hypothetical scenarios illustrating how particular standards might be applied in particular contexts, as well as an analysis of each scenario.[9]

All the above documents are valuable, but when people refer to "the *Standards*" in the field of educational measurement, they mean the *Standards for Educational and Psychological Testing*. It stands alone in terms of historical resonance and status as an official policy document for the AERA, APA, and NCME.

IMPLEMENTING THE *STANDARDS*

How, then, does the *Standards* ultimately serve to translate theory into practice? How does it govern testing—if, in fact, it does?

The document itself acknowledges its lack of mechanisms for enforcement. Nor does the Association of Test Publishers have any enforcement power over its members: "Ultimately, the test publisher is responsible for the quality of the test. However, tests used in schools, businesses or other public settings are regulated by federal and state laws" (1997–2004, under "Who sets the standards for tests?").

Thus, beyond matters that are subject to legal and governmental control (as described in the next section), any compliance with the *Standards* is voluntary. Test makers and users do have significant motivation to comply, since test information is valuable only to the extent that it is credible. However, such efforts can encounter significant obstacles.

Some of the difficulties are inherent in the discipline of educational measurement. Concepts such as validity and reliability are complex, and even within the profession there can be a lack of perfect consensus or clarity about these most important principles (Frisbie, 2005).

Problems also arise from the *Standards* itself. On the one hand, some specialists criticize it for insufficient guidance, including the abandonment of prioritization. Now that test makers are presumably responsible for all of the standards, it may be harder to hold them responsible for any particular standard (Camara & Lane, 2006, p. 36). On the other hand, at the same time that new standards are needed to address new developments in testing, the growing list becomes unwieldy.

Moreover, the *Standards* is a document written for specialists. As Camara and Lane (2006) point out, while the *Standards* conceives of "test users" as measurement professionals, there is now a much broader range of test users (teachers, parents, and policy makers) who lack formal training in testing and who may even be unaware of the existence of such guidelines.

But even full awareness of the *Standards* does not mean that decision makers will carry out its principles. In one case, the United States Citizenship and Immigration Services (USCIS) commissioned the official government advisory panel on testing to provide input on redesigning the test administered to applicants for U.S. citizenship. But in the end, the USCIS followed few of the panel's recommendations about actions needed to comply with the *Standards*—probably because of time and cost, but possibly also because a high level of technical expertise is needed to understand what the *Standards* requires (Elliott, Chudowsky, Plake, & McDonnell, 2006).

Pragmatic considerations—staffing as well as time and money—may indeed be the greatest obstacles to following the *Standards*. With the surge in accountability testing, not only did test publishers need quickly to create customized tests for each state (as well as score the tests and report results), but also they had to create modified or *alternate assessments* for students with disabilities and English Language Learners—each of which requires its own set of supporting studies and evidence (Harris, 2006). (As we will see in chapter 7, such research often involves small subpopulations and therefore may be difficult to conduct even with sufficient resources.)

What are some possible solutions? To help bridge the gap between specialists and laypersons, Elliott et al. (2006) recommend creating spin-off documents aimed at specific audiences, such as policy makers, or at specific test purposes, such as credentialing. These spin-offs would emphasize the most important concepts for the situation and translate them into lay terms, to help the reader understand why following the relevant standards is crucial.

Voluntary efforts to promote compliance with the *Standards* do exist within the test publishing industry. As Linn (2006) comments, "Some test publishers clearly pay a good deal of attention to the *Standards*" and document such efforts. He cites, for example, Educational Testing Service's (ETS's) parallel set of standards for use in auditing the company's own testing programs (see ETS, 2002). ETS's quality-and-fairness audits call upon both internal and external experts, require considerable accumulation of evidence over time, and must be repeated periodically.

Another approach to compliance is the use of external reviews and monitoring. Madaus (2001) traces the history of the Buros Institute of Mental Measurements, founded in 1938 by Oscar K. Buros (1905–1978) to improve test quality by publishing reviews of tests in annual *Mental Measurements Yearbooks* and offering consulting and auditing services. Also providing reviews of selected tests is the National Board on Educational Testing and Public Policy, affiliated with Boston College.

However, such reviews are usually voluntary and may take too long to keep up with the proliferation of new tests. Thus, Wise (2006) suggests that the most effective way to encourage compliance, at least in state or federally funded testing programs, is to encourage official requirements for compliance.

Could the measurement profession help by creating an organization devoted to reviewing tests and advising clients? The APA's past suggestions for creating a Bureau of Test Standards did not materialize; nor have suggestions for creating an official auditing agency (Madaus, 2001). Little wonder, because funding such an agency, giving it any real power, and agreeing on how it would be run are no small obstacles (Koretz, 2006).

But what about legal and governmental mechanisms? To what extent and by what means do they regulate educational testing?*

GOVERNMENTAL AND LEGAL REGULATION

Federal Influence Through an Advisory Board and Title I Funding

One way in which the federal government might—but does not—control the standards for and quality of educational testing would be through an official department or agency devoted to this mission. Such an idea has been floated a number of times over the years. For example, in 1976 the National Association for the Advancement of Colored People (NAACP, 2007) proposed creating a testing agency similar to other federal regulatory agencies in order to protect consumers of tests and other assessment procedures. Here the goal was primarily to protect examinees.

In 1990, the National Commission on Testing and Public Policy revisited this suggestion but, concerned about politicization of such an agency, suggested instead forming a nongovernmental organization for quality control, that might resemble the Consumers' Union or the Underwriters Laboratory. Neither a consumer agency nor a quality-control agency has been created.

However, since 1993, the federal government has had its own advisory panel: the Board on Testing and Assessment, which is part of the National Research Council. The BOTA's rotating membership spans a range of disciplines, and the members "advise policy makers and practitioners about the strengths and limitations of tests, as well as their appropriate design, use, and interpretation" (National Academies, 2007, p. 2).[10]

---

*Note that regulation of educational and of employment testing are not identical. Although some of the same legal statutes and constitutional protections apply to both, employment testing is addressed specifically in various requirements described by the U.S. Equal Employment Opportunity Commission (2008), especially the "Uniform Guidelines on Employee Selection Procedures" of 1978.

Many significant reports about assessment have emerged from this organization, most of which can be viewed without charge at the National Academies Press website. Despite the influence of BOTA research within the measurement profession, though, the limits of its power are suggested by the disinclination of the USCIS agency to follow advice that it specifically requested from a BOTA panel. Nevertheless, the BOTA members make numerous policy recommendations, such as a letter to the U.S. Department of Education cautioning about the feasibility and desirability of various stipulations in the RTTT Funding competition (NRC, 2009).

Without any official agency for regulating educational testing, and without direct control over the nation's educational system, the federal government still exerts some crucial types of leverage. As we have seen, states have to participate in the federal NAEP program in order to receive Title I funding, which is a relatively small part of the nation's education budget but crucial to states nevertheless. Moreover, the reauthorization of the 1965 ESEA in 2002 as the No Child Left Behind Act required states to conduct testing in order to receive Title I funds.

NCLB testing was regulated somewhat indirectly, in that the federal government established procedures for peer review audit process but did not conduct these audits. The reviewers were supposed to be experts in assessment whose feedback would help guide states as well as inform federal decisions about approval of state assessment systems (U.S. Department of Education, 2007).

Regulation Through Constitutional Protections and Legal Statutes

Whereas the NAEP and ESEA testing programs (such as NCLB) are concerned with measuring aggregate student performance, other tests are used in making important decisions about individual students (such as grade-to-grade promotion tests, high school exit exams, or college admissions tests). These types of tests invoke another kind of federal regulation, via legal and constitutional protections.

Testing programs may be subject to legal challenges if they appear to violate the rights to fair treatment guaranteed in the Fourteenth Amendment of the U.S. Constitution and the Civil Rights Act of 1964. These guarantees include due process, equal protection, and the rights of an individual to control his or her own destiny.[11]

One kind of due process is "procedural," and it implies that examinees must be given adequate notice about a mandatory testing program used for high-stakes decisions (they must receive clear and timely information about the content and consequences). Also, examinees must be able to appeal the outcomes (Parkes & Stevens, 2003).

Procedural due process was invoked in the landmark cases of *Debra P. v. Turlington* (Florida, 1979) and *GI Forum v. Texas Education Agency* (1999). In both cases, the state had recently instituted a mandatory exam for receiving a high school diploma—which is often required for employment or higher education. Legal challenges included the argument that students and teachers had not been given sufficient prior notice to prepare for the new test (Sireci & Parker, 2006). The challenge to the Florida test resulted in delaying the test for four years.

The other kind of due process is "substantive," which "addresses the purposes of a governmental process and holds that they must have some legitimate purpose and be reasonable," not "capricious or arbitrary" (Parkes & Stevens, 2003, p. 146). Being able to show that decisions were based on the *Standards* and advice of relevant experts (such as psychometricians and educators) is crucial for defending testing programs against charges of capriciousness or arbitrariness.

In addition to due process, the constitutional principle of equal protection— that "individuals must be treated equally by educational processes"—was a key factor in other phases of both *Debra P.* and *GI Forum*. The two relevant aspects are the potential for disparate impact (disproportionately lower passing rates for legally protected minority groups) and any possible discriminatory intent or intentional bias that might cause disparate impact (Mehrens & Popham, 1992; Parkes & Stevens, 2003). If passing an educational test bears on employment opportunities, the prohibitions against discrimination in Title VII of the Civil Rights Act of 1964 may also be relevant, with "adverse impact" measured by statistical criteria (see Buckendahl & Hunt, 2005, p. 149, for the three methods typically used to determine impact).

Although requiring scrutiny, the phenomenon of different passing rates on the part of different groups does not automatically mean that a test is invalid or can be successfully challenged (Parkes & Stevens, 2003). In *GI Forum v. Texas Education Agency*, the state was able to present a sufficiently well-documented and comprehensive argument for the validity of the testing program, despite the differential passing rates (Sireci & Parker, 2006). An article by an expert witness, William Mehrens (2000), explains how he used the *Standards* to evaluate the Texas diploma test.

The final important way in which federal legislation regulates educational testing has to do with students who have disabilities. They may need accommodations in the procedures or may need a modified or alternate kind of test intended to measure as nearly as possible the same proficiency as the mainstream test does. Test publishers have introduced many types of accommodations voluntarily, and these efforts have been further spurred by federal legislation.[12]

However, as Heaney and Pullin (1998) explain, accommodations and *modifications* raise another legal issue. On the one hand, the *Standards* advises *flagging* (attaching an asterisk or other notation) scores whose meaning may differ from those of standard administrations. On the other hand, in admissions testing, this practice is problematic because Section 504 regulations stipulate that educational institutions cannot ask applicants whether or not they are disabled.[13]

Regulation of Educational Testing at the State Level

State departments of education control state-mandated tests, and within the school system, districts also make decisions about testing. States do not tend to have independent regulatory agencies that monitor testing in the school system. However, with increasing emphasis on testing for accountability purposes, some states have tried to address conflicts of interest by assigning auditing responsibilities to departments separate from those responsible for the testing programs (Dewan, 2010).

Also at the state level are other regulations that can significantly affect the quality of testing programs. State officials may be under pressure or legally required to accept the lowest bids submitted by prospective contractors, including test publishers. Moreover, the time required for development and scoring becomes an issue (Brennan [2004] estimates that developing a new test usually requires at least three years). Thus, the U.S. Government Accountability Office (2009) found that considerations of cost and time, rather than assessment needs, shaped state decisions about the content of tests and the use of cheaper, more quickly scored multiple-choice items instead of essays and other constructed-response tasks.

Officials at the state level can also affect the content of state tests via the curricular standards that the officials adopt. In the example of the Texas State Board of Education's controversial standards for social science and history, the effects on Texas state tests follow logically. However, because of the Texas market's influence on textbook publishers, decisions made in Texas can affect other states' standards and tests as well. (At the least, the national outcry over the Texas standards raised a useful debate about overt attempts to define and control knowledge.)

Last, another state's law has affected nationally administered tests: the 1980 New York State "truth-in-testing law," which requires publishing tests and answers after the fact (Sack, 1991). Disclosure requirements have been scaled back somewhat since then. As the National Commission on Testing and Public Policy (1990) points out, such disclosure does not "enable examinees to evaluate the adequacy of a test as a measure of what it purports to measure, or to question how the test is used" (p. 21).

Overall, then, the picture of guidelines for educational testing and their enforcement is mixed. On the one hand, the assessment profession has reached relative consensus on a fairly mature set of criteria for making and using tests, and federal laws provide important protections for students whose lives may be affected. On the other hand, fulfilling the criteria in the *Standards* is voluntary on the part of testing organizations, and there are significant obstacles and disincentives to complying, especially the time and money required.

At the same time, educators object to what they see as negative effects on learning, or at least few benefits, from externally imposed tests over which they have little control. But in state policies on testing, political and practical considerations often outweigh pedagogical and psychometric ones.

This imperfect situation has no simple answer, but citizens, educators, specialists, regulators, and even policy makers actually do share some similar concerns, even if expressed in different language. Agreement on basic principles might help in negotiating diverse agendas.

As a first step, let us consider the root concept in testing, what might be considered the soul of assessment: validity.

Chapter IV: Key Points

- In testing, the four groups of stakeholders are citizens (students, taxpayers, advocacy organizations); educators and educational administrators; members of the measurement professions; and regulators (government officials, policy makers, and legal professionals).
- Citizens' views influence policy on testing, but they tend to focus on the quantity rather than the quality of testing. Better communication about assessment issues and greater "assessment literacy" could improve citizen input. Advocacy organizations may support very different testing policies, depending on how they believe the policies affect their own constituents.
- Educators are concerned about the impact of externally imposed testing on teachers, schools, and students. They advocate input into such testing and/or greater local control of testing. They also emphasize the kinds of resources needed to implement both internal classroom assessment and externally mandated tests. In creating the latter, test makers need to work with educators, who understand the realities of teaching and learning.
- The official consensus of the measurement profession for applying theory to practice is articulated in the *Standards for Educational and Psychological Testing*. This continually evolving series is supplemented by books, articles, and other sets of guidelines. However, the professional standards remain voluntary, without a mechanism for enforcement in the industry.
- The federal advisory board on testing is a valuable resource but lacks official power to control testing. However, the federal government exerts some control via funding that schools accept. In addition, constitutional and statutory protections regulate certain aspects of testing, especially as its use in high-stakes decisions may affect members of ethnic or racial groups and students with disabilities. Politics, budget constraints, and other pragmatic issues also significantly influence the quality of testing.

NOTES

1. These organizations include those specifically concerned with testing, such as the National Center for Fair and Open Testing (FairTest), but they also include organizations concerned with schools and educational issues in general, such as the Center on Education Policy, Public Education Network, Center for Education Reform, Council for Aid to Education, National Center for Public Policy and Higher Education, and Institute for Language and Education Policy. Also participating in the public dialogue on testing are organizations concerned with social and civil rights issues.

2. An example is this NAACP recommendation: "Place a moratorium on all High Stakes Testing Legislation until adequate resources are provided to remove the statistical significant racial disparities in the results" (2007, p. 85).

In contrast, the American Diploma Project Network—a consortium that includes the Education Trust (an organization focused on low-income and minority student achievement), Achieve, Inc., the Thomas B. Fordham Foundation, as well as educators, state officials, and business executives—advocates using exit or end-of-course exams and college-readiness assessments together with other strategies to help make high school curricula more rigorous and better aligned to higher education and the workplace (Achieve, Inc., 2009, "American Diploma Project Network").

3. Groups that support accountability testing include the National Council of La Raza (2008), an advocacy group for Hispanic citizens and noncitizens, and the Learning Disabilities Association of America (2008).

4. The Association of American Colleges and Universities commissioned this study, conducted by Peter D. Hart Associates (2008). The executives ranked "a faculty supervisor's assessment of an internship or community-based project" as the type of assessment most likely to reveal skills and learning important to working in a company; their second choice was completion of an in-depth, senior-year project and their third choice was essay tests focused on problem-solving and analytical reasoning (p. 6).

5. One example of an individual boycotting a test in the United States is Carl Chew, a middle school science teacher who refused to administer the Washington (State) Assessment of Learning (Associated Press, 2008).

6. For an official statement on what teachers ought to know about assessment, see "Standards for Teacher Competence in Educational Assessment of Students" (AFT, NCME, & NEA, 1990).

7. Some of the largest organizations encompass educators across disciplines. In addition to the NEA and the AFT are the American Association of School Administrators, the Association of American Colleges and Universities, the American Council on Education, the National School Boards Association, the Association for Supervision and Curriculum Development, National Association of Elementary School Principals, the National Association of Secondary School Principals, and other such groups. Other organizations, such as the National Association for the Education of Young Children and the National Association of Special Education Teachers, have a more specific focus.

8. The *Standards* series began in 1954 with the American Psychological Association's *Technical Recommendations for Psychological Tests and Diagnostic*

Techniques, followed in 1955 by the AERA and NCMUE *Technical Recommendations for Achievement Tests*. In 1966, the APA, AERA, and NCME jointly sponsored *Standards for Educational and Psychological Tests and Manuals*. The same three organizations have continued to publish subsequent revisions in 1974, 1985, and 1999. Since 1966, a joint committee representing the three organizations has been responsible for the documents and has solicited input and review from outside experts.

9. Formed in 1974, the Joint Committee on Standards for Educational Evaluation represents not only the AERA, APA, and NCME, but also other U.S. and Canadian organizations of educators and of measurement specialists. It has published *The Standards for Program Evaluation*, 1994; *The Standards for Personnel Evaluation*, 1988; and *The Standards for Student Evaluation*, 2003. A list of the main guidelines can be seen at the website of the Western Michigan University Center on Evaluation.

10. The NRC, part of the National Academies of Sciences and Engineering, provides independent research services to Congress, governmental agencies, and foundations, as described in National Academies (2008). BOTA also has a brochure, "Lessons Learned about Testing," useful in promoting assessment literacy for the public (National Academies, 2007).

11. According to Sireci and Parker (2006):

> Essentially, there are four routes to challenging a test in court: (a) Title VI of the Civil Rights Act of 1964 (Title VI, 1999), (b) Title VII of the Civil Rights Act of 1964 (Title VII, 1999), (c) the Equal Protection Clause of the Fourteenth Amendment (United States Constitution Amendment 14, § 1), and (d) the Due Process Clause of the Fourteenth Amendment (United States Constitution Amendment 14, § 1). (p. 29)

12. According to Pitoniak and Royer (2001), Section 504 of the 1973 Rehabilitation Act "specifically prohibits tests that discriminate against otherwise qualified candidates because of their impairments" and requires the availability of accommodations for tests with any ties to federal funding (p. 55). The 1990 Americans with Disabilities Act (ADA) applies to all companies with more than fifteen employees, in effect meaning that all test publishers must comply with its requirements.

The 1991 Individuals with Disabilities Education Act (IDEA) requires that students with disabilities have access to public education and be provided with an individual educational program. The 1997 amendments to IDEA required including such students in state and district tests with any needed accommodations or modifications.

13. Educational institutions "are not allowed to take into account the existence of a disability unless it is necessary to do so to determine whether the applicant is qualified to participate in the educational program" (Heaney & Pullin, 1998, p. 89).

SELECTED READINGS

American Educational Research Association (AERA), American Psychological Association (APA), & National Council on Measurement in Education (NCME). (1999). *Standards for educational and psychological testing.* Washington, DC: American Educational Research Association.

Brennan, R. L. (Ed.). (2006). *Educational Measurement* (4th ed.). Westport, CT: American Council on Education and Praeger Publishers. (The 1951, 1971, and 1989 editions are also of great importance.)

Parkes, J., & Stevens, J. (2003). Legal issues in school accountability systems. *Applied Measurement in Education, 16*(2), 141–58.

Popham, W. J. (2003). Seeking redemption for our psychometric sins. *Educational Measurement: Issues and Practice, 22*(1), 45–48.

In addition, visit the websites of educators' organizations, such as the NEA, AFT, IRA, NCTE, NCTM, NSTA, NCSS, CCSSO, NAEYC, NASET, etc., for their most recent policy statements on assessment.

Chapter Five

Validity

The central issue is appraisal of the meaning and consequences of measurement.

—Samuel Messick, 1989 (p. 14)

Validity is universally acknowledged as the most important concept in assessment, but what is it? For all the scholarly literature that has spun webs of theory around the idea of validity, a dictionary is still not a bad place to start.

Definitions of the word *valid* include "well grounded or justifiable: being at once relevant and meaningful," "logically correct," and "appropriate to the end in view" (Merriam-Webster, 2008). Such phrases suggest a commonsense perspective. Assessment procedures should have a well-supported justification or rationale, and they should produce meaningful information that is relevant to a particular purpose.

Moreover, the definition of *valid* as "executed with the proper legal authority and formalities" suggests that, in the realm of testing, validity includes following the *Standards* and conforming to any applicable constitutional protections or legal statutes.

Validity thus goes beyond the test materials to include contextual considerations. No matter how well constructed, a test by itself cannot be innately valid. Instead, the focus is on the information produced by a test: its scores.

Test scores are intended to have specific meanings when used in a specific way, and psychometric validity is concerned with the extent to which these intentions are fulfilled. Thus validity is always a matter of degree.

Imagine, for example, a state-mandated, end-of-course test on high school chemistry intended to determine how well students have met specified learning

77

goals. Assume that the state's learning goals for chemistry represent a research-based model of proficiency at the appropriate level; that the curriculum and actual instruction convey these concepts, knowledge, and skills; and that the tasks in the test sample important aspects of what students had been taught. To the extent that these assumptions are true, such a test might provide relevant, meaningful information about what students had learned.

Then, this information might be used in a proper way for helping make decisions about awarding credit toward the high school diploma, if the scores were considered in conjunction with other evidence, such as projects, lab reports, interim assessments, and so on.

However, context is crucial, so that validity is not only a matter of degree but also has a "contingent character" (Kane, 2006, p. 60). The very same end-of-year test could produce misleading information if the actual curriculum differed from the presumed one. And even if the test were given to appropriately instructed students, the scores could be used in improper ways, such as making direct comparisons with states that have different curricula, tests, and performance standards.

Issues related to validity can be subtle and thorny. For example, what if the state academic standards were outdated or omitted some key concepts and skills? What if most of the items in the test involved factual recall, with few requiring analysis, synthesis, or other higher-order thinking skills? In either case, the information that the scores conveyed about "proficiency" in chemistry would be similarly limited.

The larger context of the test extends both backward and forward in time. For example, the validity and possibly the legality of the testing program could be challenged, if the state-mandated test measured lab skills that some students did not have a reasonable opportunity to learn, because their high schools had meager lab facilities or none at all. (Simply deciding to exclude lab skills from the test would only degrade the meaning of proficiency.) And later, after graduating from high school, what if even those students who had done reasonably well on the test found themselves unprepared for college-level chemistry?[1]

As a final example, what if school administrators sought to evaluate chemistry teachers solely in terms of their students' test results? This use of scores would differ from the intended purpose. It would interpret the scores as measurements of teachers' proficiency, even though the scores were intended to indicate students' proficiency.

As these questions suggest, validity is complex. Investigating validity means probing all aspects of assessment procedures, especially the assumptions on which they are based. Samuel Messick (1931–1998) described the process of validation as "scientific inquiry" because it subjects "the meaning and consequences of measurement" to systematic, empirical scrutiny and research (1989, p. 14). More recently, Michael T. Kane (2006) has described it as a process of evaluating the credibility of claims about how scores should be interpreted and how they should be used. Validation is, then, a matter of critical thinking.

In this chapter, we will explore the concept of validity and specific strategies for validation, all of which continue to evolve. As we will see, validity theory addresses the scientific side of testing: "What do the scores mean?" and "Are they accurate?" It also addresses the uses of testing as a technology: "How well does it work?" Arguably, it may also address larger consequences: "How well does it serve society?"

We will also see that no single type of evidence suffices to address validity concerns; triangulation and cross-verification are needed. Thus, validation draws upon an accumulation of different approaches developed over the years.*

HOW A UNITARY CONCEPT OF VALIDITY EMERGED

An Initial Definition of Validity

Testing programs have always had to grapple with issues of meaning and accuracy, as officials for the Chinese civil service exams did when they tried to prevent cheating and preserve the intended meaning of scores. When the era of mental testing dawned, scientific methods suggested a new strategy. Just like scientists repeating their experiments, psychometricians might make their results credible by retesting examinees and obtaining consistent results (e.g., Cattell, 1890, p. 374).

However, consistency only goes so far. As Spearman (1904) emphasized, "Two points must always be carefully kept asunder": the consistency or reliability of experimental results and claims about what the results actually mean (p. 238). The problem is that consistent, reliable results are necessary but not sufficient to establish accuracy, meaning, or relevance. For example, stepping on the same scale many times and getting similar readings each time would not guarantee that the numbers were accurate. Nor would consistency show whether the person was at a healthful weight.

Thus, investigating test-score reliability branched off as one line of inquiry (see chapter 6), while investigating meaning and relevance became another. By the 1920s, measurement specialists had a term for the latter aspect of measurement: validity. In the initial definition, which focused on the scientific

---

*Although the principles of validity are certainly relevant to classroom assessment, validity investigation tends to require the larger examinee populations and greater resources of formal testing programs.

perspective, a "valid test" would be one that "really measures what it purports to measure and consistently measures this same something throughout the entire range of the test"—that is, at all score levels (McCall, 1922, p. 195).

Over the first half of the twentieth century, psychometricians and educators pursued different methods for determining validity, in terms of accuracy, relevance, and usefulness. (The methods, described later in this chapter, focused on determining how well test tasks represent educational objectives and how well test performance corresponds with "real life" performance.) However, modern validity theory began with the 1954–1955 *Technical Recommendations*. While reaffirming the importance of existing types of "validating evidence," the *Technical Recommendations* also introduced a new one.

The Concept of Construct Validity

Because the existing types of evidence could not always "indicate the degree to which the test measures what it is intended to measure," the new approach focused on the underlying reasons for examinee performance (AERA & NCMUE, 1955, p. 16). The concept of *construct validity* was particularly intended to address assessments of abstract skills and abilities, including outcomes of education akin to "psychological traits or qualities" (p. 26).

In fact, the idea came from psychology, and its proponents, Lee Cronbach and Paul E. Meehl (1920–2003), had introduced it in the 1954 recommendations for psychological tests. As Cronbach (1957) later recounted, construct validity was conceived as a way to evaluate claims about what a particular psychological test actually measured. Meehl, whose background was in the history and philosophy of science, suggested using the methods of logical empiricism.[2]

Just as a scientist would propose a scientific theory or hypothesis to predict observations, the psychologist would propose a theoretical model of a mental trait or attribute, called a *construct*.* Then the psychologist would apply the model to predict how someone possessing that trait would behave in a testing situation. Finding that test results accorded with the prediction would help support the theory.[3]

By emphasizing underlying reasons for test performance, the construct approach offered a new perspective on educational tests, especially those addressing higher-order skills. Recall the process that Tyler (for whom

---

*Examples of psychological constructs would be motivation or emotional intelligence. In education, examples of constructs would be proficiency in high school chemistry, ability to comprehend the kinds of texts used in graduate studies, readiness for the demands of college-level writing, or other abstract traits relevant to learning and academic achievement.

Cronbach had once worked as a research assistant) had laid out for creating achievement tests. It involved defining educational objectives, embodying each objective in tasks, and then specifying the "nature of the reaction to be made by the student" to each task (1934/1989, p. 57). By this means a test would obtain evidence of the extent to which students were meeting the objectives.

Now consider this process from the perspective of a construct framework. In specifying a higher-order objective such as "ability to evaluate data with reference to given criteria," Tyler was proposing a hypothetical attribute. Then, by describing correct or good responses to a task presumed to require this ability, Tyler was predicting how someone possessing that attribute would behave.

But, unlike Tyler, Cronbach and Meehl did not assume that such a test simply measured the hypothesized attribute, that is, that a student's performance indicated the extent to which he or she possessed the ability to evaluate data with reference to given criteria—and nothing else. Instead, the construct approach also required investigating other, less obvious theories or explanations for the student's performance on the test.

Thus, in keeping with Popper's model of scientific inquiry, the process of investigating an explanation for test performance includes investigating challenges or "plausible rival hypotheses." Successful challenges or alternatives to the proposed explanation weaken it, but the explanation gains credibility if it remains intact despite attempts to falsify it (Cronbach, 1988, p. 13).

As an illustration, Cronbach (1971) cited a test intended to measure the construct of reading comprehension skills. If it did, then a student's level of reading skills should explain the student's test score.

But what if students had insufficient time to complete the test, or insufficient motivation to perform well, or, on the basis of preexisting knowledge, could have guessed the answers to questions without even looking at the given material? Then the test scores would reflect other attributes, such as quickness, motivation, or topic familiarity, in addition to or instead of comprehension. Given these possibilities, test makers needed to analyze formally the kinds of "pernicious disturbing factors" and "irrelevancies" noted by earlier theorists.[4]

The idea of construct validity thus confronted fundamental questions of meaning, accuracy, and relevance in testing. Its influence has been profound.

A Unitary Concept of Validity

In 1957, developmental psychologist Jane Loevinger (1918–2008) suggested taking a more comprehensive view of construct validity. In fact, she said, construct validity, or "essential validity," actually constituted "the whole of validity from a scientific point of view" because a plausible interpretation of test scores would require a single explanation or theory about the construct that accounts for all available evidence (pp. 642, 636, 689).

In science, a proposed theory must address every type of relevant evidence. So too would a proposed explanation for performance on a test have to consider all types of validity evidence, whether supportive or not.

Not until the 1980s did the profession accept Loevinger's idea. But her vision of theory testing gave a new coherence to the idea of validity.

Considering construct validity as the whole of validity means, for example, that to claim that a test measures middle-school students' reading skills, one first needs to define a theory or model of reading proficiency and its developmental levels. This theory predicts that students at a particular level ought to be able to perform certain types of reading tasks with specified levels of difficulty. Moreover, performance on the test should be consistent with performance on other related measures of reading skills, such as relevant grades in language arts classes. The explanation of scores must also consider any inconsistencies and other factors that may affect performance.

Thus, interpreting the scores correctly requires ongoing scrutiny of evidence. Many kinds of data (such as information about changing student demographics, new research findings about the development of reading proficiency, etc.) could support, contradict, or call for revising the original theory.[5]

The apotheosis of Loevinger's view of construct validity is Messick's treatise on a "unitary validity." This chapter in the 1989 *Educational Measurement* is the basis for the 1999 *Standards* chapter on validity.

In a unitary validity, all aspects or "facets" of validity are subsumed under construct validity, which requires bringing together "any evidence that bears on the interpretation or meaning of test scores" (Messick, 1989, p. 17). Such evidence may include but is not limited to how well the test content represents construct-relevant behaviors, how well test scores correlate with performance on other measures of this construct, and the extent to which the meanings of scores remain the same across different groups of examinees and situations.[6]

Moreover, the validation process includes addressing "threats to construct validity," or ways in which a test may fail to measure the targeted construct. Messick (1989) identified two threats: first, *construct underrepresentation* such that important parts of the construct are not represented in the test; and second, *construct-irrelevant variance* such that examinees' performance on the test is affected by factors extraneous to the desired construct. In the latter case, scores are "contaminated" (p. 34).

Examples of construct underrepresentation in the high school chemistry test mentioned earlier would be omitting questions about lab skills or focusing on factual knowledge at the expense of conceptual understanding. However, as Messick noted, any test will inevitably have limitations in its coverage of the construct, and therefore multiple measures are always preferable. Hence the desirability of using projects, classroom performance, grades, etc., as well as the end-of-course test score in deciding whether the student has met the criteria for proficiency.

Construct-irrelevant variance could arise from myriad factors, such as incidents of cheating, ambiguous or poorly conceived tasks on the test, or any other influences that undermine the intended meaning of scores. For a proficiency test, construct irrelevance makes items either easier or more difficult than they ought to be. (Note, however, that poor performance by students who had not been taught the tested subject matter would be construct-relevant, because the test is supposed to measure learning. The invalidity might lie in a failure to align test materials with instruction and curriculum, or else in a failure to teach students the prescribed curriculum. In either case the intended meaning of scores would be compromised.)

Clearly, the notion of construct-irrelevant factors emphasizes the importance of context in understanding the meaning of test scores. But, as Messick further argued, if validity depends on context, then a unitary validity must also encompass the ways in which the scores are used.

The Relationship Between Score Meaning and Score Use

In fact, far earlier than 1989, such theorists as Lindquist (1936) and Edward E. Cureton (1902–1992; in his 1951 chapter on validity) emphasized that tests could be valid only in relation to particular purposes. Later, Cronbach (1971) probed this point more deeply by explaining why using tests to describe and to make decisions are not necessarily separate matters. The scientific and technological aspects of a test have a symbiotic relationship, since the intended use of scores affects how the test is designed and what it is intended to measure—that is, what the scores mean.[7]

For example, if the purpose were to make decisions about placing high school students in the college-level calculus sequence, then the focus would be narrower than if the purpose were to compare students in terms of overall proficiency in mathematics and quantitative reasoning. Hence, directly echoing the first sentence in Messick's 1989 chapter, the *Standards* asserts "validity refers to the degree to which evidence and theory support the interpretations of test scores entailed by proposed uses of tests" (AERA et al., 1999, p. 9).

By extension, if scores from the same test are to be used in more than one way, then each different purpose requires a separate validity investigation.

Such would be the case if an attempt were made to use the (hypothetical) high school chemistry test to evaluate teachers' effectiveness. In real life, an example would be a state's using a test designed for college admissions as part of a high school exit exam.*

In keeping with Cronbach 's emphasis on decision making, Messick (1989) also discusses the need for evaluating a test's "decision-making utility"—the "relative benefits derived from utilizing the test in decision making," including whether it provides necessary information worth the cost (pp. 78–80). For example, using test scores for placement or selection might be justified in terms of quantitative correlations with examinees' subsequent performance or score users' levels of satisfaction.

However, utility and efficacy are not simply quantitative matters—and they are only part of the larger constellation of consequences that surround testing, as we will explore in the last section of this chapter. Moreover, fairness depends as much on how scores are used as on how they are interpreted, which is the basis for legal challenges against certain tests used in high-stakes decisions.

"Validity is a unitary concept" has come to be measurement orthodoxy, and that very sentence has appeared in the *Standards* since 1985. Yet dissent exists. The major objection is that Messick's all-encompassing view of validity is too abstract, intricate, and ambitious to offer practical guidance for real-life validation efforts.[8] For example, in educational achievement tests, Lissitz and Samuelson (2007) favor primary emphasis on *content-related evidence*, that is, the relationship between the tasks in the test and the curriculum that the test is intended to represent.[9]

Borsboom, Mellenbergh, and van Heerden (2004) propose a radical (in both senses of the word) return to the older definition of validity: the extent to which a test measures what it purports to measure. Taking a realist stance with respect to the existence of traits or attributes, they assert that "a test is valid for measuring an attribute if and only if (a) the attribute exists and (b) variations in the attribute causally produce variations in the outcomes of the measurement procedures" (p. 1061). Validation would focus only on the causal relationship between attribute and performance.

Such rumblings may affect the ongoing evolution of validity theory. Already, concerns about practical guidance have spurred an argument-based approach to validation processes. Although the argument approach insists

---

*A subtler example is using the same test in a situation with high stakes for examinees (such as a high school exit exam) and in a situation with low stakes (such as a research study or an accountability test with consequences for teachers but not for students). Lower motivation may be associated with significant decreases in test performance (Wise & DeMars, 2005). This point is especially important when scores are used are used to establish norms or to inform policy (DeMars, 2000). It is also a reason for trying out new test items by embedding them into operational test forms rather than by giving them in obviously experimental administrations.

less on formal scientific theories than Messick did and shifts the focus from constructs to claims, it still reflects the unitary concept of validity.

THE ARGUMENT-BASED
APPROACH TO VALIDATION

Given that the unitary concept of validity is so comprehensive, any framework for systematically validating interpretations and uses of test scores has to be broad enough to encompass many kinds of evidence. Moreover, because validation is where theory has to deal with the outside world, the framework also has to address real-world criteria: fairness, utility, and worth.

Thus, the current approach to validation refers less to scientific theory testing than to the model of argumentation as used in "real-world contexts": informal logic and practical reasoning (Kane, 2004, p. 145). This approach returns us somewhat from the realm of technical abstraction to the everyday definition of "valid": justifiable, executed with the proper formalities, appropriate to the end in view.

Still, at first glance, adopting a model from the discipline of rhetoric seems surprising. However, such influential works as Stephen Toulmin's 1958 *The Uses of Argument* (cited by Kane, 2006) have portrayed scientific inquiry and knowledge building as processes of argumentation and reasoning akin to those used in legal cases.[10] Moreover, Cronbach (1988) invoked the concept of a *validity argument*, as opposed to unstructured validity research. Messick himself observed that "the justification and defense of measurement and its validity is and may always be a rhetorical art," because "the function of test validation is to marshal evidence and arguments in support of, or counter to, proposed interpretations and uses of test scores" (1988, p. 43; 1989, p. 32).

Kane built on this idea in 1992 by laying out principles for "an argument-based approach to validity," which he elaborates in his 2006 *Educational Measurement* chapter on validation. Like any argument, the validity argument assumes the existence of an audience to be persuaded and is subject to three criteria: clarity, coherence, and plausibility.

Just as with any argument, making a case for what scores mean and why they should be used for a particular purpose involves claims and conclusions. Often, these claims and conclusions cannot be absolutely verified; at most they can be shown to be "highly plausible, given all the available evidence" (Kane, 1992, p. 527). The validity argument therefore identifies specific assumptions underlying the claims; identifies alternative possible claims or explanations; then seeks evidence to support the proposed claims (especially weaker ones) and to refute the alternative claims.[11]

Although classified differently (see below), the types of evidence officially used in a validity argument also echo those of rhetoric: testimonial (citing authority), statistical, experimental, and sometimes physical. For example, evidence about test materials is largely testimonial; studies about possible sources of construct-irrelevant variance often rely on experiments; evidence about examinees' actual response processes may include physical data; and evidence always includes statistical analyses of test data, demographic data, and so on. Moreover, Kane (2006) explains how arguments about the meaning and use of test scores can embody familiar types of logic—and logical fallacies.

Not only does Kane's concept of validation as argumentation deemphasize highly theoretical constructs, it may even mean that defining such a construct is not absolutely necessary. Focusing on claims shifts the ground to the inferences and assumptions one makes in interpreting observations of examinee performance. (For an example of such claims and a discussion of how Kane's argument approach can structure the validation process without requiring a defined construct, see Chapelle, Enright, & Jamieson, 2010.)

This line of thinking is in keeping with a movement toward defining assessment of learning as drawing inferences from the evidence that examinees provide of their proficiency, rather than as taking quasi-physical measurements. This perspective actually has a long history, but its relative modesty may have left it overshadowed by the more ambitious paradigm of scientific theory testing. (Renaming everything called "educational measurement" as "educational inferences" would have interesting implications for the discipline and the profession.)[12]

As ever, validity theory and validation approaches are on the move, and thus the 1999 *Standards* does not fully align with the 2006 *Educational Measurement*. But the argument-based approach to validation helps organize what needs to be done to investigate validity, including *validity studies* focused on particular questions.

In keeping with the unitary view of validity, the argument approach also emphasizes that all parts of the assessment process are interdependent. A weak link in the test's design, administration, scoring, data analysis, or any other area could undermine the intended meanings and uses of scores.

TYPES OF EVIDENCE USED
IN A VALIDITY ARGUMENT

The *Standards* prescribes guidelines for test makers and users to fulfill their joint responsibility of marshaling and documenting a validity argument.

Echoing the theorists, it emphasizes the need to integrate old and new evidence into a coherent but not static account that "may indicate the need for refining the definition of the construct, may suggest revisions in the test or other aspects of the testing process, and may indicate areas needing further study" (AERA et al., 1999, p. 17). It also details the types of documentation needed for this account.

Categories of validity evidence in the *Standards* are test content, response processes, internal structure, relations to external *variables*, and consequences. A validity argument does not have to include all five, but it should include the evidence that is most relevant to supporting the claims. (For an example of using all five to review K–12 tests, see Ferrara & DeMauro, 2006.) A process of triangulation and cross-verification via different modes of inquiry should help strengthen the validity argument.

We will consider the first four categories of evidence in this section, then the fifth (consequences) separately, because it presents a unique set of challenges. Many of the types of evidence discussed below are explored further in subsequent chapters.

Content-Related Evidence

This category of evidence focuses on the test itself and on the testing procedures. A validity argument would use content-related evidence to investigate whether (a) the construct that the test is intended to measure is important and relevant to the intended use of test scores; and (b) the testing procedures support the intended meaning of scores. Do the test materials adequately represent the construct? Do the procedures as a whole minimize potential sources of construct-irrelevant variance?

Although content-related evidence is the most obvious starting place for investigating validity, its generally qualitative nature is problematic from the perspective of scientific theory testing. Both Loevinger and Messick struggled with the fact that even though the relevance and representativeness of test materials are obviously important to the meaning of scores, these qualities are a matter of judgment and therefore difficult to confirm or refute with empirical evidence (Messick, 1989, pp. 17, 37, 41). With this concern in mind, test makers, test users, and entities that set academic standards have been trying to make content-related evidence more empirical.

The traditional concept of content-related evidence appeared in Cureton's 1951 chapter on validity. Cureton discussed the process of creating and evaluating tests from the perspective of logical or substantive relevance to the curriculum. Determining curricular relevance would involve judging how well the test tasks serve as a representative sample—in terms of breadth, depth, and kind—of the various performances that constitute the goals of instruction.*

With the acceptance of a unitary validity, the notion of content-related evidence became more comprehensive. In the 1999 *Standards*, it includes defining the construct (for example, as a conceptual model of a proficiency) that is to be measured for a particular purpose; translating the construct into a *content domain* (a comprehensive set of behaviors, ways of demonstrating the proficiency, types of relevant performances); and then sampling the domain in the assessment procedures. Content-related evidence thus surveys the entire process of developing, administering, and scoring the test. (For more about the test-development process, see chapters 9–11 in volume 2.)

To communicate with the public, testing programs typically provide a kind of mission statement placing the construct in the context of a specific purpose. For example, the Law School Admission Test (LSAT®) is explained thus: "It provides a standard measure of acquired reading and verbal reasoning skills that law schools can use as one of several factors in assessing applicants" (LSAC, 2008, ¶ 1). An interesting and helpful variation is the "portrait" of a student who meets the Common Core State Standards for college and career readiness in reading writing, speaking, listening, and language (CCSSI, 2010a, p. 7).

Such statements and sketches are the front door behind which unfolds the development process. The initial stage involves defining more fully the construct and content domain (which often tend to blur together). It can include reviews of research literature, analyses of curricula, input from committees of experts, and surveys of educators, practitioners, etc., about the nature and relative importance of particular knowledge and skills. Using data and research conclusions is one strategy for trying to make the construct and content domain more "evidence-based" and empirical in nature (a point emphasized in the Common Core State Standards project, for example).

In many cases a domain that is the focus of interest for an educational test is depicted in terms of academic standards. However, some educators and researchers are concerned that standards as typically defined can lead to curricular goals that are incoherent and unrealistic, and in turn to tests with the same qualities.[13]

Thus, there is increased interest in "vertical alignment" of standards across grades. In a more fundamental departure, new process-oriented approaches

---

*Cureton distinguished such logical relevance from "face validity," which is not an official kind of validity. It refers to a superficial resemblance between test tasks and real-life tasks that does not necessarily indicate content validity. As an example, he cited a test that appears to cover relevant subject-matter topics but does not address cognitive skills that are important educational objectives (p. 671). On the other hand, "face invalidity," such that the tasks appear unrelated to the construct, would be a problem in educational tests, as opposed to psychological tests.

depict domains as cognitive models, domain-mastery models, or learning progressions that represent how students develop expertise in the particular discipline (see NRC, 2005; Gorin, 2006; Leighton & Gierl, 2007; Corcoran et al., 2009; CCSSI, 2010b).

This big-picture perspective matters in making an argument about the validity of test content. As Lindquist (1951) noted, "The decisions which are made preliminary to actual test construction are, from the broadest point of view, far more important or crucial than those which follow" (p. 120).

Eventually, however, the construct and content domain are necessarily reduced to a smaller, lower-level sampling, in a process that Koretz (2009) describes (pp. 4–7). The resulting plan is embodied in *test specifications* or *blueprints* according to which testing programs assemble interchangeable versions of a test.

Testing programs often conduct reviews and analyses of the test specifications and of actual tests built from them in order to provide evidence about how the chosen topics, skills, and tasks represent the content domain. *Alignment studies* map the test questions to academic content standards and types of cognitive demands. These studies may include surveying teachers about the extent to which actual instruction is aligned with the content standards. Often such studies emphasize consistency among judgments about alignment, to enhance the sense that the process is empirical. Nevertheless, it is still not a matter of science, and there is the danger that an item may have only a superficial relationship to a targeted standard.[14]

Content-related validity evidence also extends to rationales for the ways in which examinees' responses are scored and the scores are communicated to test users. The validity argument would consider such matters as: rules for assigning scores, use of norming samples, methods for establishing performance categories and *score scales,* and ways in which scores from different tests are linked. (See chapter 8.)

Then, just as content-related validation should explain strategies used to promote construct representation in the test materials, so too should it address the strategies used to minimize construct-irrelevant factors. This evidence includes protocols for maintaining test security and for writing items to avoid culture-specific concepts and unclear or overly complex wording. (See chapter 7.) For tests used in low-stakes decisions, evidence would include any incentives, statistical adjustments, and data selection used to address the effect of low motivation (Wise & DeMars, 2005).

Last, as Koretz (2009) explains, validation should revisit test content to see how actual testing may have affected it. If the test is used in high-stakes decisions, teachers and schools may have changed instruction to focus on the anticipated skills, knowledge, and types of tasks in the test. This "reallocation" may in turn change the test content from a sample representing a larger, richer domain of proficiency to a sample representing a much narrower domain. Then score inflation may occur without real improvement—especially if the topics and tasks in the test become predictable. Using a separate measure as a check on test scores may help identify such problems.

Evidence About Response Processes

As Cronbach and Meehl (1955) first suggested, one way of investigating whether a test is measuring the targeted construct would be to observe the examinee's "process of performance" (p. 289). Thus, this category of evidence addresses the question: what are examinees really doing? Answering this question, which can involve both quantitative and qualitative approaches, is especially important for diagnostic tests intended to identify particular strengths and weaknesses in cognitive skills.

To study response processes, researchers may interview examinees afterward, observe examinees taking the test, and/or ask examinees to think aloud while completing the tasks. They may turn these observations into "case studies" of individual examinees' experience. Researchers may even track examinees' eye movements or take images of examinees' brains in the process of working on the tasks (Gorin, 2006; Mangels et al., 2006).*

Another approach is proactive: to define the construct from the outset in terms of the cognitive processes necessary for performing the required tasks and then design the test items to reveal these processes (for example, as multistage simulations) (Gorin, 2006; Leighton & Gierl, 2007). This approach relies on *cognitive task analysis,* derived from studies of how experts or novices actually perform workplace tasks, to identify the knowledge and strategies that people at particular levels of proficiency use to perform certain types of tasks (Mislevy & Huang, 2006). (See Baker, 2009, slide 40, for an example of deconstructing a mathematics task.)[15]

However, there is a trade-off, as Leighton and Gierl (2007) note. The more detailed and empirically based the tasks, the more specific and defensible they are in capturing cognitive processes, but at the same time, this very detail and concreteness can narrow the set of knowledge and skills assessed and require extensive research.

Response processes also include those of *raters* (readers, judges) who score constructed-response tasks in a test. Validity research could include interviewing and observing raters, to see if they are actually using the specified criteria to evaluate examinees' responses.

---

*For an example of a study of response processes, see Threlfall, Nelson, and Walker (2007). They observed and interviewed ninth-grade students taking a prototype test of ICT skills, in order to investigate sources of difficulty relevant or irrelevant to the intended construct—which, they acknowledge, is a new concept, not fully defined. Sources of construct-irrelevant difficulty appeared to include insufficiently clear instructions and demands on other subject knowledge.

Evidence About Internal Structure

This category of evidence is decidedly empirical, as it compares the statistical data from actual test administrations against predictions about how examinees will perform. A central question is whether test *dimensionality*, the "minimum number of examinee abilities measured by the test items," appears to be in line with predictions (Tate, 2002, p. 181). How many distinct constructs, or dimensions, is the test intended to measure, and how many is it actually measuring?

Usually a test that reports a single overall score is intended to measure one overall construct (for example, quantitative skills). However, unidimensionality is to some extent a fiction, because the central construct usually has subsidiary components (for example, ability to perform particular kinds of mathematical operations or reasoning). If *subscores* are used, they reflect such components. If the test is instead explicitly multidimensional, it may have separately scored sections, such as quantitative and verbal (Tate, 2002).[16]

How would data show that the test is unidimensional, if such is the intention? In statistical terms, an examinee's performance on individual items should correspond with his or her overall performance. Thus, for example, one would expect that the more difficult a selected-response item is, the higher the overall test scores of those students who do choose the correct answer. Actual data from the test should reflect both the intended *difficulty* of items and the intended test dimensionality. (See chapter 6 for an explanation of ways in which item difficulty can be estimated.)[17]

An extension of this principle is used in analyses of *differential item functioning* (DIF), which can indicate unwanted multidimensionality—that is, measuring something other than what was intended. DIF occurs when different groups of examinees (e.g., men, women, ethnic minorities) with similar overall scores on the test perform in systematically different ways on an item. The analysis looks at how examinees at each overall score level performed on a particular item to see if the item appeared to be harder or easier for examinees as categorized by ethnicity, gender, language, or other characteristic. (See chapter 7 for more about DIF.)

Data about reliability of test scores and sources of measurement error would also be included in this area. (See chapter 6 for more about reliability information.)

Relations to Other Variables

As the category name suggests, this kind of empirical evidence draws on information outside the test. Do the data about "external variables"—that is, other relevant measurements of examinees' performance—support or undermine the test's claim about measuring a particular construct?

In fact, this quantitative approach to validation originated with the very beginning of mental measurement. To find whether Cattell's psychophysical tests of college freshmen predicted their future academic performance, Wissler used Pearson's new methods of computing *correlation coefficients* to make quantitative comparisons of performance across measures.*

Spearman (1904), who emphasized the use of correlations among phenomena as a way of finding meaning, improved on Wissler's methods by taking into account errors of observation. These methods paved the way for validity investigation focused on examining how test scores correlate with results from *criterion* measures.

In principle, Cureton (1951) explained, such inquiry would involve comparing how students perform on tasks in a test with how they perform on related tasks in real life—the "ultimate criterion." Thus, when Wissler compared students' test scores to subsequent grades, the grades served as the criterion measure for real-life academic achievement.

Insofar as Wissler was investigating how well Cattell's tests predicted future course grades, he was investigating what would come to be called "predictive validity," "predictive accuracy," or *predictive evidence.* Even today, college admissions tests estimate predictive accuracy for college grades, albeit using more sophisticated mathematical techniques than simple correlations. (See note 9, chapter 7; but also see Atkinson & Geiser, 2009, pp. 15–18, for an argument against emphasizing prediction.)

However, as Cureton's description suggested, test performance could also be compared to a contemporary or concurrent criterion measure rather than a future one. *Concurrent validity* studies can also be used "to validate a proxy measure that would be cheaper, easier, or safer than the criterion " (Kane, 2006, p. 18). Although predictive and concurrent criterion comparisons were once considered distinct, they are based on the same principle and are now both classified as criterion-related evidence.†

In the area of intelligence testing, Terman investigated both kinds of criterion-related evidence. He attempted to show that the Army Mental Tests measured "a soldier's value to the service" by comparing soldiers' test scores with officers' ratings of men and with official U.S. Army classifications (1918, pp. 182–84). Later, in 1922, he launched the first—albeit flawed—

---

*A simple correlation coefficient indicates the linear relationship between two different variables (such as an individual's scores on two different tests). The correlation coefficient indicates the extent to which the two variables move together with each other, both in direction (positive or negative) and in amount. The scale for correlation coefficients goes upward from -1 (completely negative or inverse correspondence) to 0 (no correspondence) to +1 (completely positive or perfect correspondence).

†A clear example of a concurrent validity study is an investigation by Lee (2002) into using a laboratory-based driving simulator to assess performance of drivers over age sixty, as a cheaper and safer alternative to an actual road test. Lee scored volunteers' performance on both the simulator (the proxy measure) and the road test (the criterion), and then she examined the correlations, as adjusted for sources of measurement error, between the two sets of scores for each driver. Of course, the ultimate criterion would be real-life driving performance over time.

longitudinal study, amassing decades' worth of data on children who had received high scores on his intelligence tests (Leslie, 2000).[18]

Soon, so great became the emphasis on viewing validity as the statistical correspondence between test and criterion scores that the correlation coefficient was named a *validity coefficient*. A 1946 text on educational measurement even asserted "In a very general sense, a test is valid for anything with which it correlates" (Guilford, p. 429; quoted in Angoff, 1988, p. 20). Such a statement suggests that validity evidence could include correlations with an unrelated, irrelevant criterion—the meaning of test scores would not matter as long as they were useful for a certain purpose. For this reason, critics such as Borsboom et al. (2004) argue against using any criterion correlations for validation.

In the ideal, any criterion measure used to judge the accuracy and usefulness of test scores ought to "exemplify a measurement procedure clearly superior to (i.e., more relevant and precise than) that embodied in the test" (Ebel, 1961/1996, p. 217). But a superior measurement procedure or even a relevant one is not always available, and trying to establish the validity of the criterion measures would lead to an "infinite regress" (p. 213). Hence the common use of grades as a criterion, even though they can be subjective and inconsistent.

Still, the *Standards* cautions that the value of a test-criterion relationship depends on how relevant, reliable, and valid the criterion measure is with respect to the same construct on which the test focuses (AERA et al., 1999, p. 14).

Other information from external variables would be *convergent* and *discriminant evidence* about whether the test is measuring the intended construct. Internal analyses of test dimensionality show only the number, not the nature, of dimensions, so that even a unidimensional test might not be measuring the intended construct. Researchers would hope to find similar results from other measures intended to assess similar constructs (convergent evidence), as well as dissimilar results from measures intended to assess dissimilar constructs (discriminant evidence) (AERA et al., 1999, p. 15).

Techniques for collecting such evidence originate with the "multitrait multimethod matrix " introduced by Campbell and Fiske (1959). The basic principle is to use at least two different methods to measure two different constructs, then determine whether measurements of the same construct correlate more highly with each other than with measurements of other constructs. For example, scores on a test of quantitative skills should correlate more highly with grades in math courses or other quantitatively oriented disciplines than with test scores in verbal skills or grades in English courses. Both halves of the investigation are important: similar results for similar constructs, dissimilar results for dissimilar constructs.

Another type of external variable involves the conditions of a particular assessment procedure. For example, researchers conduct experiments to see whether or not a test is undesirably *speeded*, that is, whether time limits affect how examinees perform on a test that is not intended to measure how quickly the examinee can work (Lu & Sireci, 2007). To investigate the robustness of the construct and possible sources of construct-irrelevant variance, researchers may vary the topics, tasks, item formats, raters, and so on, and observe the effects on scores (Messick, 1989). Research on an *"N*-effect " even suggests that increasing the number (*N*) of students or perceived competitors taking a test in the same venue can decrease motivation (Garcia & Tor, 2009).

Last in the "other variables" category, the validity argument must address the extent to which results from localized validity studies apply to other settings and situations. Obviously, the populations and conditions in the validity samples should be as representative as possible of those for which the test is intended. With sufficient amounts of data, meta-analyses of existing validity studies may support using the test within a specified range of other situations (AERA et al., 1999, pp. 15–16).

CONSEQUENCES AND VALIDITY

In 1988, Cronbach urged that validation "link concepts, evidence, social and personal consequences, and values" (p. 4), while Messick emphasized making "judgmental appraisals" of consequences as well as "empirical appraisals" of evidence (1988, p. 41). Such statements and new attention in the 1985 *Standards* to the needs of particular groups (speakers of foreign languages or disabled examinees) reflected growing awareness of how testing affects individuals and society. Moreover, the intensified use of testing as a means toward reforming education raised the obvious question of whether or not this time-consuming and expensive strategy actually benefited students.

Messick's 1989 chapter built on this trend by including as a new aspect of validity the "potential or actual" social consequences arising from test interpretation or test use. Frederiksen and Collins (1990) extended this approach for educational tests by proposing an overarching concept of *systemic validity*: the extent to which testing "induces in the educational system curricular and instructional changes that foster the development of the cognitive skills that the test is designed to measure" (p. 5). Shepard (1993) suggested that validity standards be modeled on Food and Drug Administration standards, in which scientists are "responsible for evaluating both the theoretically anticipated effects and side effects of any product before it is rendered 'safe and effective' and released for wide-scale use" (p. 426).

These questions can be examined by classifying consequences as Brennan (2006) proposes: "intended and unintended, positive and negative" (p. 8). The obvious starting point is intended positive consequences: the anticipated benefits of testing. For example, if the explicit purpose of a testing program were to improve instruction and promote learning, then validation would include demonstrating that these outcomes actually occur and can be attributed to the program.

Addressing unintended and negative consequences is a murkier area, analogous to dealing with undesirable side effects of a medication.

To begin with, measurement observations always carry value implications. Numerical scores and labels such as "proficient," "85th percentile," "below the mean," and so on, are not neutral. The observer effects of testing—defining individual identity or worth—are exactly what Hanson (2000), Garrison (2004), and Berlak (2000) criticize.[19]

Other types of negative outcomes can include undesired effects on curricula and instruction, differential impact on certain groups of examinees, cheating and test coaching that subvert the meaning of scores, and misuse of scores by unauthorized entities. An obvious and too common example of misuse is ranking states or school districts according to scores from college admissions tests (Brennan, 2006).

Still, it is not easy to anticipate all the possible consequences of testing— nor is it simple to assign and enforce responsibility for them.

Often, test makers may be best able to collect information about test effects and explain it to test users. Test publishers have an obligation to provide evidence and rationales for intended uses of tests and to warn against potential misuses of test scores. But validity standards can only hold test publishers accountable for consequences within their control. Many are not, short of withdrawing the test.

According to the *Standards,* test users (such as states) are jointly responsible for the validation process and hence often share responsibility for consequences (AERA et al., 1999, p. 11). Yet the only enforcement mechanisms are legal ones. Linn (1998) comments that only "the judicial system or ballot box" can force policy makers who mandate testing to demonstrate its efficacy (p. 29). Hence perhaps the justice system could set the rules for evaluating social consequences (Langenfeld & Crocker, 1994). On the other hand, Elliot (1987) makes a cogent argument that the adversary system is inherently incapable of framing the best possible policies on test use; if remedies are needed, they must be legislative.[20]

Evidence about consequences for examinees is particularly important when courts consider challenges to tests used in high-stakes decisions. The validity argument must address questions about statutory and constitutional protections, including adequate notice, sufficient curricular preparation, and accommodations and modifications for examinees with disabilities or limited English proficiency (Sireci & Parker, 2006).

There are efforts to make evaluation of consequences more systematic. Mehrens (2002) suggests sources of evidence relevant to K–12 tests: curricular changes, effect on teacher morale and behavior, effect on student motivation and self-image, gains in learning, and public perception.

An example of such research is offered by Hamilton, Stecher, Marsh, McCombs, Robyn, Russell, Naftel, and Barney (2007), who examine the impact of accountability tests via "case study" classroom observations and surveys and interviews of teachers and administrators repeated over several years. In a different vein, Goertz, Oláh, and Riggan (2010) studied teachers' actual use of data from interim assessments and its effects on instruction and achievement. (For more about how test purposes, uses, and consequences interrelate, see chapter 8 and see chapter 9 in volume 2.)

Yet conflating test consequences with scientific accuracy in the validation process has mixed consequences itself. On the one hand, it helps hold claims about benefits up to empirical scrutiny and facilitates cost-benefit analysis. It could lead to positive actions, such as involving policy makers, educators, parents, and students, in designing and validating a test that will affect them (Ryan, 2002). And it might reframe validity in school tests as "educational value" so that "a test is valid to the extent that you are happy for teachers to teach toward the test" (Wiliam, 2000, p. 117).

On the other hand, many experts—despite agreeing that consequences absolutely should be considered in decisions about test use —argue that viewing consequences as part of validity causes decision makers to confuse the accuracy of score interpretations with the effects of test uses (Popham, 1997; Koretz, 2008). The problem is that score interpretations can be quite accurate but then misused.

The ongoing debate can be seen in comments on the subject from members of the NCME (2010). Some members argue for a clear distinction between justifying the meaning of scores and justifying the uses of scores, perhaps calling the former "validity" and the latter "utility." Others argue that surgically separating the two is not possible and not even desirable, since consequences might be deemphasized.

This issue is one that BOTA could certainly address, but part of the problem may be that testing has no agency for regulation or consumer protection, as many other industries do. The larger problem of consequences is one that cannot be solved within the profession; it involves citizens, educators, and government officials as well. As an example of a step forward, the RTTT assessment competition required the consortia to explain plans for determining whether the intended effects on institutions and individuals are being achieved (see SBAC, 2010, p. 88).

Perhaps requiring, or at least offering guidelines for, testing programs to create a kind of "environmental impact report" as part of the development process would also be helpful. As more research about consequences accumulates, there should be a sounder basis for predicting effects of particular types of testing, finding ways to minimize negative effects, and considering the range of alternatives. In turn, having to formulate a preliminary document about consequences might encourage programs to make proactive improvements.

For now, validation is officially supposed to address efficacy for the stated purpose and anticipated ancillary effects, to the extent that these are within the control of test makers and test users. The *Standards* distinguishes between issues "within the technical purview of validity" from those of "social policy" (AERA et al., 1999, p. 16).

Table 5.1. Elements of a Validity Argument

Questions	Reasoning and Evidence
Why give the test; what information is it intended to provide? What are the claims about score meaning and use?	• The need for information about particular knowledge and skills in order to make a particular kind of decision • Potential benefits beyond those of other available measures • Overview and detailed description of construct, domain, and claims
How do the assessment procedures (test content, format, administration, scoring) promote the accuracy and intended meaning of the information?	• Methods and sources used in determining construct, domain, and score use (research, surveys, expert input, etc.) • Support for decisions that underlie the test specifications • Rules/procedures for writing, reviewing, assembling, and scoring test items; qualifications of persons involved • Alignment studies that include instruction and curriculum • Strategies to minimize specific sources of construct underrepresentation and of construct-irrelevant variance
How closely do actual response processes match the intended ones?	• Tasks designed to reveal steps in cognitive processes • Observations of examinees and raters as they work • Interviews with examinees and raters afterward
How well do statistical data match the planned internal structure of the test?	• Factor analyses comparing intended with actual test dimensionality for different population groups • Correlations among the different sections of the test • Procedures for analyzing item difficulty and discrimination • Procedures for analyzing differential item functioning

(continued)

Table 5.1. *(Continued)*

Questions	Reasoning and Evidence
How well do relationships between test scores and data from external sources support the intended use and meaning of scores?	• Relevance, reliability, and validity of criterion measure(s); correspondence between test scores and criterion scores • Comparisons with convergent and discriminant measures • Generalizability of local validity studies to other situations • Effects of varying different conditions of the test
How well are the consequences of test use anticipated and addressed?	• Acknowledgment of potential negative consequences • Compliance with legal rights and protections • Strategies and protocols for fairness and accessibility • Empirical research on actual outcomes and effects
Is there sufficient guidance for examinees and test users?	• Who is tested, who uses the test, in what kinds of decisions • Complete, accessible test-familiarization materials • Limitations of the test; types of supplementary measures • Warnings against specific misuses of test scores
How clear, coherent, plausible, and complete is the entire validity argument?	• Provides separate argument for each proposed use of scores • Includes counterevidence and addresses threats to validity • Covers all aspects of technical quality (reliability, etc.) • Documented in accordance with the *Standards* • Addresses any significant test revisions

A validity argument should, then, offer varied and compelling types of evidence on both scientific and technological aspects of testing. It must both convincingly support and responsibly qualify claims about the meaning, relevance, accuracy, and usefulness of test scores.

Chapter V: Key Points

- Validity is not an inherent property of a test, nor is it an absolute. It is the extent to which theory, reasoning, and evidence together support the intended meaning and use of scores. Validity is not only a matter of degree but also a matter of context.
- The construct approach, introduced in 1954–1955, proposed scientific theory testing as way of establishing validity. How well does the construct (a theory about a mental attribute, such as proficiency in an academic subject) explain the ways in which examinee perform? A unitary concept of validity posits that construct validity is the overarching framework for all validity evidence. Conversely, the construct theory must address all relevant evidence.
- The *Standards* requires testing programs to present a logically coherent validity argument for claims about what the test scores mean and how they should be used.
- Different kinds of evidence may support or weaken the argument. One is content evidence, which focuses on judgments about how the construct is defined and how well the test materials and procedures serve to represent that construct. Another is evidence about relations to external variables, such as the extent to which performance on the test corresponds with performance on criterion measures of the same construct. Other evidence can include statistical analyses comparing predicted and actual test data, as well as studies of what examinees are actually thinking and doing while they complete the tasks in the test.
- In advocating a unitary validity, Messick also included the consequences of testing as a facet of validity. Other experts believe consequences should be evaluated separately from the meaning and accuracy of scores. Test makers and/or users do have a responsibility to minimize negative effects of using the test as intended and to support claims about efficacy.

NOTES

1. The topic of opportunity to learn is further explored in chapter 7, but note that the possible illegality would come from a state's requiring students to meet standards for which the state has not provided adequate resources. If the test were a licensing test for a profession, there would be no legal requirement to demonstrate that all examinees have sufficient opportunity to learn the tested knowledge and skills.

2. Cronbach was a member of both the 1954 and the 1955 *Technical Recommendations* committees. This point is significant because their documents contradicted some of Cureton's ideas about validity in the 1951 *Educational Measurement*. Cureton (1951) had warned against ascribing "causal or explanatory implications" to test performance—against defining "abstract concepts" beyond what could be empirically observed (pp. 641–43). It may also be significant that Cureton is not listed as a member of the 1955 Committees.

3. This process might sound somewhat solipsistic. A relativistic perspective might see construct validity as no more than a matter of agreement between the test and a version of socially determined reality held by its makers and users (Messick, 1989, p. 24).

4. In 1918, E. L. Thorndike emphasized that accurate and useful test results could not be obtained without using methods to eliminate "certain pernicious disturbing factors, notably unfair preparation for the test, inequalities in interest and effort, and inequalities in understanding what the task is" (pp. 21, 23). Soon after, McCall (1922) discussed ways in which language and test-question formats could introduce irrelevancies and extraneous difficulties, such as complex wording of math problems, unfamiliar question types, speed of handwriting, and fatigue (pp. 198–200).

5. Thus, for example, if Yerkes had used his demographic data to explore the hypotheses that the scores on the U.S. Army Mental Tests were affected by cultural knowledge, English proficiency, and testing conditions, he might have revised his theory that the scores indicated innate intelligence and nothing else.

6. Validity generalization means that it is not necessary to do a new validity study for each different group of people, as long as they can be considered members of the population represented by the group used in the validation study (M. J. Zieky, personal communication, June 4, 2010).

7. Lindquist cautioned that "if a test is 'valid,' it is valid for *a given purpose*, with a given group of pupils, and is valid only to the degree that it accomplishes that specific purpose for that specific group" (1936, p. 21). According to Cureton, "The essential question of test validity is how well a test does the job it is employed to do" (1951, p. 621).

8. See Shepard, 1993, p. 427; Brennan, 2001c, p. 12; Borsboom et al., 2004, p. 1061; and Lissitz and Samuelsen, 2007, p. 427.

9. In contrast, Embretson (2007) objects to privileging content-related validity evidence in part because deemphasizing constructs and external relationships would make it more difficult to identify and address sources of construct-irrelevant variance (for example, imprecise or confusing wording on a mathematics question) (pp. 451–52).

10. Toulmin (1958) called informal logic "generalized jurisprudence," and he suggested that "argumentation can be compared with law-suits, and the claims we make and argue for in extra-legal contexts with claims made in the courts" (p. 7). Alluding to the central role of argumentation in science, he noted that the great figures in natural science "have transformed not only our beliefs, but also our ways of arguing and our standards of relevance and proof" (p. 257).

11. Referring to "claims and conclusions" deliberately simplifies Kane's approach. In fact, he proposes an "interpretive argument" as the rhetorical counterpart of a scientific theory, that is, the framework for interpretation and use of test scores. The interpretive argument "specifies the reasoning involved in getting from the test results to the conclusions and decisions based on these results" (2006, p. 25). In turn, the validity argument scrutinizes the interpretive argument.

The reason for simplifying Kane's terminology is that the similarity of the terms can be confusing.

12. The early origins of this perspective can be seen in writings by Tyler, who repeatedly used the term "evidence." Perhaps the clearest recent statement is from Mislevy, Steinberg, and Almond (2003): "In educational assessment, we observe what students say, do, or make in a few particular circumstances and attempt to infer what they know, can do, or have accomplished more generally. A web of inference connects the two" (p. 3). This idea is also suggestive of generalizability theory (see chapter 6).

13. The American Federation of Teachers (AFT, 2008b) offers explanations and illustrations of what makes "strong" standards (e.g., specific, explicit, detailed, with attention to both content and skills) and "weak" standards.

14. The Council of Chief State School Officers (2008) provides a brief overview of two models for conducting alignment studies: the "Surveys of Enacted Curriculum" model developed by Andrew Porter and the "Webb Model," developed by Norman Webb. For more about the latter, see Webb (2006).

For a more detailed treatment of alignment studies, see the 2007 issue of *Applied Measurement in Education* that is devoted to the topic (vol. 20, no. 1). Other resources are Crocker (2003), who describes a range of research on content representativeness (p. 8), and Popham (2007), who suggests procedures specifically aimed at judging the instructional sensitivity of a test intended for accountability purposes.

15. See Clark and Estes, 1996, for the origins of this approach. For more examples, see Embretson (1998) and Mislevy, Steinberg, and Almond (2003). Embretson discusses the development and tryout of abstract-reasoning items using various analyses of response processes; Mislevy et al. apply the concepts of evidence-centered design to large-scale language testing. In keeping with Kane's idea of interpretive arguments, the latter approach starts by identifying claims one wants to be able to make about aspects of students' knowledge and skills, then designs tasks to capture evidence relevant to the claims.

16. For an example of a study that identified "computation" and "applications" as distinct but related constructs in mathematical skills, and that also showed each construct as having high correlations with reading skills, see Thurber, Shinn, and Smolkowski (2002).

17. The methods used to explore test dimensionality are based on the techniques of factor analysis that Spearman invented to examine correlations among various measures of students' intelligence. In essence, his single g factor suggested that these measures were unidimensional, capturing the same construct.

18. Not only was the sample of over 1,000 children unrepresentative of the general population, but also Terman did not establish and track a control group, nor did he maintain distance from his subjects, the "Termites." The important legacies of Terman's study were the conceptual precedent that it set and the amount and variety of data collected about the subjects' lives (Leslie, 2000). An intriguing fact: Lee Cronbach took Terman's test in 1921 and was one of the subjects of the study.

19. Taking a postmodern perspective, Berlak (2000) says that including consequences as part of the validation process actually subverts the assumptions of the entire measurement enterprise:

> If the validity of an educational measure cannot be determined without the intervention of human moral, educational and/or political judgments which the experts now admit, no scientific or technical process can exist for establishing the validity of a test on which its claims of fairness and objectivity rest. (p. 193)

20. Langenfeld and Crocker (1994) acknowledge that legal decisions about assessment have diverged from professional standards for assessment by focusing only on criterion and content evidence. However, they urge that courts work together with measurement professionals, because testing is a sociopolitical matter and "the legal system is in a unique position to effectively adjudicate and articulate underlying values supporting test usage" (p. 161).

Elliott (1987) investigated two cases that both involved using scores from intelligence tests to place students into special education: *Larry P. v. Riles* (1972) and *Parents in Action in Special Education (PASE) v. Hannon* (1980). The first case ruled against this use of scores and the second case, rejecting the first as a precedent, ruled in favor. Elliot argued that such influences as contemporaneous events, judges' personalities, relative strength of the opposing sides' resources, and so on determined the outcome rather than any scientific considerations. Thus "courts provide an unusually inappropriate forum for the resolution of complex social science issues" because they prevent responsible sharing of information and disinterested debate among experts (p. 202).

SELECTED READINGS

Borsboom, D., Mellenbergh, G. J., & van Heerden, J. (2004). The concept of validity. *Psychological Review, 111*(4), 1061–71.

Chapelle, C. A., Enright, M. K., & Jamieson, J. (2010). Does an argument-based approach to validity make a difference? *Educational Measurement: Issues and Practice, 29*(1), 3–13.

Haladyna, T. M. (2006). Roles and importance of validity studies in test development. In S. M. Downing & T. M. Haladyna (Eds.). *Handbook of test development* (pp. 739–55). Mahwah, NJ: Lawrence Erlbaum Associates.

Cronbach, L. J. (1971). Test validation. In R. L. Thorndike, (Ed.), *Educational measurement* (2nd ed., pp. 443–507). Washington, DC: American Council on Education.

Kane, M. T. (1992). An argument-based approach to validity. *Psychological Bulletin, 112*(3), 527–35.

Messick, S. (1989). Validity. In R. L. Linn (Ed.), *Educational measurement* (3rd ed., pp. 13–103). New York: American Council on Education and Macmillan Publishing Company.

Mislevy, R. J., Steinberg, L. S., & Almond, R. G. (2003). On the structure of educational assessments. *Measurement: Interdisciplinary Research and Perspectives, 1*(1), 3–62.

Chapter Six

Reliability

Determination of reliability is as much a logical as a statistical problem.

—Robert. L. Thorndike, 1951 (p. 570)

Imagine, for a moment, two siblings named Val and Billie, who happen to work together.

Val has long been a theoretician of science and psychology, but in recent years, this multifaceted, restless thinker has also been studying legal issues and become more of a social activist. Val is always demanding to know, "What do these scores really mean?" and "Should we be using them in that way?"

Billie, the geekier sibling, tends to be immersed in data, equations, and algorithms. Billie is always fussing, "Wait a minute—just how sure are we about these scores?"

Idealistic Val and meticulous Billie squabble at times over professional turf, yet in the end, they can't manage without each other.

Val is, of course, validity as described in the previous chapter. Billie is reliability, or the consistency of test scores. (Just like validity, reliability is a characteristic of scores, not of tests by themselves.) Over the years, Billie has been wrestling with a problem inherent in the act of observation or measurement.

That problem is that observations of the same quantity—even a physical quantity such as the weight of an object—often differ. No single observation is likely to be definitive or perfectly consistent with all other observations; instead, each is likely to be somewhat affected by "noise," accidental inconsistency, or unpredictable error. Hence *error of measurement,* "error of observation," and "measurement error" do not refer to mistakes in procedures but to an unavoidable fact of life.

R. L. Thorndike (1951) succinctly defined the yin-yang duality of reliability and error: "Wherever there is reliability in some set of measurements there is also some degree of unreliability. The two are cut from the same pie, being always present together, the one becoming more as the other becomes less" (p. 561). Therefore, understanding and quantifying either one helps us to understand and quantify the other.

In this chapter, we will look at three psychometric frameworks on which testing programs draw to address issues of error and reliability. They are *classical test theory*, which largely dates from the early 1900s; and *generalizability theory* and *item response theory*, which both emerged in the 1960s–1970s. We will need to wade into some technical waters, but only far enough to see why certain concepts are significant and how they are interrelated.

CLASSICAL TEST THEORY

Of the three psychometric frameworks, classical test theory (CTT) can be used in the broadest spectrum of testing situations, especially those involving fewer than several hundred examinees. Shaped by Charles Spearman in the early 1900s and highly refined by the 1950s, this body of mathematical concepts and models is pragmatic and focuses on actual performance, not underlying constructs. Yet CTT has influenced psychometrics for a century and is the foundation on which newer approaches have been built.*

Measurement Error and True Scores

In turn, CTT itself builds on the tradition of scientific measurement of a physical quantity. This connection is not surprising, given that the early psychometricians viewed measuring the mind as an extension of measuring natural phenomena.[1]

The basic concept of measurement error was introduced by Galileo Galilei (1564–1642), and Carl Friedrich Gauss (1777–1855) devised formal methods to handle this problem (Traub, 1997; Johnsen, 2005; Walker, 2007). Both men were concerned about inconsistency and imprecision in astronomical observations.

In considering how to reconcile the differences among astronomers' estimates of the distance from the center of the Earth to a particular star, Galileo reasoned that any given astronomer was equally likely to overestimate as to underestimate the distance. Therefore the errors in many such estimates (miles over and miles under the "true" distance) would eventually tend to cancel out one another.

---

*Harold Gulliksen (1903–1996) asserted that "nearly all the basic formulas that are particularly useful in test theory are found in Spearman's early papers" (1950, p. 1). His own 1950 *Theory of Mental Tests* and Lord, Novick, and Birnbaum's 1968 *Statistical Theories of Mental Test Scores* are considered authoritative works on CTT.

Much later, in 1809, Gauss offered a mathematical proof that if one were to add up all observations of a physical quantity, then divide this sum by the number of observations, the result—the mean or mathematical average—would be the best estimate of the "true" value. The more observations, the more precise the estimate.

Thus scientists use both logic and mathematics to deal with errors in their observations of the same quantity (a distance, volume, humidity level, etc.). Usually they are concerned with a physical quantity that exists independently, even though observations of it are affected by the measuring *instruments*, such as telescopes, graduated cylinders, hydrometers, and so on.

But in psychometrics, the focus turns to a quantity that is neither physical nor independent of the measuring instrument. This quantity is the number representing an examinee's performance on a particular test, which CTT calls the examinee's *observed score* or actual score.

As a type of observation, a test score is subject to error, so that it may be "too high" or "too low." CTT assumes that the basic principle for estimating a physical quantity still applies: taking the average of many observations helps reduce the amount of error.

In theory, then, to help cancel out the errors of measurement, examiners conducting assessment procedures could repeat or replicate their observations, just as scientists repeat observations and experiments in order to increase confidence in the results (Brennan, 2001a). By taking the average of an examinee's score over many (ideally, infinite) interchangeable or parallel versions of the test, the examiners would obtain the best estimate of the examinee's performance on that test—a *true score*. However, this assumption requires that the examinee's performance remain utterly unchanged, with no additional learning or forgetting.

A true score is thus a mathematical abstraction, an "expected" or projected mean score for a particular person, at a particular time, on a particular test—not a metaphysical or Platonic truth (Lord, Novick, & Birnbaum, 1968; Haertel, 2006). It is somewhat like the average weight a person would obtain by stepping on the same scale again and again over the course of an hour.[2]

Moreover, although reliable, a hypothetical true score is not necessarily valid in terms of accurately representing what scores from that test are intended to mean. It is only free of measurement error.*

---

*Despite being completely consistent and reliable, a true score might be inaccurate as an indication of the construct being measured. There might be sources of invalidity in the assessment procedures, such as underrepresentation of the domain, questions that measure constructs other than the one intended, physical or linguistic barriers, and so on. Because this kind of error would have a consistent effect on an examinee's score—it would bias the examinee's score in one direction and would not be cancelled out by retesting—it is called *systematic error*.

However, a particular source of invalidity (such as a misscored multiple-choice item or untrained raters) can affect different examinees in different ways. If test makers can predict or identify the problem, they can adjust the measurement procedures and/or the scores.

Logically, then, the difference between an examinee's observed score and true score is the error of measurement. Spearman's 1907 formula puts this logic into mathematical terms: an observed score X is a combination of the true score T and the "error score" E, that is, $X = T + E$. (The value of E would be negative if X were too low, positive if X were too high, or zero if X were free of *random error*.)

An examinee's test score is thus a Thorndikean pie sliced into two portions: reliability and error. Unfortunately, we do not know how big each portion is—but as we will see, CTT offers ways to estimate their size.

Types of Random Error in Testing

First, however, we need to look more closely at measurement error. It is what would cause an examinee's scores over infinite retests to fluctuate up and down from the examinee's true score. It thus causes unpredictable, undesirable *variance*—that is, the dispersion of these scores from their mean.

But what, in turn, causes measurement error? It arises from "random, temporary, unstable characteristics" of the examinee or instrument (Haertel, 2006, p. 68). Hence it is considered to be random error. CTT stresses this randomness, because it is the basis for a useful assumption: the measurement errors that occur in test scores are not correlated with one another or with the examinees' true scores.

Random error in testing can be caused by chance factors of two types. One type is related to the testing occasion, as when an examinee's temporary fatigue, level of motivation, lucky guesswork, or unlucky guesswork introduces "error from time sampling." In theory, increasing the number of testing occasions and taking the mean score would reduce error from the occasion.[3]

But there are also chance factors related to the instrument: any particular set of items chosen to represent the content domain introduces "error from content sampling." For example, some questions on one version of a test might happen to coincide with areas in which an examinee is strong; given another version of the test, the examinee might not be so fortunate. Moreover, each test item has its own characteristics that may elicit "idiosyncratic reactions" from different examinees (Haertel, 2006, p. 70). For example, one examinee might consider a particular essay question intriguing; another examinee might consider it tedious.

In theory, again, increasing the number of items in a test could help cover more of the domain and thereby reduce error from sampling. In addition, it would reduce the effect of any one particular item on the overall test score.[4]

One other type of instrument-related error occurs in tests that use constructed-response tasks. The score that an examinee receives for his/her response may be affected by whichever rater(s) happen to score the response. In theory, this kind of error could be reduced by having many raters score the response and taking the average score. (See the section on rating processes later in this chapter.)

Of course, these kinds of random, chance factors are not the only influences on test scores. The largest influence, or source of variance, should be the extent to which examinees have the relevant knowledge and skills. But a test maker trying to quantify the reliability of a test's scores has to decide how to define reliability. The test maker must choose whether to include a given factor in the reliability portion of the score (consider it as part of the true score), to include it in the error portion, or even to ignore it.

Statistical Concepts in CTT

In order to see how these decisions are made in practical terms, it is helpful first to understand some of the statistical concepts that CTT combines in powerful ways to express relationships among observed scores, true scores, and error scores.

Distribution (or frequency of values) refers to the overall shape of a set of data points as plotted on an x-y graph. One could plot many types of data sets, such as a group of examinees' observed scores on a test, the same examinees' error scores, or the hypothetical set of observed scores that a single examinee would obtain after retaking the test many times.

In a *normal distribution* such as Gauss described, the shape is a "bell curve" centered on the mean. (See Figure 6.1 for an illustration.) Here about half the data points lie symmetrically on either side of the mean. More of the data points lie close to the mean than lie far from the mean, with the peak at the mean.[5] In theory, the set of scores that an examinee would obtain from infinite retesting would take this kind of shape. Also in theory, one might expect that test scores for a very large population of examinees would be normally distributed, although the reality may look different.

Because distributions have many possible patterns, it would be helpful to be able to describe exactly how a set of data points spreads out on either side of its mean—whether the data points tend to cluster tightly around the mean or disperse widely from it. The *standard deviation* (*SD*) expresses the dispersion of the data set in terms of the units used to measure it (such as units in a test's score scale). The smaller the *SD*, the more tightly the data points cluster around the mean, and vice versa. (See Figure 6.1.)

CTT applies the concepts of distribution and standard deviation to a set of error scores, whether for an individual hypothetically retaking a test many times or for a very large group of examinees actually taking the test a single

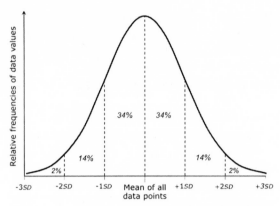

Figure 6.1. Normal distribution and standard deviations. The graph shows a "bell curve" of normally distributed data points. In this distribution, 68 percent of all the data points lie within ±1 *SD* of the mean; 95 percent lie within ±2 *SD*; and 99.7 percent lie within ±3 *SD*.

time. Because the errors are both positive and negative values, this set is distributed around its mean of zero (which is the amount of error in a true score). The question then becomes: to what extent do the error scores vary from their mean? For example, if they are widely dispersed from their mean, then the observed scores will contain large amounts of error.

The answer to this question is a *standard error of measurement (SEM)*, defined as the standard distribution of the error scores for a particular test. It is estimated based on the consistency and distribution of observed scores for a group taking the test.[6]

The *SEM* is expressed in units of the test's score scale (for example, 5 out of 100 points). For a test's *SEM*, smaller is better. The more tightly the error scores cluster around their mean of zero, the less error an examinee's score is likely to contain.[7]

Often the *SEM* for a test is depicted as *score bands* (or *error bands*) around a score on the test's scale, to give a better sense of the amount of positive or negative error that may affect an examinee's score. In score bands, the observed score is assumed to be close to the examinee's true score, and the bands reflect a hypothetical set of observed scores normally distributed around the true score. (See Figure 6.2.)

This method is used to suggest, tentatively, that there is a 68 percent probability that a score band extending from 1 *SEM* below to 1 *SEM* above the examinee's score will include the examinee's true score. By lengthening this band at both ends, so that it reaches from 2 *SEM* below to 2 *SEM* above the examinee's score, there is a 95 percent probability that the score band will in-

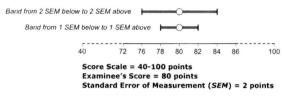

Figure 6.2. Score bands showing error in a test score. Tentatively, there is a 68 percent probability that the lower band includes the examinee's true score, and a 95 percent probability that the upper band includes the examinee's true score.

clude the true score. (In the example, the 68 percent band spans about 78 to 82 on the score scale, and the 95 percent band spans about 76 to 84 on the score scale.) Thus the wider the band, the more likely it includes the true score.[8]

Harvill (1991) calls score bands an "adequate approximation" of score precision for an examinee when the reliability of the group's scores is "reasonably high" and the examinee's score is not distant from the group's mean score (p. 186). Still, as he emphasizes, the possibility remains that a person's true score does not lie within the score bands.

Last, CTT brings the concept of correlation to bear upon the reliability of scores from a particular test given to a particular population of examinees. (Conceptually, this reliability is the ratio of observed score variance to true score variance.) By definition, estimating this reliability requires more than one score. As Brennan (2001a) explains, "To get direct information about consistency of performance, at least two instances are required. That is, replications in some sense are necessary to estimate reliability" (p. 295). But without retesting examinees, how is it possible to obtain additional scores?

In 1910, working separately, Spearman and William Brown (1881–1952) each offered a way to simulate two independent measurements or replications from a single test. If the test had a sufficient number of items, it could be treated as two parallel half-tests—for example, by sequentially assigning every second item to a half-test. The two parallel half-tests constitute two replications, each of which produces a half-test score (Reynolds, Livingston, & Willson, 2006).

Spearman and Brown recognized that a correlation coefficient—a *reliability coefficient*—could express the extent to which scores in these two replications tended to vary together. The Spearman-Brown approach also provided a formula for "prophesying" the number of test items needed to reach a certain level of reliability. As time went on, other methods would be devised for engineering replications to obtain reliability coefficients (see the next section). Thus there is not just a single formula for a reliability coefficient.

Yet however it is calculated, a reliability coefficient in CTT always indicates the consistency of scores for a particular group of examinees who took a particular test, not for any one member of this group. It indicates how strongly the group's scores vary systematically together across two replications of the test. It indicates the extent to which individuals tend to score above the group's mean or below the mean on both replications, such that their performance in relation to one another remains consistent.

As with other correlation coefficients expressing the relationship between two variables, a key word is "variables." The more variation in scores across the group of examinees, from high to low scores, the higher the reliability coefficient (and vice versa). This fact is one reason, apart from informational utility, why it is desirable to create a test that elicits a full range of scores from examinees.

Because reliability coefficients are used in calculating the *SEM*, the former affects the latter. The higher the reliability coefficient, the lower the *SEM*. It makes sense both logically and mathematically that the greater the consistency in a group's scores, the less error likely to be present in individual scores. Moreover, any type of error considered in the reliability coefficient is also reflected in the *SEM*.

Different Types of Replications = Different Types of Reliability

While replications are necessary to investigate the consistency of scores, both the quantities and logical meanings of reliability statistics depend on the type of replications that are used. The same testing program could compute multiple reliability coefficients and *SEM*s and could specify more than one type of true score, depending on how sources of reliability and error are defined (Haertel, 2006). Thus, although reliability is like validity in being a property of test scores, it is not a unitary concept in the way that construct validity is (Brennan, 2001a).

The first, most obvious type of replication is a test-retest approach. Repeating precisely the same test on different days would, in theory, help quantify error related to time sampling and help answer the question, "How consistent are the examinees' scores over different testing occasions?" It would provide what Cronbach (1951/1996) called a *coefficient of stability,* as a more precise term for a reliability coefficient reflecting only the stability of scores over some period of time (p. 258).[9]

This approach is not common in educational testing. In contrast to psychological testing, educational testing is usually concerned with an examinee's proficiency at a certain point in time rather than with a trait assumed to be stable over time. Moreover, the effects of memory and practice would mean that the measurements were not independent, and thus reliability coefficients would be "artificially inflated" (Reynolds et al., 2006, p. 92). And, even apart from expense, it would waste an opportunity: giving exactly the same set of items a second time would mean that the test makers could not observe the effect of content sampling by varying the set of items.

A second approach to replications is to use parallel test forms to quantify the amount of error related to content sampling. Test makers build alternate versions of the same test, with the same number of items, format of items, topics, cognitive skills, and statistical characteristics.[10] Giving both forms on the same day would produce a kind of reliability coefficient that Cronbach (1951/1996) named a *coefficient of equivalence*. It addresses the question, "How consistent are examinees' scores across different sets of items representing the same domain?"

Best of all might be to administer parallel forms several days apart, if one could ensure that examinees remained exactly the same in terms of not learning or forgetting about the relevant material. This strategy would presumably result in a lower but more appropriate reliability coefficient, because it would include both error related to content sampling and error related to time sampling (Haertel, 2006, p. 70). It would yield "a coefficient of stability and equivalence" (Cronbach, 1951/1996, p. 258).

Giving parallel or alternate forms separated by several days would demand significant time, money, and other resources. Therefore, reliability estimates are usually computed for single administrations of one test form. Yet even here, reliability can be defined in different ways under different methods, producing different data.

The earliest method, the split-half approach using the 1910 Spearman-Brown formula, divides one test form into two smaller test forms that can function as if they were parallel tests. Meeting the statistical requirements can be difficult, and the coefficients can differ depending on how the items are grouped (Cronbach, 1951/1996, p. 258). However, if time limits are a significant influence on performance, using separately timed split halves is the best way to estimate alternate-forms reliability without having to administer two complete test forms to the same examinees.

A different concept of parallel measurements was introduced in 1937 when Kuder and Richardson devised formulae that would become known as KR-20 and KR-21 (Traub, 1997). Assuming that items can be scored as correct/incorrect (in a *dichotomous* manner), these formulae compute reliability coefficients based on all the hypothetically possible ways of splitting the test to produce parallel halves. This approach better reveals the consistency of examinees' performance across items; hence the term *internal consistency* (Reynolds et al., 2006). In practice, an internal consistency coefficient is a good estimate of an alternate-forms reliability coefficient.[11]

Later, in 1951, Cronbach offered a more general formula for a coefficient of internal consistency that could also be used with test items having more than one possible score (*polytomous* items, such as essays with a 0–6 scale). He called it *coefficient alpha* or α (hence *Cronbach's α* or *Cronbach's alpha*). Here the coefficient is "the mean of all split-half coefficients resulting from different splittings of a test" (p. 257). Later conceptions also loosened the requirements for strict parallelism, but Cronbach's alpha is still frequently used.

The general principle, then, is that to identify and estimate the error contributed by some aspect of the measurement procedures, the procedures must replicate this aspect in a systematic manner. If students take a test on only one occasion, then the reliability coefficients and *SEM* include only error from content sampling. They reflect only equivalence or internal consistency, not stability, so that error bands or score bands suggest a range of performance on different sets of items rather than on different occasions. As Feldt and Brennan (1989) say, "Artful manipulation of the data from a single testing occasion cannot alter this basic fact" (p. 110).

Reliability and Error in the Rating Process

Returning to the principle that adding (good) items to a test can improve score reliability, it is evident that tests using constructed-response tasks, such as essays, tend to start out at a disadvantage. Usually such tests contain fewer items than tests using only selected-response questions, so that the amount of error from content sampling or examinee/task interaction is likely to be greater.

In addition, constructed-response introduces a new source of error: the rating process. Because individual raters can vary in their judgments, the measurement of a response could vary depending on which rater happened to score the response. However, if each response is scored by more than one rater, with examinees' responses assigned randomly across raters, then the rating process is a form of replication from which one can estimate an amount of random error. (In large-scale testing programs that use constructed-response tasks, a typical arrangement is to have each response scored by two raters who cannot see each other's scores.)

Reliability data can then include *interrater reliability*, usually defined as the average consistency of raters' scores for the same response. It addresses the question, "How likely is it that any given response would be scored in the same way if it had been scored by a different set of raters?"

Testing programs typically report average levels of agreement either for all the constructed-response tasks in the test or else by type of task. These interrater reliability statistics are expressed as percentages or as types of correlation coefficients.

However, different methods for calculating agreement statistics can affect both their amount and meaning. First, "agreement" of raters' scores with one another can be defined in different ways: exact agreement only (both raters give the same score) or exact plus adjacent (both raters give the same or adjacent scores). Second, the calculations may or may not take into account the effect of chance agreement, possibly also the severity of disagreements. Third, the method used for resolving scores that disagree can affect, even distort, the overall statistics on interrater agreement.[12]

A major theme in the history of constructed-response testing has been a drive to enhance interrater reliability by using standardized tasks and procedures that promote uniformity in raters' use of the scoring criteria. (Increasing the number of raters per response also reduces the amount of error, but significantly adds to time, expense, and staffing needs.)

Yet anyone who scores examinees' responses quickly gains a different perspective on interrater reliability. While consistency in raters' judgments is generally desirable, it is always less important than validity—than giving the "right" score, the most defensible score, in terms of the scoring guidelines. To take an extreme example, a group of raters could achieve perfect agreement by making a pact to ignore the *scoring guide* and instead give an arbitrary score of 3 (on a scale of 6) to all responses, regardless of responses' merits or defects. But most of the scores would probably be wrong. (See chapter 11 in volume 2 for more about scoring constructed-response tasks.)

GENERALIZABILITY THEORY

As we have seen, CTT implies that different sources of error can affect the reliability of test scores and that measurement procedures can be replicated in various ways, via different test forms, different raters, different occasions, etc. A later framework, generalizability theory (GT), pursues these implications, by offering ways to investigate specific sources of error and the effects of specific types of replications. GT loosens some of CTT's restrictions and even envisions a new harmony between reliability and validity. (One might irreverently think of GT—an offspring of the 1960s—as the hippie version of staid CTT.)

Primarily used for research purposes, GT can help test makers design procedures so that they optimize score reliability ("dependability" in GT) given the available resources, such as raters or testing time. GT is especially helpful for designing tests that involve constructed-response tasks. However, it requires control over experimental procedures, extended data collection, and specialized software applications.[13]

GT Is Developed to "Liberalize" CTT

Although GT was not introduced until the 1960s–1970s, psychometricians had already recognized the need to analyze score variance and measurement error in greater depth than CTT could accommodate. In keeping with his emphasis on reliability as a logical problem, R. L. Thorndike (1951) provided a table enumerating "possible sources of variance in score on a particular test," such as examinee-task interaction, subjective ratings, and temporary circumstances affecting the examinee. He noted that techniques for *analysis of variance* (ANOVA) might help quantify these sources—that is, how much variance was contributed by each of the variables (pp. 564–73).*

But rather than just look at the different components of test-score variance after the fact, one might instead investigate the different influences on test scores by dissecting the measurement process itself. Cronbach began to do so in 1951 when he emphasized that different types of observations yielded different estimates and meanings for score reliability (i.e., equivalence or stability or both). And it was, in fact, Cronbach who went on to develop GT with other colleagues.

It is not surprising, therefore, that like Cronbach's construct approach to validity, GT reflects a process-oriented scientific paradigm in which an "investigator" stipulates a theory, designs experiments, collects data via a test, and modifies the data-collection design (i.e., the test design) accordingly.

In 1963, Cronbach, Rajaratnam, and Gleser proposed revisiting classical ideas about reliability, just as Cronbach and Meehl had done with older ideas of validity. CTT's requirements for statistically parallel observations, such as parallel test forms or raters, were difficult to satisfy in real life and perhaps unnecessary. Instead, a "liberalized" concept of reliability would allow the investigator to specify observations (such as raters) that were interchangeable, even if they were not strictly equivalent replications (pp. 272, 282). This approach would reflect the essential purpose of reliability, that is, to generalize from available observations to other possible observations of the same type.

Cronbach, Gleser, Nanda, and Rajaratnam then refined and amplified GT, culminating in 1972 with *The Dependability of Behavioral Measurements: Theory of Generalizability Scores and Profiles*. This book is still a central work on GT, although the psychometric model has undergone some further refinement and development since the 1970s (as described in Brennan's 2001b *Generalizability Theory*). The techniques of GT include but go beyond ANOVA. Especially significant has been the creation of the GENOVA software, begun in the 1980s, to facilitate statistical computations for GT applications.

---

*Like quite a few other aspects of mental measurement, analysis of variance techniques actually originated in the discipline of biology. Introduced by geneticist and statistician Ronald A. Fisher (1890–1962) in the 1920s, ANOVA techniques are used to divide observed variance into constituent parts.

An Assessment Procedure Contains a Faceted
Universe of Observations

GT makes its case for looking at the big picture and permitting some flexibility in the measurement process thus:

> The decision maker is almost never interested in the response given to the particular stimulus objects or questions, to the particular tester, at the particular moment of testing. Some, at least, of these conditions of measurement could be altered without making the score any less acceptable to the decision maker. That is to say, there is a universe of observations, any of which would have yielded a usable basis for the decision. (Cronbach et al., 1972, p. 15)*

Having opened up the strict replications of CTT to the looser, interchangeable observations of GT, Cronbach et al. (1972) accordingly broadened the concept of a CTT true score to a *universe score*, the mean score across all the various types of acceptable observations or replications. Thus a person's theoretical universe score is analogous to the true score in CTT, but the number of tasks, raters, or occasions can be changed or other acceptable alterations made (Brennan, 2000).

To specify parameters for a universe of observations, the investigator classifies certain types of observations as *facets*—the factors that are sources of variance in the measurement procedure. For example, with the examinees (called "persons" in GT) constituting the object or focus of measurement, the facets designated as influences on a person's scores could include the raters, types of tasks, and occasions.† Interactions between two categories (e.g., person and task) can also be facets. Each particular instance of a facet (a kind of task, a test form, a testing date, a group of raters, etc.) is a *condition* or observation that could be replicated via acceptably interchangeable, independent observations.

The investigator embodies these decisions in an experimental design specifying all the facets (factors influencing scores). In this generalizability study, or "G study," the investigator can manipulate, control, or ignore each facet systematically (Shavelson et al., 1989). To estimate how much error a facet contributes to a person's test score, the investigator engineers at least two

---

*The terminology of decision making pervades the 1972 book on GT. It reflects the mid-1900s influence of decision theory, which Cronbach and Gleser had explicitly applied to psychometrics in 1957. The idea is that classifying examinees' level of skills, knowledge, or abilities is always a decision-making process. Dependability or reliability therefore involves the likelihood that the decision would be the same if the process were to be replicated.

†Assuming that the examinee is the object of measurement, the person facet should provide the largest source of score variance, because scores are supposed to vary from one person to the next. The "person effect" is the universe-score component of the observed score, analogous to the true-score component of an observed score (Shavelson, Webb, & Rowley, 1989, p. 924).

conditions of the facet (such as two raters, two occasions, etc.), then compares the scores obtained to see how consistent they are.

A G study thus helps to determine the number of conditions (observations)
per facet that will optimize reliability/dependability. If a facet contributes
little error, then one might reduce the number of conditions; if a facet contributes a large amount of error, then one might increase the number of conditions (Marcoulides, 1999).

With this information, the test designer can allocate resources strategically
to address the largest sources of error. If, for example, more error comes from
content sampling (tasks) than from time sampling (occasions), then adding
items would increase dependability more than adding testing occasions. Another possibility in a G study would be to compare two versions of a facet
(such as two groups of raters, each trained by a different method) and find
out which version produced more reliable scores. In either case, the findings
would help design procedures to strengthen a particular kind of score interpretation or achieve a certain statistical goal for reliability.

GT also offers the "principle of symmetry" positing "that any facet in a
design may be regarded as the object of measurement" and function as the
universe-score part of the observed score (Shavelson et al., 1989, p. 928).
Thus, for example, rather than focusing on individual students as the object of
measurement, the investigator might focus on the schools that these students
attend. From this perspective, the students become a source of measurement
error in the schools' scores.

Using GT to Design Testing Procedures

Many examples of G studies have to do with designing constructed-response
assessments, since adding even one or two more items (such as another half-
hour essay) or another rater per response entails significant time and expense.

One example is a G study that was aimed at determining the number of
constructed-response test items and raters needed for a history test. In keeping with what is typically found, adding items was a more effective way to
improve test-score reliability than was adding more raters per response. The
analysis of error variance in such studies tends to show that the interaction of
examinees with particular tasks contributes more error to the observed score
than do the raters who evaluate the responses (Baker, Abedi, Linn, & Niemi,
1996).

Other studies have explored which proposed item types might best enhance
score reliability. Yin and Shavelson (2004) used G studies to determine which
of two types of concept-map tasks would have more reliable scores and thus
be preferable for summative assessment (i.e., students' scores count toward a

grade or other important decision). For a language-skills test, Lee and Kantor (2005) considered not only the numbers of tasks and raters but also the types and combinations of tasks that would help maximize score reliability.

Test designers can also use GT to investigate the effect of interpreting scores in alternate ways. GT distinguishes between *relative decisions* having to do with differences between persons and *absolute decisions* having to do with specified levels of performance. A relative decision ranks persons in relation to one another; an absolute decision considers the person's performance in relation to prescribed criteria for quality. Relative decisions are usually presented as scores along a continuous scale; absolute decisions usually divide the scores into performance categories via *cut scores,* that is, the score or borderline at which one category changes to another, such as pass versus fail (Marcoulides, 1999).

GT can be used to investigate how choosing relative versus absolute score decisions would affect score reliability, because each type of decision treats error differently. For relative decisions, a *generalizability coefficient* is analogous to a reliability coefficient; for absolute decisions, the analogue of a reliability coefficient is called an *index of dependability*.

GT thus calls attention to a new reliability question. For relative decisions, the question is how likely examinees would be to obtain the same numerical score with a different test form, day, rater, or other factor. But for absolute decisions, the question is how likely examinees would be to obtain the same category with a different test form, day, or rater—that is, "How reliable are the classifications?"

The question is especially important when an examinee's numerical score is just above or below a cut. Therefore testing programs that classify numerical scores into performance levels need to estimate the reliability of classifications, using methods such as those offered by Livingston and Lewis (1993). The higher the coefficient(s), the greater the probability that examinees would remain classified in the same categories upon taking the test again.[14]

A final point about GT is its close relationship with validity (not surprising, given Cronbach's role in both arenas). For example, when GT involves defining acceptably interchangeable observations from a content domain, it can blur the line between reliability and validity, because how the content domain is sampled is also a validity issue (Brennan, 2000, pp. 9–10).

This point is illustrated by Shale (1996) in his argument for applying GT to assessments of writing skills. Under GT, equally acceptable samples of writing performance might span multiple modes, such as expository, narrative, and persuasive. If a test includes at least two writing tasks to promote reliability, then abandoning the parallelism of CTT for this broader definition of interchangeable tasks could also enhance validity, by representing the construct of writing skills more fully.

In this way GT aspires to bring reliability closer to validity. Defining a universe of acceptable observations that would permit inferences about a person is relevant to the meaning of scores, not just to their quantitative consistency. On a more modest level, GT certainly calls attention to the conceptual aspects of replication and reliability and the many forms they can take in measurement.

ITEM RESPONSE THEORY

At the time that GT was being formulated, a third psychometric framework was presented by Frederic M. Lord (1913–2000), Melvin R. Novick (1932–1986), and Allan Birnbaum (1923–1976) in the 1968 *Statistical Theories of Mental Test Scores*. This new approach would later be called item response theory (IRT) and, made more accessible by Lord's 1980 *Applications of Item Response Theory to Practical Testing Problems*, would become widely used in large-scale testing.

It is worth drawing attention to the era in which IRT emerged because, like GT, it has clear connections to the 1950s–1960s developments in validity theory. Even though Lord et al. viewed construct validity as a "difficult and controversial subject" not yet fully explicated, they concurred that "for scientific purposes, the most important characteristic of a test is its construct validity" (pp. 278–79).

Unlike CTT or GT, IRT assumes the existence of latent or hidden psychological constructs underlying examinees' observed performance on tests. Lord et al. (1968) referred to a construct as a *latent trait* and to their approach as "latent trait theory": "Any theory of latent traits supposes that an individual's behavior can be accounted for, to a substantial degree, by defining certain human characteristics called traits, quantitatively estimating the individual's standing on each of these traits, and then using the numerical value to predict or explain performance in relevant situations" (p. 358). The theory proposed a new model describing in mathematical terms how an examinee's mental traits were related to patterns of responses.

Assume that the trait or construct of interest is essentially unidimensional.[15] In that case, the basis of the IRT mathematical model is a single continuum or scale that quantifies the trait as a variable, of which a person possesses some amount or level.[16] This amount exists independent of any test used to measure the trait (unlike a true score, which by definition has to do with performance on a test).

Nonetheless, the amount of the trait helps "predict or explain performance" on a test. In the case of a test that is composed of selected-response items, intended to measure some ability or proficiency, IRT relies on estimated "ability levels" to predict the probability that an examinee will answer any item correctly. (Examinees of equal ability would have the same probability, regardless of the item's content.)

How are ability levels estimated? This question is answered in more detail below, but the basic assumption is that "as people possess more ability, they are more likely to be able to complete successfully a task requiring that ability" (R. M. Thorndike, 1999, p. 19). Thus, the more difficult the task, the more likely that a successful response indicates a higher level on the continuum of ability or proficiency. Conversely, succeeding for the most part only on easy tasks would indicate a low level of proficiency.

Quantifying Item Difficulty and Discrimination (in CTT)

In contrast to CTT, which focuses on overall test scores, IRT focuses on individual tasks or items—in particular, on the relationship between levels of proficiency and probability of responding successfully to a task at a particular level of difficulty.

Nonetheless, CTT is helpful in understanding how IRT establishes relationships between task difficulty and proficiency levels. Constructing tests in CTT does require attention to how examinees perform on the individual items. Of interest are each item's difficulty and *discrimination*, statistical characteristics studied in *item analysis* procedures.

In CTT, the difficulty of a selected-response item is expressed in terms of the percentage of examinees answering the item correctly. A high *p value* suggests that the item is easy for most examinees and a low *p* value that it is difficult for most examinees. This information helps test developers select items for parallel test forms with similar overall difficulty levels (Haladyna, 1999).[17]

However, *p* values in CTT are not fixed. They refer to a specific group or sample of examinees taking a particular test. For example, if a new, more proficient group takes this test, the *p* values for some items may be higher, meaning that the items are easier for this new group.

Next, analyzing item discrimination requires that one view the item in the context of the whole test. Discrimination is the item's "ability to sensitively measure individual differences that truly exist among test-takers" such that examinees "who chose the correct answer should have an overall high score on the test, and those who chose the wrong answer should have an overall low score on the test" (Haladyna, 1999, p. 166). In CTT, the relationship between examinee performance on an item and on the overall test is expressed as a correlation coefficient. Higher positive correlations indicate items that are more helpful in discriminating among examinees on the basis of proficiency, as defined by overall test performance.*

While CTT item statistics for difficulty and discrimination are certainly useful, their dependence on a specific examinee group is a drawback, as one cannot guarantee that proficiency levels, score distributions, or item statistics will remain the same across groups. In CTT, constructing a new parallel form with statistical characteristics equivalent to those of previous test forms involves making predictions, not necessarily accurate, about how future groups of examinees will perform on items.

Establishing Item Parameters in IRT

Although methods exist for adjusting the total test scores to reflect differences in populations (see chapter 8), Lord et al. (1968) recognized the desirability of being better able to predict item difficulty and discrimination characteristics. Knowing these characteristics or *item parameters* would not only help in creating parallel test forms but also make it possible to enhance reliability and precision of measurement. Rather than having to rely on statistics that change from one group of examinees to the next, the ideal would be to have items with characteristics remaining "approximately invariant" across groups (p. 354).

Using IRT methods, test makers attempt to establish item parameters by conducting "calibrations" in which a pool of test items is experimentally administered to examinees. The goal is to map each item in the pool onto the latent trait's continuum or scale so that each item has an established difficulty level corresponding to a point on that scale. Easier items would be placed lower on the latent-trait scale. The more difficult the item, the higher its position on the scale. (This trait continuum is labeled by the Greek letter *theta*, θ. The θ scale is translated into conventional score scales for reporting the scores.)

In essence, calibrating items requires two things: "a group of [items] that are distributed over the entire continuum and a group of examinees, necessarily quite large, whose abilities cover the same range" (R. M. Thorndike, 1999, p. 24).

---

*Although CTT item analysis typically involves selected-response items with one or more "correct" answers, it is also possible to analyze the difficulty and discrimination of constructed-response items that are scored along a rating scale. Note that an analysis of an item's discriminating power usually excludes that particular item from the total score.

At minimum, all IRT models estimate a difficulty parameter (*b* value) for each item, which corresponds to the trait level best measured by that item. This approach is often called a Rasch model after Georg Rasch (1901–1980), who devised it in the 1960s in an effort separate from that of Lord, Novick, and Birnbaum.

Two-parameter IRT models also estimate a discrimination parameter (*a* value), indicating how well the item differentiates those who have the corresponding *b* level from those who do not. Three-parameter models include a "pseudoguessing" parameter (*c* value), indicating the probability that persons with a trait level below the item's difficulty level would choose the correct answer by chance or guess (Hambleton, 1989, pp. 153–5/6).

In IRT, the item parameters are depicted on *x-y* graphs as S-shaped *item characteristic curves* (ICCs). For multiple-choice items, the ICC shows the probability that examinees at specified trait levels will answer the item correctly. With a scale of probability as the vertical axis and the scale of trait levels as the horizontal axis, the graph relates item difficulty to trait levels: the more difficult the item, the higher its trait-level *b* parameter. The graph should show that examinees whose θ (trait level) is exactly at the level of the item's difficulty have a 50 percent probability of answering correctly (Hambleton, 1989).[18]

Once an IRT model with item parameters has been established for a particular test, statisticians can analyze how well data from ongoing test administrations fit the model. Problems with fit may lead to revising items or dropping them from the pool.

IRT Makes Adaptive Testing Practical

As modern as IRT may seem, it actually illustrates once again how some current-day practices arose from earlier ideas. It is a bit poignant, perhaps, that psychometricians envisioned IRT-like methods and applications long before the computer technology existed to make them feasible.

In 1925, Thurstone devised a way to place the Simon-Binet intelligence-test items on an age-graded scale, thus relating performance on each item to chronological age. Clinicians could administer items in order of increasing difficulty, then determine the highest level of item the child could answer correctly (Bock, 1997).

R. M. Thorndike (1999) describes how in 1926 his grandfather, E. L. Thorndike, took the significant next step of creating a trait-based scale independent of any specific population. Thus "a person's standing on the trait was given by the scale value of the items they had a 50-50 chance of passing," just as in IRT (p. 26). However, E. L. Thorndike's individually administered intelligence test was impractical for mass use.

Although Lord et al. (1968) did not allude to these precedents, they too saw the potential for individualized—but automated—administration that trait-based IRT offered. Writing in the same decade that saw the first trip to the moon, they imagined "examinees sitting at individual computer consoles on which they directly record their responses," making possible "sequential selection of items, such that each examinee is administered a test composed of items that at each stage of the testing are chosen so as to contribute as much as possible to the estimation or decision at hand" (p. 320).

Such a vision has been realized in the computer-adaptive testing (CAT) now used in many large-scale testing programs.* The software administers a series of items, starting with items of easy to middle difficulty. Correct responses lead to more difficult items and incorrect responses trigger easier items. This customized test form can mostly concentrate on items at the examinee's approximate trait level, thereby minimizing items much too easy or much too hard to contribute additional information. (Items may also be grouped as "testlets" rather than presented individually.)

Adaptive testing departs from the CTT requirement for parallel test forms, because the set of items given and their difficulty level produce a customized test for each examinee. The higher the examinee's proficiency, the more difficult the set of items administered (Hambleton, 1989).

Such an approach revives the medical metaphors used in the early 1900s to depict mental measurement. Embretson (1999) compares the IRT process of estimating trait levels to the process by which a clinician uses probing questions to diagnose a condition. In effect, the software program asks: "Given the properties of the items and knowledge of how item properties influence behavior (i.e., the IRT model), what is the most likely trait level to explain the person's responses?" (p. 9).

The measurement advantages of IRT adaptive testing are significant. First, parallel test forms need not be created—although large pools of test items across all difficulty levels are needed. Second, adaptive tests can be shorter than parallel test forms, because "standard errors are smallest when the items are optimally appropriate for a particular trait score level and when item discriminations are high" (Embretson & Riese, 2000, p. 18). Third, an estimate of precision called a "test information function" is associated with each trait level, regardless of changes in test population (Embretson, 1999).[19]

A different argument advanced for adaptive testing is that it makes the testing experience more satisfying for students because they are working on items at their actual skill level (SBAC, 2010, p. 36). Note, however, that in the adaptive process, examinees do not just receive items that they are likely to answer successfully. Most examinees will also routinely encounter items that they cannot answer successfully.

---

*For a list, see the CAT Central website at http://www.psych.umn.edu/psylabs/catcentral/.

Even in nonadaptive testing, IRT methods for estimating item parameters can be helpful. IRT is commonly used in large-scale educational testing programs to create pools of items with known statistical characteristics, from which test developers can select items to create test forms according to desired specifications (Yen & Fitzpatrick, 2006).

At the same time, IRT does not solve all reliability issues and has limitations even beyond its requirements for large numbers of examinees, large numbers of items for CAT, and sophisticated software. As R. M. Thorndike (1999) points out, "IRT has little to say on the matter of the psychological theory underlying a test and general matters of test design" (p. 27). That is, IRT posits the existence of an underlying trait or proficiency but does not explain its nature or how students develop it. Nor can IRT replace GT in identifying sources of error and investigating ways to design measurement procedures.

Moreover, when IRT is used in adaptive testing, the concept of replications that underlies reliability becomes ambiguous, according to Brennan (2001a). He urges that, where possible, IRT models be applied "with at least two independent instances of the measurement procedure" (p. 305).

MAKING A RELIABILITY ARGUMENT

Each psychometric framework has, then, certain advantages and disadvantages. For example, CTT tests usually require fixed test forms, whereas IRT permits adaptive testing. Yet CTT methods are still widely used, especially in small-scale testing.[20] At the same time, GT can help optimize test design in terms of reducing error.

Thus, each approach may be useful at a certain stage of test development (Daniel, 1999; Hambleton & Jones, 1993). A large-scale testing program could use CTT for initial analysis of item statistics, then GT to decide about types of tasks, numbers of raters, numbers of tasks, and so on. Later, the program could use IRT methods to establish item parameters and offer adaptive testing. CTT and IRT can also be used simultaneously as cross-checks. Table 6.1 shows how the frameworks address reliability issues in different ways.

With all these ways of handling measurement error, what is a principled approach to reliability? It is not simply to produce the highest possible reliability coefficient.

First, the type of reliability matters: given the purpose of the test, is content sampling or time sampling more important (or are both necessary)? Second, the theoretically most accurate coefficient, reflecting both equivalence and stability, would be numerically lower than a coefficient reflecting only one type of reliability. Third, certain disciplines, such as writing proficiency, require using constructed-response tasks in a test, even though scores will not attain the level of reliability that might have been possible using only selected-response items.

Table 6.1. Psychometric Frameworks Compared

Classical Test Theory	Generalizability Theory	Item Response Theory
Focuses on an examinee's observed performance and the error of measurement	Focuses on concepts of reliability, sources of variance, and ways to reduce error	Uses probability to estimate the amount of an underlying trait possessed by an examinee
• An examinee's true score is the projected average score over infinite retesting • The actual, observed score combines the unknown true score and some unknown amount of error • The standard error of measurement (*SEM*) is an estimated range for the amount of error in a score	• Investigator specifies a universe of observations with facets such as tasks, ratings, and occasions • A universe score is the person's true score for that universe • Analysis of variance: how much each facet contributes to total variance and to error in observed scores	• Posits a continuum of levels for the underlying (latent) trait or construct, which exists independent of the test • Via calibration, each item is assigned a difficulty level on this continuum • An examinee's patterns of correct/incorrect responses are used to estimate the examinee's trait level, or θ
Item statistics and test-score reliability coefficients refer to a particular population	Test-score dependability is based on specified interchangeable observations: the "conditions" for each facet	In theory, an item's parameters and each examinee's θ are sample-free (they do not refer to a group or a test form)
Reliability can be calculated for test-retest and parallel forms; internal consistency calculated via KR, split-half, or coefficient α	For relative decisions, a generalizability coefficient; for absolute decisions involving categories, an index of dependability	As in CTT, an internal-consistency coefficient can be calculated for a set of items (though different examinees may take different sets of items)
A test *SEM* or conditional *SEM*s are used to estimate precision of individual scores	Can calculate different *SEM*s for relative decisions or for absolute decisions	Provides a test information function for each θ level to indicate precision of the individual score
Total error is estimated but sources are undifferentiated	The total error is broken down by source (by facet)	Error is not differentiated as in GT, but it may be smaller than in CTT
Item difficulty is a *p* value; discrimination compares performance on item and test	Can use CTT or IRT methods for estimating item difficulty and discrimination	Item difficulty is on the θ scale; item discrimination can be calculated for any θ level

Classical Test Theory	Generalizability Theory	Item Response Theory
CTT (vs. IRT) can be used for smaller groups of examinees, has simpler calculations, and is easier to understand	Requires larger numbers of examinees than basic CTT and the ability to conduct a series of tightly controlled studies	Requires hundreds or thousands of examinees; large pools of items across all levels of difficulty; and complex software
Useful across a range of testing situations, including small-scale or one-time	Useful for deciding how to design testing procedures to enhance the reliability of scores	Useful for computer-adaptive testing, which may permit shorter tests with more precise scores

Beyond these technical issues, various critics have voiced concerns about focusing too much on reliability. They charge that standardized tasks designed to promote consistency in how examinees perform, as well as scoring protocols dictating that raters evaluate responses in a uniform manner, privilege reliability at the expense of validity.

One concern is that the quality of assessment suffers, because the tasks limit the skills that can be tested and because important sources of evidence about learning, such as student-created portfolios or projects, do not lend themselves to the standardization that promotes score reliability. Moreover, raters independently scoring anonymous work do not have the opportunity to understand the full context of a student's proficiency, to negotiate judgments about the work with other raters, or to give students feedback tailored to individual needs and circumstances (see Moss, 1994; Shale; 1996; and Huot, 2002, regarding these issues).

It is not just critics of standardized testing who see the privileging of traditional reliability as a problem for validity. Even the *Standards* notes that steps toward greater flexibility in assessment methods may well increase the types and amount of measurement error but may at the same time address crucial validity concerns such as construct underrepresentation (AERA et al., 1999, p. 26).

But the primary concern is that assessment practices focused too much on reliability can undermine good instructional practices (Moss, 2004). Such is the effect that Hillocks (2002) discerns in case studies examining how different types of writing assessments affected writing instruction.

As a goal and value in testing, then, reliability calls for a nuanced approach that to the extent possible enhances rather than detracts from validity.

If reliability is indeed more a matter of logic than of statistics, one might follow the excellent suggestion that "reliability, like validity, consist of an argument supported by evidence" (Parkes, 2007, p. 2). Parkes urges that the reliability argument consider the underlying values, the meaning, the purpose, and the context of reliability; the definition(s) of a replication; and the required tolerance, that is, "How reliable is reliable enough for this decision?" This approach would take into account the potential trade-offs involved in efforts to improve reliability.

Although the 1999 *Standards* does not call for a reliability argument, the idea fits well with its recommendations. The information that programs are to supply alludes to various reliability issues, such as:

> identification of the major sources of error, summary statistics bearing on the size of such errors, and the degree of generalizability of scores across alternate forms, scorers, administrations, or other relevant dimensions. It also includes a description of the examinee population to whom the foregoing data apply. (p. 27)

The *Standards* also emphasizes the need to optimize precision of measurement in test scores that have serious consequences. Context is crucial, as is preserving the intended meaning and usefulness of scores (see Kane, 1996, for some practical strategies). But in absolute decisions, there is also the question of whether to err on the side of screening examinees in or screening them out. This point has clear policy implications in situations such as exams for high school graduation.

Taken together, the criticisms of pursuing reliability, the complexities of depicting reliability, and the consequences of error indicate the need to step back from the test and think about the meaning of reliability in a larger context. Such a reframing of the question is in the spirit of GT but pursues its implications further.

For example, one might explore more conceptual notions of replication, rather than just the traditional structural replications (i.e., test forms, raters, etc.). Thus, one might look for "commonalities and trends" in the performance of interest over a period of time, and probe the qualitative reasons for inconsistencies in that performance (Parkes, 2007, pp. 4–5). Indeed, Messick (1989) emphasized that the validity, like science, is primarily concerned with accounting for consistency in behaviors or responses.

A broader view of reliability would mean "converging evidence" or "evidence of different types that support the same inference" (Mislevy, 1996, p. 8). Thus one might move toward the postmeasurement perspective, admitting into the universe of observations other types of samples, such as portfolios and projects, as well as test performance.

Another way of reframing reliability is to consider that in the everyday world, "reliability" and "dependability" both connote "trustworthiness." Providing complete information about measurement error and its effects on test scores is more likely to increase public confidence than is making vague claims about measurement precision, argues Newton (2005). However, simply offering the data may not be the most helpful approach. Each testing program could also provide a summary of its reliability argument, written to be accessible to the public.

Reliability is, then, about candor, communication, and integrity as much as it is about psychometric frameworks, procedural replications, and statistical calculations. At the same time, those technical considerations involve continually defining "reliability" through choices about types and numbers of observations. Thus reliability, with its many meanings, bears on validity in subtle as well as obvious ways.

Table 6.2. Elements of a Reliability Argument

Questions	Reasoning and Evidence
What kinds of reliability and error are most relevant to the intended meaning and use of scores (and subscores, if these are reported)?	• For scores intended to indicate proficiency in a domain, reliability in terms of content sampling is a priority • For scores intended to indicate a trait or characteristic assumed to be stable over time, reliability in terms of time sampling is a priority • For scores used to categorize examinees by performance levels, reliability of classifications is a priority • For scores based on raters' judgments, consistency in rating is a priority • Corroborating evidence from measures other than the test may be relevant
How is error from content sampling addressed?	• Specifications indicate how each test form samples the domain (number of items per area, total number of items) • Statisticians choose appropriate methods for estimating coefficients of equivalence or internal consistency, or IRT test information function
Is error from time sampling (occasion) addressed; if so, how?	• If not addressed, reasons (type of construct, G-study results showing that occasion is not a major source of error, etc.) • If addressed, then the number and scheduling of test-retests or alternate forms, as well as estimates of reliability across replications
How do test materials address any reliability issues specific to constructed-response?	• G-study conducted to identify portion of error contributed by tasks (content sampling) as well as by raters, occasion, etc. • To the extent feasible, the test design uses the types and numbers of tasks (and raters) shown to be optimal in the G-study

(continued)

Table 6.2. (*continued*)

Questions	Reasoning and Evidence
How do the scoring procedures address any issues specific to constructed-response?	• The procedures promote rater agreement on scores but clearly privilege accuracy and validity of scores over reliability • Definition(s) of interrater reliability and score agreement are specified • Statistics on rater agreement incorporate the probability of chance agreement and the severity of disagreements
Are the various reliability issues and information communicated clearly to examinees and test users?	• Major sources of error are explained and quantified • Score bands presented in units from the test's score scale • Terms related to reliability are explained • Type(s) of coefficients identified: stability, equivalence, internal consistency, dependability of classifications, etc. • If different scores are being compared, the error in both scores is considered • The population(s) to whom reliability statistics apply are specified
How clear, coherent, plausible, and complete is the entire reliability argument?	• Explains types of reliability important to the test's purpose and how they are addressed while maintaining validity • Offers all relevant statistics (e.g., *SEM*s, test information function, reliability coefficients, index of dependability) • Identifies the underlying methods, conditions, groups, etc. • Gives generalizability coefficients for facets (forms, raters, etc.) • Explains how the degree of reliability is sufficient to support the intended interpretations and uses of scores • Is documented in accordance with the *Standards*

Chapter VI: Key Points

- In measurement, reliability and error (inconsistency) are complementary parts of a whole. In CTT and GT, any observed or actual test score likely contains some amount of random error that makes it differ from a hypothetical, completely reliable true or universe score. Increasing the number of observations (in terms of test items, test forms, test occasions, or raters) can help increase reliability and decrease error, because the errors in scores that are "too high" and "too low" eventually tend to cancel out one another.
- The logical meaning of reliability data depends on the types of observations or replications used to obtain them. Comparing scores from two testing occasions addresses stability over different occasions. Comparing scores from split-half, coefficient alpha, etc., addresses equivalence over different samplings of content.
- A reliability coefficient describes consistency of test scores for groups. A standard error of measurement indicates the (im)precision of individuals' scores. Interrater percentages or coefficients indicate the extent of consistency in raters' judgments of a constructed response, such as an essay.
- CTT, GT, and IRT all address reliability and error, but each has its own assumptions, features, advantages, and disadvantages. (See Table 6.1 for details.)
- Enhancing reliability of scores helps support their intended meaning. Yet too great an emphasis on the types of tests and scoring protocols that optimize reliability may undermine validity if it constricts the skills and knowledge that are taught, learned, and assessed.
- Each testing program should ideally have a reliability argument that presents its rationales for choosing particular reliability strategies as well the relevant evidence and data.

NOTES

1. In the discussion of CTT that follows, I am particularly indebted to suggestions from S. A. Livingston (personal communication, May 26, 2010).

2. In a detailed critique of CTT and of the idea that different tests could be parallel, Borsboom (2005) describes the true score as "the disposition of a person to generate a particular kind of score," without any deep causal implications (p. 45). It pertains only to a single point in time. Although the concept of infinite retests suggests repeated administrations over time with a "brainwashing" between each administration, "the term 'brainwashing' must be taken to mean that the subject is restored to his original state—not only with respect to memory, learning, and fatiguing effects, but with respect to time itself" (p. 25).

3. These two categories follow the distinctions made by Reynolds et al. (2006, pp. 89–90) because they are helpful in understanding basic concepts of replication. However, other authorities classify error in different ways. The 1999 *Standards* views random error as either internal or external to the examinee.

4. However, Cronbach (1951/1996) cautioned that increasing score reliability by lengthening a test can have disadvantages, if the additional items give only redundant information. It might be preferable to have items that offer new information (p. 266).

5. As Feldt and Brennan (1989) point out, it is commonly supposed that CTT requires normal distribution of true scores, observed scores, and error scores. Although such a distribution is helpful for various computations, it is not absolutely necessary. See their list of the major assumptions in CTT, pp. 108–9.

6. The formula for an *SEM* in CTT is: "Subtract the test reliability from one, take the square root of that difference, and multiply the square root value times the standard deviation of the test scores" (Harvill, 1991, p. 182.). Here "test reliability" refers to the reliability coefficient, a statistic expressing the consistency of observed scores for a group of examinees taking the test.

7. Harvill (1991) notes that because a test's scores may not be equally reliable at all levels, it is more precise to calculate "conditional" *CSEM*s rather than just one *SEM* for the entire score scale (pp. 183, 186). However, because the *CSEM* tends not to vary much except at the very high and very low ends of the score scale, and because most groups of test takers include relatively few examinees at the extreme ends of the score scale, the *SEM* tends to be very similar across groups (personal communication from S.A. Livingston, May 26, 2010).

A complication is that the score level at which the *CSEM* appears to be largest and smallest depends in part on whether one is looking at raw or scaled scores (see the glossary for definitions). As a practical matter, if a testing program reports *CSEM*s, one can see the relevant numerical values.

8. The assumption that the observed score is likely to be near the true score is based on the probability that an examinee's hypothetical set of observed scores would be normally distributed, with 40 percent of the observed scores containing no error and being equal to the true score. Score bands using the *SEM* actually suggest a probable range for observed scores around a specific true score.

Again, the stated probabilities in score bands are tentative. See Gulliksen (1950) for more about why one can calculate probabilities that all persons with a particular true score are likely to have an obtained score within a certain range ($T \pm SEM$), but there is less certainty that all persons with a particular observed score would have a true score within a specified probable range ($X \pm SEM$) (pp. 17–22).

Here is another way to think about why score-band probabilities are so tentative: in solving the equation $X = T + E$, knowing only the value of X leaves the value of T unknown. But knowing only the value of T would give the average of all possible Xs and hence indicate the probable distribution of all Xs.

9. Borsboom (2005) points out that this approach cannot distinguish between situations in which the construct remains stable and those in which the construct does not (as in when students gain proficiency between two testing occasions). The stability is instead statistical, in the ranking of examinees (p. 26).

10. According to Feldt and Brennan (1989), strictly parallel forms would produce the same distribution of observed scores for a very large population of examinees, would vary together in the same ways, and would both vary in the same way with respect to any other measure that is not a parallel form. However, in most cases, parallel forms would need only equal means and variances (p. 108).

11. Both this observation and the preceding observation about separately timed split-halves come from S. A. Livingston (personal communication, May 26, 2010).

12. As Reynolds et al. (2006) point out, simply computing the percent of agreement for all raters across all responses gives an overestimate of interrater reliability. Why?

Raters may assign the same or adjacent scores purely by chance, just as they might assign discrepant scores by chance. Thus, one preferred method is to use the "Cohen's kappa" formula, which "subtracts the chance agreement from the observed agreement" in order to calculate the true agreement (Reynolds et al., 2006, pp. 256–58). This approach gives a more realistic but lower estimate of interrater reliability.

S. A. Livingston cautions that definitions of chance agreement rely on assumptions about how scores will be distributed (personal communication, May 26, 2010). For a discussion of interrater reliability and some modifications to the Cohen's kappa computation, see Powers (2000). He suggests using a "weighted kappa" that also takes into account the extent or seriousness of score disagreements between and among readers.

It should also be noted that if the method for resolving discrepant scores involves discarding an outlying score, then interrater agreement statistics may be "artificially inflated" (Johnson, Penny, & Gordon, 2000, p. 136). Cherry and Meyer (1993/2009) go so far as to say that this "tertium quid" procedure of discarding an outlying score both violates reliability theory and produces a reliability coefficient that is likely to be "largely meaningless" (pp. 39–42).

13. Applying GT to data from operational programs can be problematic, for example, when the actual assignment of responses to raters does not follow the assignment that an investigator would like to prescribe (S. A. Livingston, personal communication, May 26, 2010).

14. Livingston and Lewis (1993) and Harvill (1991) also investigate issues of accuracy in classifications. One can stipulate the desired performance levels in terms of true scores, then calculate the probabilities that a person with a particular true score would be likely to obtain a particular actual score.

15. IRT models can be built to accommodate multidimensional constructs, but for the sake of simplicity, the present discussion assumes a unidimensional model.

16. However, Lord et al. (1968) were careful to caution that it was still necessary to investigate validity by means of correlations with criterion measures and both convergent and discriminant evidence.

17. For a large-scale test that uses fixed test forms, an overall average 50 percent correct (0.50) across the examinee population is considered desirable. It helps bring about a good fit of data with normal score distribution, such that the average score is around the middle of the score scale. It optimizes the measuring efficiency of the test, for the following reason.

An overall test difficulty lower than 0.50 would mean that the average score was below the middle of the designated score scale. Such a test would be too difficult for the population and would not differentiate well among the lower-proficiency examinees, whose scores would all be clustered at the bottom. Conversely, much higher than 0.50 would mean that the test was too easy for the population and therefore of little use in differentiating among higher-proficiency examinees.

Items with p values of around 0.50 are very useful, because they are the most likely to differentiate among examinees. However, one would not want to create a test form composed solely of such items, because although it would efficiently separate examinees into upper and lower halves, it would not differentiate well among examinees in either half.

18. For the sake of simplicity, this discussion focuses on conventional right/wrong multiple-choice items. For multi-answer items, such as those rated on a score scale (e.g., an essay with a 0–6 scale) IRT treats each level as if it were an item with its own characteristic curve.

19. In adaptive testing, IRT focuses more on precision of individual scores than on reliability coefficients for group scores, since the test "form" is different from one individual to the next. However, as Daniel (1999) notes, adaptive testing using IRT may include computation of internal-consistency coefficients. Having a reliability coefficient is important if inferences are to be made about groups rather than individuals.

20. For example, Hogan, Benjamin, and Brezinski (2000/2003) analyzed almost 700 tests from the APA *Directory of Unpublished Experimental Mental Measures*, which covered tests appearing from 1991 to 1995 in professional journals of education, psychology, and sociology. They found that the coefficient alpha from CTT "was the overwhelming favorite among types of [reliability] coefficients" (pp. 61, 64). Obtaining adequate sample sizes for GT and IRT can be a challenge; statisticians have been working on methods to apply these frameworks to smaller populations.

SELECTED READINGS

Borsboom, D. (2005). *Measuring the mind: Conceptual issues in contemporary psychometrics*. Cambridge: Cambridge University Press.

Brennan, R. L. (2001a). An essay on the history and future of reliability from the perspective of replications. *Journal of Educational Measurement, 38*(4), 295–317.

Embretson, S. E., & Hershberger, S. L. (Eds.). (1999), *The new rules of measurement: What every psychologist and educator should know*. Mahwah, NJ: Lawrence Erlbaum Associates.

Kane, M. T. (1996). The precision of measurements. *Applied Measurement in Education, 9*(4), 355–79.

National Council on Measurement in Education (NCME) website, modules in the ITEMS section: Traub, R. E., & Rowley, G., L. (1991). *Understanding reliability*; Harvill, L. M. (1991). *Standard error of measurement*; and Hambleton, R. K., & Jones, R. W. (1993). *Comparison of classical test theory and item response theory and their applications to test development*.

Parkes, J. (2007). Reliability as argument. *Educational Measurement: Issues and Practice, 4*(26), 2–10.

Shavelson, R. J., Webb, N. M., & Rowley, G. L. (1989). Generalizability theory. *American Psychologist, 44*(6), 922–32.

Chapter Seven

Fairness and Accessibility

There is still no statistic that can prove whether or not a test item or a test is fair.

—Michael J. Zieky, 2006 (p. 361)

In contrast to validity and reliability, for which the *Standards* gives official definitions, fairness is a term that "is used in many different ways and has no single technical meaning" (AERA et al., 1999, p. 74). Determining what fairness means in specific circumstances, and how to achieve it, can be as difficult in the realm of testing as in education, law, and other spheres of activity that directly affect human lives.

Devising impartial and equal procedures does not necessarily mean treating all people exactly alike. Nor, as Rawls (1971) pointed out, does formal or procedural justice necessarily bring about substantive justice. For example, even a fair trial may result in the "wrong outcome" of convicting the innocent or exonerating the guilty. Procedural justice cannot exist in a vacuum: "Only against the background of a just basic structure, including a just political constitution and a just arrangement of social and economic institutions, can one say that the requisite just procedure exists" (p. 87).

Attaining complete fairness in assessment procedures would require that the world in which they exist be a just one. Nevertheless, test makers and users—like people who work in the judicial system—need to strive for procedures that are as fair as possible.

In this chapter, we will explore psychometric strategies for promoting fairness in the technical sense. They involve controlling aspects of test content, context, and scoring; using statistical analyses to investigate whether or not a

133

test is measuring all examinees in the same way; and removing various kinds of physical and linguistic barriers.

Despite this wide range of strategies, there are limits. Fairness does not always require demonstrating that examinees have sufficient opportunity to learn; this criterion applies only to certain kinds of tests. Moreover, fairness does not require equal outcomes, in terms of similar scores across gender groups, ethnic groups, socioeconomic groups, and so on (AERA et al., 1999, pp. 75–76). Even the most scrupulous efforts toward procedural justice in testing cannot ensure equality of outcomes.

FAIRNESS AS A TECHNICAL CONCEPT IN TESTING

Long before construct validity was conceived or construct-irrelevant variance had a name, specialists in educational measurement recognized that extraneous factors could undermine the intended meaning of test scores. In 1936, using language that would later enter the fairness vocabulary, Lindquist cautioned against taking statistics for item difficulty and discrimination at face value, because test items could become "non-functioning" if they drew upon irrelevant or unintended response processes.

Initial attempts at tracing construct-irrelevant variance to examinees' differing backgrounds focused on intelligence testing. In 1951, Eells, Davis, Havingurst, Herrick, and Tyler surveyed earlier studies as far back as 1911 and conducted their own analysis, which identified "cultural bias in test items" as "differences in the extent to which the child being tested has the opportunity to know and become familiar with the specific subject matter or specific processes required by the test item" (p. 58, quoted in Camilli, 2006, p. 235). Such differences could also affect scores in achievement tests, but they are not mentioned in the 1951 *Educational Measurement* or the 1954–1955 *Technical Recommendations*.

It is no coincidence that awareness about cultural effects on test performance took root during the next decade, during which the 1964 Civil Rights Act and 1965 National Voting Rights Act became law and the 1966 Equality of Educational Opportunity Survey was conducted. Adding fuel to the fire was Arthur Jensen's 1969 article on boosting IQ and scholastic achievement, which not only perpetuated the view that intelligence is unitary and largely hereditary but also suggested that genetic factors could account for differences in IQ scores between European Americans and African Americans.

In the second edition of *Educational Measurement*, R. L. Thorndike acknowledged that the use of test results from economically disadvantaged students and minority groups was under increasing attack and that "neither the definitions of fairness nor the stock of evidence on which judgments of fairness can be based are in very satisfactory condition at the present time" (1971b, p. 12).[1] By 1974, the *Standards* asserted the need to "investigate the possibility of bias in tests or in test items" for ethnic and gender groups (pp. 43–44), and the 1985 edition included chapters on testing people with limited proficiency in English and people with disabilities. Today fairness has its own section in the *Standards*.

According fairness a status akin to that of validity and reliability is, then, a relatively recent development. Just as the body of laws, statutes, and court rulings focused on equity and opportunity has grown since the Civil Rights era, so too has the body of research, technical standards, discussion, and debate about how to achieve fairness in assessment.

However, when Cole and Moss wrote on "Bias in Test Use" in the "Theories and General Principles" section of the 1989 *Educational Measurement*, they did not dwell on political, legal, ethical, or social aspects of bias. Instead, agreeing with Messick (1989), they presented the topic as an extension of validity theory—thereby offering an illustration of how societal concerns can influence scientific considerations.[2]

A "context-based construct validation" would emphasize how the use of test scores in a particular context—of persons, settings, and purposes—affects the meaning of those scores (Cole & Moss, 1989, p. 203). Contextual effects leading to different meanings for different examinees are a technical problem, called bias.

In keeping with this approach, the *Standards* carefully circumscribes its technical requirements for fairness. The overarching principle is to promote comparable score meanings for examinees regardless of their gender, race, ethnicity, disability, or linguistic background, by ensuring "lack of bias" and "equitable treatment in the testing process." To remove bias, one must address any deficiencies in a test or test use that "result in different meanings for scores earned by members of different identifiable subgroups" (AERA et al., 1999, p. 74). Bias undermines validity; it introduces systematic error into certain examinees' scores.

FAIRNESS STRATEGIES FOR TEST CONTENT, CONTEXT, AND SCORING

Thus the question of fairness in testing is reframed to a significant extent as one of validity and reliability. By this means the notion of procedural justice is aligned with the traditional concerns of measurement.

The first question is, then: do the measurement procedures themselves contribute to differential performance among examinees? Are some groups of examinees advantaged or disadvantaged by any of the following:

- the definition of the construct;
- the concepts, language, and format of the items;
- the context in which the test is presented; or
- the way in which examinees' responses are scored?

After all, as Cronbach (1971) pointed out, constructs themselves are culturally determined; they are "deliberate creations" that cultures choose to organize experience into categories (pp. 462, 464). Even concepts of proficiency in math vary from one culture to another.

Test makers must proactively address possible causes of differential test performance, in addition to analyzing test data and background information about examinees (as described below). The goal is to combine both approaches in an iterative process for improving fairness.

However, even though empirical evidence informs efforts to prevent test bias, proactive fairness strategies are not an exact science. They also reflect contemporary sensibilities, educated guesses, and consensus among those involved in the testing process. Indeed, statistical findings about possible item bias often fail to correspond with reviewers' judgments about the same items (Cole & Zieky, 2001).

Fairness Guidelines for Test Content

Early attempts to prevent bias in test materials began with "minority reviews" of tests prior to publication. By the 1970s, the process as conducted at Educational Testing Service included written guidelines and covered women as well as ethnic groups. In 1980 these voluntary reviews became mandatory.

ETS's approaches to fairness reviews are of particular interest because they have become increasingly comprehensive and the guidelines are available to the public. As part of the audit process, each testing program has to create a detailed fairness plan. Specific rules are in such documents as the *Guidelines for Fairness Review of Assessments* (2009a), *Guidelines for the Assessment of English Language Learners* (2009b), and *International Principles for Fairness Review of Assessments* (2009c). Annual ACT fairness reports also outline guidelines and protocols (e.g., ACT, 2008). Although the 1999 *Standards* does not require fairness guidelines and procedures (despite such implications in Standards 3.5, 3.6, 7.4, and 7.7), they seem a reasonable expectation by now.

Since fairness guidelines from ACT and ETS are readily available at the respective websites, we will consider just the major conceptual points (see also McNamara and Roever, 2006, pp. 130–37). Both companies' documents emphasize the importance of ensuring that diversity (gender, ethnicity, geography, etc.) is represented in the people who are involved in defining the construct, designing the test, and writing and reviewing the items. As appropriate, the test material should also reflect the diversity of our society.

Assuming that such input, along with relevant research, has already helped frame the construct to be measured, the ETS *Guidelines for Fairness Review* (2009a) then explicitly connects fairness with avoiding cognitive, affective, or physical factors that may cause construct-irrelevant variance. In the cognitive category is unnecessarily difficult language, as well as any topics that call upon knowledge or skills other than those intended. (For example, urban students taking a math test might be disadvantaged by a word problem that assumed familiarity with agricultural terms or concepts.) Affective strategies include avoiding unnecessarily controversial or offensive material, avoiding stereotypes, and using appropriate terminology for individuals or groups. The physical category incorporates principles of universal design, as discussed later in this chapter.

The guidelines do, however, distinguish between "skills" and "content" tests. The former refers to cross-disciplinary skills such as writing or quantitative reasoning and the latter to discipline-specific content, such as biology or history. Skills tests rarely call for covering particular topics in the questions. However, content tests must include material "important for valid measurement of the tested subject, even if that material would otherwise be out of compliance with the guidelines," because it is controversial, upsetting, and so on (ETS, 2009a, pp. 6–7).

Thus, for example, the topics suitable for testing writing skills would differ from those suitable for testing proficiency in U.S. history. Essay topics for a writing test should not focus on violence, crime, abortion, or other emotionally charged subjects that could distract the examinee from fully displaying his or her writing skills. In contrast, as appropriate, a history test might include questions about the origins of the Vietnam War, controversial Supreme Court rulings, divisive problems in contemporary society, and so on.

Although this distinction is helpful, fairness guidelines still pose an inherent challenge: how to provide test materials that reflect diversity but are free of potentially construct-irrelevant factors. Certainly specific decisions about topics and texts can be contentious. Since scholars, scientists, novelists, poets, and artists do not create their work with test-fairness criteria (or other test needs) in mind, test developers often have to exclude authentic texts and images that are otherwise engaging and worthwhile.

At the same time, extreme cautiousness has its own costs. For example, an uproar arose in New York State when a parent found that reading passages on a state test had been significantly altered from the original literary texts, without the authors' consent, to meet guidelines on potentially offensive content (Kleinfield, 2002). This episode led to an agreement to adapt texts only in length, that is, to use unedited excerpts. Still, too often, avoiding sensitive topics and texts can produce tests that are more bland or sanitized than the materials used in actual classrooms—thereby limiting the test's ability to represent the domain.

Ultimately, no set of guidelines can encompass every consideration that may affect the fairness of test content. To the extent possible, test developers need to look at the test from the examinee's point of view. Such empathy does not mean eliminating legitimate difficulty but rather trying to understand how examinees may perceive the directions, tasks, and scoring criteria. To this end, it is helpful to study response processes and collect detailed feedback from field tests (experimental administrations prior to the operational administration). Consulting former examinees might also be useful.

Fairness in Contextual Matters

Fairness strategies encompass not just test materials but also the entirety of the testing process, in order to give all examinees "comparable opportunity to demonstrate their standing on the construct(s) the test is intended to measure" (AERA et al., 1999, p. 74). Aspects of comparable opportunity include appropriate testing conditions (see the discussion of accommodations below); confidential reporting of scores accompanied by information needed to interpret them accurately; and the opportunity to become familiar with and prepare for the test.

With regard to this last point, test makers have an obligation to provide sufficient free and low-cost materials for students to understand fully the test's purpose, use, content, format, directions, procedures, and scoring criteria. Offering disclosed items and tests is highly desirable, so that students can practice beforehand. Some test makers and test users hold test-familiarization workshops for students from underrepresented groups, and, although not prescribed or even mentioned in the *Standards,* test makers and schools frequently offer need-based assistance with test fees.

A corollary to the principle of comparable opportunity to prepare for the test is the necessity for test makers and users to maintain complete security over undisclosed, "live" test materials. At the same time, examinees have a reciprocal obligation: "Any form of cheating, or other behavior that reduces the fairness and validity of the test, is irresponsible, is unfair to other test takers, and may lead to sanctions" (AERA et al. 1999, pp. 79–80).

Apart from these relatively obvious matters of context, increasing attention is being paid to a different type of preparation: the psychological frame of mind with which examinees approach the test. Such research is particularly concerned with addressing score differences among groups. It focuses primarily on the possibility, first proposed by Steele and Aronson (1995), that performance can be influenced by an examinee's self-perception as a member of a particular demographic group.

From prior research about effects of prejudice, Steele and Aronson believed that undertaking a test presented as an intellectual task might cause students who identified with a historically oppressed group to feel a "threat of confirming or being judged by a negative societal stereotype—a suspicion—about their group's intellectual ability and competence" (p. 797). In their experiments, they found that describing a graduate-level test of verbal skills as diagnostic of intellectual ability, or activating group stereotypes beforehand, could adversely affect the performance of examinees from a negatively stereotyped group.

Despite their academic success in the past, the examinees under a stereotype-threat condition (in this case, African American undergraduates at Stanford University) appeared to work less efficiently and effectively. Steele and Aronson further suggested that students who care most about the skills being tested, and whose self-regard is linked to possessing those skills, might be the most deeply affected.

Since 1995, many additional studies have investigated stereotype threat, although almost always under experimental conditions. (For a very comprehensive resource on this research, see the Reducingstereotypethreat.org website.) The experiments have had mixed results, with findings of some effect from stereotype threat focused on ethnic identity, gender, age, or socioeconomic status (Wicherts, Dolan, & Hessen, 2005; McGlone & Pfiester, 2007). But few groups appear to be immune. Even high-achieving Caucasian male engineering students did worse on a difficult math test when told that the study was investigating Asians' superior mathematical skills (Aronson, 2004).

In their own experiments, Wicherts et al. found that threat conditions particularly affected performance on the most difficult part of a test. One possibility is that negatively stereotyped examinees fall into a counterproductive cycle as they focus on avoiding failure rather than on trying demonstrating their competence (Smith, 2004).

Yet stereotype threat does not make examinees slacken their efforts; they try even harder (Aronson, 2004). In fact, stereotype threat can actually improve the targeted group's performance on easy tasks. Moreover, a group conditioned to expect superior performance by its own members may experience "stereotype lift " for difficult tasks.

Of several possible strategies for addressing negative effects of stereotype threat, one might be to "vaccinate" students before the test. For example, African American or female students who were first taught about the phenomenon of stereotype threat, then exposed to some version of it, performed as well on difficult tests as those in the no-threat condition (McGlone & Pfiester, 2007).

A second approach—emphasizing examples of achievement relevant to the examinee—might be more widely applicable across age groups, especially if stereotype lift applies. For example, reading essays about women's success in quantitatively oriented fields appeared to improve female students' performance on a math test (Altermatt & Kim, 2004).[3]

A third strategy—teaching self-empowerment techniques—spans a variety of approaches. Some address group membership; for example, one study found that African American and Latino students improved performance when taught to envision academic success for their future "possible selves" as congruent with their racial-ethnic identities and as attainable through specific behaviors (Oyserman, Bybee, & Terry, 2006). Mentoring programs using Dweck's method—teaching students that intelligence is malleable with effort—improved performance across all groups (McGlone & Pfiester, 2007; Aronson, 2004).

Among the various studies, though, few have focused on operational conditions. One that did examined correlations between performance on the GRE General Test and conditions at testing centers (Walters, Lee, & Trapani, 2004). In these observations, proctors' gender and ethnicity did not seem to affect examinees' performance; examinees tended to perform better at large, busy testing centers; and a warm, friendly atmosphere did not enhance performance. As Walters et al. suggest, it is possible that in operational settings, feeling anonymous is preferable and the drive to perform well outweighs other considerations.

Indeed, research has not yet shown that stereotype threat is a major cause of score differences. Nevertheless, Wicherts et al. (2005) maintain that if a test has differential score outcomes by subgroup, and if experiments show that the relevant subgroup's scores can be changed by manipulating stereotype threat, then stereotype threat may indeed cause measurement bias.

Beyond addressing the possibility of stereotype threat, other approaches to reducing score gaps among groups might include assessing a broader range of relevant cognitive and noncognitive constructs; minimizing reading and writing requirements via computer technology; attempting to enhance examinee motivation; using portfolios; and providing extensive test-familiarization (Sackett, Schmitt, Ellingson, & Kabin, 2001). Results have been mixed so far, but Sackett et al. advocate exploring the first two strategies in particular. An example in college admissions is the "Kaleidoscope" method, which includes tasks and rubrics for evaluating attributes such as creativity and "wisdom," and which appears to avoid differential performance by ethnicity (Sternberg, 2010).

The popularity of quizzes and puzzles suggests one other possible strategy. Why do people enjoy these challenges but dread taking academic tests? Perhaps encouraging students to see a connection and take educational tests as a sort of "serious play" could help students display their knowledge and skills to better advantage. At the same time, creating test material that is intellectually engaging might also help.[4]

Fairness in Scoring Procedures

Scoring of selected-response items is essentially automatic and usually does not raise fairness or validity issues, since all examinees have the same choices available and since each answer choice is either right or wrong. One exception is when an examinee marks or otherwise selects answers in a way that violates the directions, such as circling bubbles instead of filling them in. To help prevent misunderstandings, test directions include sample items illustrating how examinees should indicate their answer choices.

The other exception—a rare one—occurs when the items are misscored, either because of a problem in automated processes or because of a flaw in the item itself. Testing programs clearly have to raise the scores of examinees who were incorrectly penalized. More debatable, from a fairness perspective, is the usual policy of leaving scores untouched when examinees accidentally benefit from a scoring error.

Scoring of constructed-response tasks raises a wider range of issues, because examinees can respond in different ways and, in turn, raters can give these responses different scores. Many of the strategies for promoting fairness and comparable meaning of scores are obvious: removing names or other identifying information from responses; distributing responses randomly to raters; specifying the scoring criteria in written guidelines and illustrating the criteria with sample responses; setting requirements for raters' qualifications and scoring performance; and training and monitoring raters in order to ensure that they are applying the prescribed criteria.

But deeper fairness issues are ambiguous. If the very point of using constructed-response tasks is to permit divergent responses, is there an inherent contradiction in scoring all responses with exactly the same criteria? A perpetual problem is how much latitude to give examinees for unusual approaches, and conversely how much latitude to give raters in exercising their own judgment.

One can also question the methods used for resolving disagreements between two raters' scores via a third score. In theory, simply averaging

all the raters' scores would minimize the effect of any idiosyncratic evaluation and produce the most reliable score. But also in theory, privileging an
experienced third rater's score (by averaging it with the closest other score)
produces the most accurate and valid score.

Other difficult fairness problems, as Baldwin (in press) discusses, include
the extent to which examinees taking tests of writing skills should be penalized for including memorized essay templates and examples; and whether
programs that use a single rater for most of the responses, with a small
percentage double-scored to check accuracy, should alter the score of any
response that happens to receive a different second score. (For more on fairness issues in scoring, see Baldwin's article and see chapter 11 in volume 2.)

FAIRNESS STRATEGIES THAT
RELY ON STATISTICAL ANALYSES

Complementing the qualitative fairness strategies described thus far are
statistical strategies. Still focusing on validity, these quantitative approaches
investigate the possibility that a test's scores might have different meanings
for subgroups within a population of examinees. Differential item functioning
(DIF) focuses on internal evidence from test data; *differential test functioning (DTF)* often considers external evidence by comparing test scores with
performance on criterion measures.*

Although not introduced into testing programs until the 1980s, both types
of analyses are now established practice. Each assumes that a test's examinee
population can be classified in subgroups (such as ethnicity, gender, economic status, first/best language, even school district) indicating shared experience or other characteristics that might conceivably affect performance.[5]

Like other validity research, DIF and DTF analyses should begin early in the
test-development process and continue throughout the life of the test. Where
possible, statistical indications of differential functioning should be addressed
before the items become operational and the scores count—hence another
reason for *pretesting*. The preferred method is to include some untried items in
operational test forms, then omit these items when calculating the official scores.

Differential Item Functioning

As explained in chapter 6, a basic psychometric principle is that examinees at a similar level of proficiency with regard to a given construct

---

*Differential item functioning and differential test functioning are only statistical observations.
Determining whether an item or test meets the technical definition of bias—that is, whether it has
systematically differential validity for different subgroups—is a separate step.

should perform in similar ways on an item measuring that construct. That is, examinees with a similar overall test score or θ level should have a similar probability of correctly answering a particular item (or of getting a particular score on an item that uses a scale, such as an essay). Validity studies routinely investigate the extent to which test data fit this internal-structure model.

DIF analyses assume that the same measurement principle should hold true when one breaks down the examinee population into defined subgroups —for example, by gender. Comparisons between subgroups should reveal the same logical relationship between overall test performance and performance on individual items. If not, then the item may be measuring examinees in different ways, by capturing construct-irrelevant factors.

Usually comparisons involve a *reference group* and a *focal group*. For example, if men were designated as the reference group and women as the focal group, then each item would be examined in terms of how women and men with similar overall performance on the test responded. The item should be equally easy or difficult for both groups at any given level of test score or, but if disparities are observed, then the item is scrutinized for possible bias. Such comparisons can also be made for multiple subgroups, resulting in multiple sets of DIF statistics per item.*

In practice, various methods are used for DIF analyses.[6] DIF studies can also be conducted across groups of similar types of items and across tests, an approach that is helpful in uncovering patterns of problematic content or format. However, traditional DIF analyses may be unsatisfactory if a test contains only constructed-response tasks.[7]

DIF analysis may reveal negative trends in an item (i.e., the focal group has lower than expected scores compared to the reference group) or positive trends. The trends may be more or less pronounced. Thus, for example, analyses may categorize positive DIF and negative DIF each in three levels of magnitude (Zieky, 2003).

DIF can even be nonuniform in an item. For example, the members of a focal group whose scores are in the lower part of the scale might display a negative trend while those whose scores are in the higher part of the scale display a positive trend. IRT methods are particularly helpful in investigating whether the same trend exists throughout the entire scale (Waller, Thompson, & Wenk, 2000).

A new approach in DIF analyses is to redefine the idea of a reference group so that it is no longer a particular subgroup, such as males or Caucasians. In a "DIF dissection " method, the reference group is the total examinee population

---

*Again, these are disparities relative to overall performance. Simply finding that more men or more women correctly answered a given item would trigger further examination but not necessarily mean that the item functioned differently according to gender.

or "melting pot." Then, each subgroup, including those that represent interactions of ethnicity and gender (e.g., Asian American females, African American males, etc.) serves as a focal group (Zhang, Dorans, & Matthews-López, 2005).

Supplementing DIF analyses with examinees' feedback can be particularly helpful in discerning possible causes for differential group performance. Such feedback may also identify meaningful subgroups of examinees other than the conventional demographic categories, thereby offering new observations and insights.[8]

Differential Test Functioning

Item-level analyses are relatively straightforward, insofar as they tend to rely on a readily available frame of reference for investigating differential subgroup performance. That frame of reference is examinees' total scores or estimated θ levels.

But what about test-level differences among subgroups? What if subgroups have different average test scores, different distributions of test scores, or different passing rates? According to the *Standards*, fairness does not require that overall passing rates be comparable across groups, nor do score differences across groups necessarily demonstrate that a test is biased or unfair (AERA et al., 1999, p. 75). Fairness does, however, require that tests, like items, function in the same way across different groups. Tests should exhibit *measurement invariance*, or "measure the same attribute in the same way in different subpopulations" (Borsboom, Romeijn, & Wicherts, 2008, p. 76).

One approach to investigating whether or not systematic error is occurring in the form of differential test functioning (DTF) does not require any external frame of reference. Instead, the comparisons between and among subgroups are made via IRT *test characteristic curves* showing the relationship between estimated levels of the proficiency and expected observed scores. If the test characteristic curves differ for two subgroups, then DTF may exist (for more detail, see Waller et al., 2000, pp. 130–31).

It is also common to use external validity evidence (criterion-related, convergent, and divergent) as a frame of reference for subgroup performance. Following the approach introduced by R. L. Thorndike (1971a), subgroup performance on a "predictor" test is compared with that on the criterion, such as grades, passing rates for credentialing exams, job ratings, teachers' ratings, evidence from research literature, etc. Do scores on the predictor test align with performance on the criterion in the same way across subgroups, as opposed to overpredicting or underpredicting performance?[9]

Yet some experts are skeptical about how well external evidence can reveal DTF. A criterion such as grades will be somewhat unreliable, biased, or influenced by factors other than those the test is intended to measure (Koretz, 2008).

Further, Millsap (1997) makes the case that a mathematical "duality paradox" exists. Unless the actual distribution of the construct is exactly the same in each of the different groups, then measurement invariance (systematic accuracy in measuring the construct) cannot coexist with predictive invariance (systematic accuracy of prediction), and it may be necessary to choose one over the other. (See also Borsboom et al., 2008, for more about this problem.)[10]

Combining DIF and DTF Data With Other Information

Despite such concerns, it is generally accepted that testing programs large enough to permit DIF and DTF analyses should conduct them, then use the data to improve assessment procedures and to issue any necessary cautions about scores.

Procedures for revising, rejecting, or accepting items that exhibit DIF involve considering both the quantitative magnitude of the effect and any qualitative reviews of the item's content. In the end, "judgment of fairness is based on whether or not the difference in difficulty is believed to be related to the construct being measured" (Zieky, 1993, p. 340).[11]

At the level of the overall test, differences in average scores across subgroups raise questions about causes, meaning(s), and effects, but again, they may or may not indicate differential test functioning and differential validity.

On the one hand, subgroup score differences may indeed mean that the test is measuring secondary constructs, other than or in addition to the intended construct. Tests of mathematical skills that rely heavily on word problems illustrate this point. Such items can make the test more difficult for students who have limited proficiency in the language of the test, even though language proficiency is not the intended construct. The question then becomes: could measurement be improved by reducing the linguistic demands?

On the other hand, score differences may indicate actual variance in proficiency levels, especially for groups who have received different instruction. For example, students who took higher-level math courses or who had the most qualified teachers might well perform better on a state math test than students who did not. Higher scores for the former group could accurately reflect higher levels of learning. As Koretz (2008) emphasizes, "Bias is an attribute of a specific inference, not of a test. . . . A difference in scores entails bias only if it is misleading (again, for a particular inference)" (pp. 262–63).

To illuminate possible causes of differential performance, testing programs must collect and analyze background information about examinees. For example, studies reported in the ACT Technical Manual (2007) associate higher ACT scores with more years of high school, higher GPAs, and higher educational goals, such as taking more English and math courses or planning to attend college (pp. 63–68). Further analyses also suggested that different levels of academic preparation resulted in differential performance, regardless of background. Such findings would be expected for a test intended to be sensitive to the effects of instruction.

At the same time, the ACT research also noted some disparity, by gender and ethnicity, in the scores' predictive accuracy for college grades. Using test scores together with high school GPA seemed to reduce these disparities (ACT, 2007, p. 107).

Other examples of background research include a study suggesting that language proficiency might affect predictive accuracy for the SAT. Across subgroups, scores were least predictive of first-year college GPA for examinees whose best language was not English (Mattern, Patterson, Shaw, Kobrin, & Barbuti, 2008). Systematically considering alternate hypotheses for score differences and the relevant evidence is certainly part of construct-oriented validation.[12]

Again, though, different validity considerations have to be balanced together. For example, DIF analyses have frequently shown that on average, male students tend to do better on multiple-choice items and female students tend to do better on constructed-response items (Zenisky, Hambleton, & Robin, 2004; DeMars, 2000). This observation would suggest including both types of question formats in a single test. But test designers also have to ensure adequate representation of the targeted knowledge and skills. Moreover, if the test is not intended to measure writing skills, then using essay formats to benefit female students would introduce construct-irrelevant variance.[13]

STRATEGIES FOR PROMOTING ACCESSIBILITY

The fairness strategies described thus far strive to equalize the test material and testing conditions across groups. However, making tests accessible to students who have disabilities or diverse linguistic backgrounds can mean reframing "equality" as "equity." Fairness may entail leveling the playing field by removing construct-irrelevant obstacles in the testing procedures—or it may require moving to a more appropriate playing field, via modified or alternate testing that produces different information about the examinee. How should these decisions be made?

The first principles to which test makers and users must turn are the relevant laws, statutes, and constitutional protections. Second are professional measurement guidelines and practices, as well as findings from research. Third are policy considerations, which, as Phillips (2002) points out, ought to include doing "what is best for the student in the long as well as the short run" (p. 131).* Yet translating these principles into specific actions is no simple matter, especially given the diversity of disabilities and of linguistic backgrounds across the millions of students in the United States.

Addressing the Needs of Students With Disabilities (SWD)

Figures from the U.S. Department of Education show that in the 2003–2004 school year, almost 14 percent of students aged three to twenty-one were in federally supported programs for the disabled (Institute of Education Sciences, 2008a). Of these 6.6 million students, half were categorized as having "specific learning disabilities" and a quarter "speech or language impairments," with "mental retardation" as a separate category. Fewer than one eighth of the students had purely physical disabilities. In brief, disabilities related to cognitive processes are far more common—a fact that makes accurate assessment of learning all the more complicated.

Both constitutional protections and legal statutes bear upon the needs and rights of students with disabilities (SWD). Legislation includes Section 504 of the 1973 Rehabilitation Act; the 1975 Education for All Handicapped Children Act (EHA), later the 1990/1997/2004 Individuals with Disabilities Education Act (IDEA); the 1990 Americans with Disabilities Act (ADA); and the 1965 Elementary and Secondary Education Act (renamed NCLB in 2002). These acts have promoted including SWD in mainstream education as well as in NAEP and in state-level and district-level testing—with some positive consequences for expectations, instruction, and performance, according to Ysseldyke, Dennison, and Nelson (2004).

Particularly significant for testing is the IDEA. It requires that processes of evaluating students for disabilities incorporate information from parents and be nondiscriminatory and that an individualized education program (IEP) appropriate for a particular student's disability (or disabilities) be developed (Taylor, 2006). Usually, the types of accommodations prescribed in a student's IEP apply both to instructional and assessment situations.[14]

It should be noted, though, that neither diagnosis nor prescription are straightforward. Policies and criteria for identifying and classifying disabilities are inconsistent across local areas and states (Koretz, 2008). New approaches to identifying and addressing learning disabilities, via Response to Intervention, are continuing to change the landscape. Then, even among students categorized with the same disability, types of accommodations can vary widely (see the long list cited by the NRC, 2004b, p. 37). For example, some students with visual impairments can read enlarged text; some can read Braille; but many can do neither.

---

*Most educational testing differs in this respect from licensing tests, in which protecting the public usually take precedence (as in bar exams, teacher licensing, medical licensing, etc.).

Turning to psychometric literature, one finds that the *Standards* first addressed the subject relatively recently—in 1985—although accommodations and modifications of tests for students with physical disabilities had been available for a number of years. Today, since the purpose of altering testing processes or test content is to minimize the effect of irrelevant attributes, making such changes involves a sequence of decisions based on the relationship between the construct being measured and the student's particular disability (AERA et al., 1999, p. 101).

Decisions: Accommodation, Modification, or Alternate Assessment?

To begin with, no accommodation at all may be desirable or needed if the purpose of the test is to diagnose the existence or extent of a disability—or if the particular disability would not affect performance on the test.

Next, certain kinds of necessary accommodations, such as a large-print test version or technological assistance with responding, may have no bearing on the construct and thus allow the student to take a test intended for the general population without changing the meaning of the score. Such adjustments may involve: the format in which the test is presented; the means by which examinees respond (for example, using an amanuensis or voice-recognition software); the test timing (allowing additional time or breaks); and the test setting (for example, placing a student who has attention deficit disorder in a separate room) (AERA et al., 1999, pp. 101–3).

If such accommodations do not suffice, then obtaining comparable scores may not be feasible. Instead, a problematic part of the test may be omitted, or an alternate test or evaluation method may be employed. Some possibilities include giving a test designed for a lower grade level, reviewing relevant academic work, or evaluating the basic skills needed to learn the subject matter (Phillips & Camara, 2006, p. 749). Such approaches may offer useful evidence about what a student with a learning disability actually can do.[15]

Complexities in Determining Whether or Not the Construct Has Changed

Devoting attention and resources to the needs of students with disabilities represents true progress. However, alterations to testing procedures can also raise questions about validity, reliability, and fairness.

These questions are exemplified in two of the most common practices: giving an examinee extra time to complete the test or reading the text of the test aloud. Not only are students with cognitive disabilities (the largest category of disabilities) often granted extra time, but so too are students whose other types of accommodations, such as using Braille or a spoken version of the test, inherently require extra time.

Extra time appears to improve the performance of both SWD and nondisabled students, although the former benefit more. Such findings could suggest some score inflation for SWD, according to the principle that a test accommodation should increase scores only for students who need it, not for other students (Sireci, Scarpati, & Li, 2005, p. 458).[16] Countering this point, Sireci et al. suggest that the standard time limits might be too stringent for students in general. Nevertheless, there are both practical and theoretical arguments against relaxing all time limits.[17]

Reading the test aloud is particularly problematic in reading-skills assessments because, for students who cannot read text, one cannot simply remove construct-irrelevant obstacles. Changing the presentation changes the construct from reading skills to listening skills instead.

Less clear is the extent to which reading aloud may change the construct in other disciplines. For example, Sireci et al. (2005) found that reading aloud raised scores on math tests for SWD but did not have consistent effects for other subject areas. A concern that Phillips (2002) notes is whether low-achieving students are disadvantaged because they, too, might benefit from a spoken presentation. Then again, even if reading aloud improves test scores, in the long run it might adversely affect those students who actually could learn to read independently, even if at a low level.

Nomenclature and Research

Many experts concur with Phillips and Camara (2006) that, as a starting point toward greater consistency and clarity, "accommodation" should refer to "nonstandard test administrations that produce comparable scores" and "modification" refer to those "that produce noncomparable scores" (p. 744). Although deciding which changes are accommodations and which modifications may be difficult, this distinction emphasizes considering whether and how such changes affect validity and fairness.[18]

So far, research about accommodated, modified, or alternate testing does not provide complete guidance. Even designing studies is difficult, because accommodations are so often individualized. Then, the existing research findings are often "contradictory," and, according to the authors of the NRC report (2004b), the usual method of looking at how scores change with accommodations is insufficient to establish the comparability of scores. More validity evidence is needed in the categories of test content, response processes, and correlations with external criteria.[19]

Given the incomplete state of knowledge about the subject, Koretz and Barton (2004) warn that "current policy is therefore based partly on unsubstantiated assumptions," such as assuming that very few students need alternate assessments, that accommodations specified in IEPs are optimal, and that performance standards for general education are necessarily appropriate for most students with cognitive disabilities (p. 54).

Many teachers of special education classes seem to concur, at least if one judges by comments in teachers' forums. Moreover, when students have profound cognitive disabilities, devoting efforts primarily to academic goals, however limited, may seem less helpful than focusing on emotional well-being and skills needed to function in life. In certain cases, even the concept of standardized academic assessment may be questionable. (For a vivid description, see Otterman, 2010.)

There is an inherent dilemma. Systematizing solutions to accessibility problems in learning and assessment is urgent, for the sake of validity, reliability, fairness, and efficiency. But generalizing solutions across different students and situations could be counterproductive if these solutions do not meet an individual's actual needs.[20]

While research and evidence accumulate and policies evolve, recommended strategies for assessment are to specify the physical and cognitive skills necessary for taking any test before deciding on alterations; to use the least intrusive alterations possible; and to monitor how the changes in testing procedures affect individual students (Bolt & Thurlow, 2004, pp. 149–50). The good news is that with so much attention now focused on these issues, knowledge ought to grow rapidly. For example, the 2010 RTTT included grants to two separate state consortia to develop alternate formative and summative assessments for students with significant cognitive disabilities—with all assessments mapped to modified versions of the Common Core Standards.

Addressing the Needs of Students With Diverse Linguistic Backgrounds

In many ways, U.S. students whose best language is not English have assessment issues similar to those for SWD. Here, too, the population is large and diverse; the methods for identifying students' needs and the criteria for testing alterations are inconsistent; the comparability of test scores from standard and altered testing conditions depends on the extent to which alterations change the construct; and research findings do not yet provide definitive answers or solutions. Here, too, experts call for going beyond simple observations of score changes to investigate all the five types of validity evidence. (For specific methods, see Sireci, Han, & Wells, 2008; and Wolf, Kao, Herman, Bachman, Bailey, Bachman, Farnsworth, & Chang, 2008.)

The interests of several million students with varied linguistic backgrounds are at stake. According to the National Clearinghouse for English Language Acquisition (2008), during 2005–2006, over five million of about fifty million students in pre-K to grade twelve were "English Language Learners " (ELL), also known as "Limited English Proficiency " (LEP) students. Although about 80 percent of ELL students speak Spanish, the NRC (2004b) lists forty other languages from Albanian to Yup'ik.

Because ELL are in a "reversible" condition, they are not protected by disability-specific statutes (Phillips & Camara, 2006). Relevant legislation includes Title VI of the Civil Rights Act of 1964 and Titles I and VII of the ESEA, which require that states report separate data on ELL as well as SWD, but federal legislation does not regulate their education as IDEA does the education of SWD. Thus, there is no federal requirement for ELL to have an individual education plan, and state and local policies about educational services and testing procedures for ELL can differ widely.[21]

Another complication is that research on how examinees' language proficiency affects measurement validity has underscored the effects of diverse cultural backgrounds as well. This point is a subtheme in the *Standards*: assessment of ELL must take into account not just linguistic factors but also cultural values, assumptions, customs, and knowledge bases—hence the importance of promoting cultural diversity among the people who define the construct and develop or review the test materials.

Starting in 1985, the *Standards* has distinguished between tests of language proficiency and tests in other subject areas. Language-proficiency tests should not cover just reading but also writing, listening, and speaking if possible (AERA et al., 1999, p. 99). Moreover, tests of English-language proficiency need to assess "academic" as well as everyday language in order to capture students' mastery of the language skills needed in the classroom (Wolf, Kao, Herman, et al., 2008).

For tests in other subjects, standards relevant to ELL include minimizing possible threats to test reliability and validity from linguistic differences; conducting validity research on the meaning of test scores across different linguistic groups; and either providing evidence of score comparability across standard and modified administrations or else providing the information for appropriate test use and interpretation (AERA et al., 1999, pp. 97–99). (For a detailed discussion of implementing standards in the test-development process, see *Guidelines for the Assessment of English Language Learners*, ETS, 2009b.)

Some changes in test content or procedures that address the needs of ELL overlap with those used to address the needs of SWD, but accommodations for tests other than those of language proficiency can also include specifically linguistic support (see NRC, 2004b, p. 39, for a full list). Common alterations in state assessments are extended time, small-group administrations, bilingual dictionaries or customized glossaries, test items and/or directions read aloud in English, and dictation to a scribe in English.

More intensive approaches include translating the existing test into different languages, using an interpreter, developing an alternate test form intended to measure the same construct in a different language, or creating dual-language tests (with versions side by side). Translation or interpretation might seem obvious solutions, but even highly competent renditions can introduce unintended differences in content and difficulty (Phillips & Camara, 2006). Thus, the *Standards* suggests that the alternate-form option may be preferable, and Wolf, Kao, Herman, et al. (2008) report favorable response from students to dual-language editions of tests.[22]

Once again, as with assessment issues for SWD, there are multiple complications, not the least of which is that assessing ELL is politically charged. In addition, determining what is construct relevant is not always easy. For example, the sciences depend heavily on specialized terms, so that mastering the terminology is part of learning discipline-specific knowledge.

Universal Design for Learning and for Assessment

In architecture, the concept of "universal design" means removing barriers and making buildings and furnishings accessible to all users. Universal design for learning (UDL) and for assessment (UDA) is similarly intended to improve access and participation for SWD and ELL, to permit "valid inferences about their performance," and even benefit other students. In short, the goal is "better tests for everyone" (Thompson & Thurlow, 2002, under "Applying Universal Design to Assessments").

Increasingly studied and implemented by test makers, UDA is a proactive strategy for preventing or minimizing construct-irrelevant barriers. Some of the specific UDA recommendations, such as ensuring that constructs are precisely defined, are part of accepted principles for test design. UDA then goes on to emphasize avoiding unnecessary or distracting graphics or illustrations; offering "simple, clear, and intuitive instructions and procedures"; promoting "maximum readability and comprehensibility" via "plain language" and clear, legible formatting; and minimizing any physical challenges (Thompson, Johnstone, & Thurlow, 2002, under "Elements of Universally Designed Assessments"; see also ETS, 2009a, pp. 36–39).*

Researchers are beginning to examine actual effects of UDA. Studies show mixed but somewhat encouraging results from giving students plain- or modified-language versions of tests (Wolf, Kao, Herman, et al., 2008, pp. 36–39). As of 2008, Wolf, Kao, Griffin, et al. found that only one state listed simplified language as a permitted accommodation, but if elements of UDA can be shown to reduce the need for such customization without compromising validity, they will become established practice.[23] Indeed, both the SBAC

---

*Kopriva (2000) describes in detail the characteristics of plain language, which include familiar or common words; repeated nouns rather than pronouns; repeated wording rather than paraphrases; simple sentence and paragraph structures; and active rather than passive voice (pp. 32–35). See also ETS, 2009a, pp. 46–54, for other guidelines and examples of accessible language.

(2010) and PARCC (2010) assessment proposals specifically call for planning and incorporating accessibility features into test design and development from the very outset.

OPPORTUNITY TO LEARN

It might seem that fairness includes ensuring that students have full and equal opportunity to learn any knowledge and skills on which they are tested. Indeed, the *Standards* emphasizes that tests used in making decisions about student promotion or graduation should cover "only the specific or generalized content and skills that students have had an opportunity to learn" (AERA et al., 1999, p. 146). The legal cases described in chapter 4 have established this principle.

Yet the *Standards* itself points out three problems with the idea that technical requirements for fairness go beyond establishing that test materials are aligned with curriculum and instruction. Ascertaining each individual's actual opportunity to learn is difficult; measuring some constructs may require students to work with unfamiliar material; and allowing very low-performing examinees to pass on the basis of insufficient opportunity undermines the meaning of a test or diploma (AERA et al., 1999, p. 76). (Opportunity to learn is not considered a determinant of fairness in testing for employment, credentialing, or admissions.)

As the NRC (2002a) report *Achieving High Educational Standards for All* and a multitude of other evidence show, students do not now have equal or complete opportunities to learn in the broader sense that goes beyond the domain of a particular test. And even the most impeccable assessment procedures cannot ensure an equitable K–12 education with sufficient resources and instruction by highly qualified teachers. Without sufficient support and services for low-performing students, "better tests will not lead to better educational outcomes" (NRC, 1999a, pp. 2–3).[24]

But some testing does, at least, bring to light the inequities that exist within and beyond the school setting.

Many external factors are correlated with achievement gaps, such as low birth weight, environmental hazards, substandard nutrition, excessive television watching, and family circumstances (see Barton & Coley, 2009; Berliner, 2009). Addressing these problems requires larger societal and political efforts.

To address inequities within the educational system, one proposed strategy is to institute formal opportunity-to-learn (OTL) criteria and evaluations—that is, to focus on educational inputs as well as test outcomes. The criteria cover such areas as teachers' qualifications and professional development; safety and adequacy of physical facilities; currency of learning materials; alignment of actual instruction and curricula with standards; and nurturing classroom environments (Ysseldyke, Thurlow, & Shin, 1995).

Table 7.1. Strategies for Promoting Fairness in Assessment

Avoiding Test Bias

- Involve representatives of diverse constituencies in test design and development.
- Define the construct (important knowledge, skills, proficiencies) precisely. Investigate issues in the construct that may be related to gender, culture, language, or disability.
- Align test content with actual curriculum and instruction, not just the prescribed standards.
- Establish and adhere to guidelines for fairness reviews and universal design, which are intended to minimize construct-irrelevant variance in the content, language, and format of a test—but do not avoid construct-relevant material or difficulty. Specify the prerequisite physical and linguistic skills.
- If the test involves constructed-response tasks, remove identifying information from student responses and train raters to apply scoring criteria in a uniform manner.
- Provide complete information needed for score users to understand the meaning of scores and to use them appropriately in decision-making processes.

- Conduct analyses of differential item functioning (DIF): for each item, do examinees at the same level of proficiency respond in the same way regardless of their demographic background? Establish rules for omitting, revising, or including items that exhibit DIF.
- Conduct analyses of differential test functioning (DTF): does the test measure a construct in the same way across demographic groups, even if the groups' average scores differ? Compare test scores with performance on criterion measures to investigate whether the test has different predictive validity for certain groups. Collect convergent and divergent evidence to investigate whether any score differences arise from a secondary or irrelevant construct or from actual differences in proficiency.
- Collect contextual data about examinees' background and educational experiences in order to promote unbiased, accurate inferences from scores. Collect qualitative feedback from examinees to understand how they perceive specific aspects of the tasks.

Treating Examinees Equitably in the Testing Process

- Adhere to constitutional protections and legal statutes pertaining to all students, as well as to those specifically addressing the rights and needs of SWD and ELL.
- Provide sufficient test-familiarization materials free of charge and additional materials at low cost.
- Maintain test security and ensure that policies on cheating are clearly communicated.
- Investigate possible relationships between stereotype threat and test performance as well as the effectiveness of various preventative strategies.
- Determine how accommodations in an IEP apply to the particular assessment that a student is taking.
- Determine which adjustments to testing procedures and/or content may be needed for SWD and ELL. Should any scores be flagged because they are not comparable to scores produced under standard conditions? If so, what guidance should be added for score users to understand the scores?
- Conduct validity research about how accommodations, modifications, and alternate assessments affect the meaning and use of scores for SWD or ELL and how they affect the students themselves.

Voluntary OTL standards were part of the Goals 2000 legislation (now defunct), and they continue to be advocated on the state level (UCLA, 2003). Concerns about costs and possible lawsuits have kept them from being widely implemented or mandated. How to define the criteria precisely but flexibly and how to collect the necessary information (teachers' records, visitors' observations of classrooms, etc.) pose challenges—but the goal of equity is worth pursuing, for reasons beyond differential test performance (Schwartz, 1995). As a starting point, Zau and Betts (2008) suggest ways to identify at-risk students and provide evidence-based interventions that would benefit the students and, ultimately, the larger community.[25]

Fairness is, then, a complex intersection of psychometric concepts, cultural ideals, and stark realities. Yet even if educational assessment—like the legal system—cannot solve societal injustices, it can model better practices. Test makers and users can set an example by committing time, energy, and resources to the pursuit of fairness in research, design, and development. As Messick (1992) observed,

> Validity, reliability, comparability, and fairness are not just measurement principles; they are social values that have meaning and force outside of measurement wherever evaluative judgments and decisions are made. (p. 2)

Chapter VII: Key Points

- Fairness in assessment involves values and "procedural justice" ultimately contingent on circumstances beyond the realm of measurement. The technical requirements for fairness in educational testing are lack of bias, equitable treatment in the testing process, and alignment of test content with curricula and instruction. Full opportunity to learn for individuals and equal outcomes for groups are not technical requirements for fairness.
- Bias refers to differential meanings of scores depending on an examinee's membership in a defined group—that is, systematic error in scores caused by construct-irrelevant variance. Fairness guidelines and protocols for test content, testing conditions, and scoring processes are intended to minimize potential sources of bias and to reflect the diversity of society.
- Statistical investigations for possible item or test bias (whether for or against a group) extend the methods used to investigate validity for the examinee population as a whole. These methods involve analyzing test data to see if the item or test is measuring all examinees in the same way as well as comparing test scores with performance on criterion measures.
- Decisions about altering test procedures to meet the needs of students with disabilities or English-language learners require asking: Are the changes "accommodations" that do not also change the construct and meaning of scores? Are the changes "modifications" that affect the construct and the meaning of scores—and if so, how? Is an alternate, nonequivalent assessment a better way to get information about what the examinee can do?
- More research and evidence are needed to evaluate the efficacy and consequences of particular testing accommodations, modified testing, and alternate assessments.

NOTES

1. In a separate, pioneering article, "Concepts of Culture Fairness," R. L. Thorndike (1971a) explored defining test fairness in terms of correlations with a logically relevant criterion performance, such as the correlation of scores on an employment test with subsequent job performance. For hiring and admissions, he proposed a proportional approach with qualifying scores set for each group such that the proportion of each group succeeding on the test would match the proportion succeeding on the criterion measure. Today, however, it is illegal to use different cut scores for different groups in selection processes.

2. In his chapter on validity in the same volume, Messick (1989) emphasized the importance of investigating "the role of context in test interpretation and test use" and "the extent to which a measure displays the same properties and patterns of relationships in different population groups and under different ecological conditions" (pp. 14–15).

3. In a related point, having peers from one's own group present during the testing process might be beneficial. As in other studies, Beaton, Tougas, Rinfret, Huard, and Delisle (2007) found that, when taking a math test, women placed by themselves in a group of men performed worse than the male students, whereas women in a gender-balanced group performed as well as the male students.

4. Introducing humorous touches in the test content might also seem to reduce anxiety, and when students are asked, they tend to agree. However, a review by McMorris, Boothroyd, and Pietrangelo (1997) of research on humor in educational testing reveals that benefits and drawbacks depend on various situational factors. Thus the usual practice is to take the safer course and avoid humor.

5. Traditional categories may be unsatisfactory; thus a study conducted by Wendler, Feigenbaum, and Escandón (2001) examined the effect of allowing students to designate more than one racial/ethnic category on a demographic question that they answered after taking the SAT I: Reasoning Test. (When registering, the students had filled out a questionnaire permitting selection of only one category.)

Permitting multiple categories had little effect on mean DIF statistics. Most students selected the same category they had selected originally, even if they added other categories as well.

6. The two general categories are (a) IRT methods, which compare item parameters, item response functions, or likelihood ratios; and (b) observed-score methods, such as standardization and Mantel-Haenszel statistics. See Camilli (2006), pp. 236–43; and McNamara and Roever (2006), pp. 113–22.

7. This problem especially affects tests that contain only one or a very few constructed-response tasks. Attempts to address it are discussed in a study by Broer, Lee, Rizavi, and Powers (2005) that focused on the GRE Analytical Writing measure. Since this section of the GRE had only two essay tasks, the total score in the section did not give as reliable a frame of reference as would the total score on a multiple-choice test. Broer et al. decided to compare performance on each essay with a composite score incorporating the score on the other essay and the score on the GRE Verbal Reasoning Section.

For a review of approaches to DIF analysis in constructed-response tasks, see Penfield and Lam (2000).

8. In studying feedback on a science test, Fox (2003) found differential performance for low- to mid-level examinees: between those who did and did not like the topic on which the test focused. DIF analysis has even proven helpful in identifying format-related problems that arose when a test was administered via computer rather than in paper-and-pencil mode (Anderson & DeMars, 2002).

9. The relationship between performance on the predictor test and on the criterion measure is expressed not as a correlation coefficient but as a "regression equation" or "regression line." A simple coefficient cannot show whether a test has equal predictive validity throughout the score scale for two or more subgroups (AERA et al., 1999, p. 82). Moreover, the regression equations or lines can show whether the original test is over-predicting or underpredicting success for any subgroup (see Camilli, 2006, pp. 230–31).

10. Borsboom et al. (2008) explain why, even when a test is measurement-invariant, differential prediction or "selection variance" is mathematically inevitable, if the groups have different mean scores and if the same passing score is applied to everyone. For groups whose distribution and mean lie higher on the θ scale, the test has more true positives and false negatives. The opposite happens to groups whose distribution and mean lie lower on the scale. Thus the test "does better in accepting members from the group with higher mean ability, and it does better in rejecting members from the group with lower mean ability" (see pp. 81–85).

11. Zieky (2003) notes that items exhibiting DIF initially are removed from computing the total score of the test in order to make it less likely that the total score is a biased frame of reference.

12. For example, DeMars (2000) found that in one high school exit exam, differential performance of ethnic subgroups had more to do with differences among schools than among subgroups per se.

See Kobrin, Sathy, and Shaw (2007) for an example of the theory-testing process. They examined subgroup differences for the SAT Reasoning Test™ over twenty years by tracing historical trends, comparing these to trends in other assessments measuring similar constructs, and weighing possible explanations.

13. This last point is made by M. J. Zieky (personal communication, June 11, 2010). Zenisky et al. (2004) caution against excluding important material because of differential performance. Analyzing a high school science test, these authors found that content such as technology or earth science tended to favor males, as did multiple-choice items containing maps, diagrams, and other visual or spatial materials.

14. Usually, but not always. For example, accommodations provided under an IEP may not apply when students with cognitive disabilities who are not "otherwise qualified" for a high school diploma take a required graduation test (Phillips & Camara, 2006, p. 744).

15. For links to many resources on alternate assessments, see the website of the National Alternate Assessment Center at http://www.naacpartners.org/Default.aspx. Sheinker and Erpenbach (2007) describe criteria to be applied to alternate assessments for students with cognitive disabilities, as well as relevant types of evidence.

Shaftel, Yang, Glasnapp, and Poggio (2005) explain one possible approach to designing and investigating an alternate assessment for lower-performing SWD, by modifying the mainstream curricular standards, simplifying the test, and offering support such as definitions of key terms. The modified test was linked with the mainstream test by administering some of the items to both disabled and nondisabled students who had taken the mainstream test.

16. This principle is formally called the "interaction hypothesis":

> The *interaction hypothesis* states that (a) when test accommodations are given to the SWD who need them, their test scores will improve, relative to the scores they would attain when taking the test under standard conditions; and (b) students without disabilities will not exhibit higher scores when taking the test with those accommodations. (Sireci et al., 2005, p. 458)

To take one example, MacArthur and Cavalier (2004) conclude that using voice recognition software or dictating to a scribe did not change the meaning of scores on a writing test, because they improved essay quality for high school students with learning disabilities but not for those without such disabilities.

17. From the classroom perspective, Phillips (2002) cautions against greatly increased or unlimited time for test taking, which can mean less time for actual instruction; moreover, if "one of the goals of education is to help students automate skills so that they are readily available for use," then such an approach would obscure important information about students who need a great deal of extra time (pp. 126–27).

18. Phillips and Camara (2006) list evidence and criteria for classifying a change in testing procedures as an accommodation or a modification (p. 745). Hollenbeck (2002) discusses the issue in depth and offers a sample flowchart for making decisions (p. 416).

19. Koretz and Barton (2004) note that, among other types of investigation, conducting DIF analyses for SWD is often infeasible because of the variety of types of accommodations and the small numbers of students who may use these accommodations for a particular test (p. 40). Moreover, DIF analyses would not answer the question of whether the entire test is problematic for SWD.

20. As Cavanaugh (2008) reports, the governing board of NAEP continues to make efforts towards bringing more consistency to state policies on accommodations for disabled students. Variation in policies limits the usefulness of national data on performance of disabled students.

On the other hand, Hollenbeck (2002) advises that decisions about accommodations, modifications, or alternate tests be targeted to individuals—and be investigated anew for each particular test, rather than simply extrapolated from past research findings.

21. For more information about how different states assess the English-language proficiency of students and use accommodations for other types of tests, see Wolf, Kao, Griffin, Herman, Bachman, Chang, and Farnsworth (2008). Decisions about accommodations are usually left up to the district or schools.

22. For a description of how one state, Oregon, has implemented ELL accommodations and modifications in statewide assessments, see Durán, Brown, and McCall (2002). Understanding the extensive efforts that went into accommodations/modifications for just a single ELL population (Spanish-speaking students) helps one appreciate the challenges of addressing the needs of multiple ELL populations.

23. For example, Abedi and Lord (2001) found that simplifying the language of some NAEP math items appeared to benefit both ELL students and low-achieving students in basic math classes, without affecting the performance of high-achieving students in more advanced classes.

24. The real inequities go beyond what is captured in the usual data. For example, Winerip (2009) visited an inner-city high school to observe a well-paid and highly experienced math teacher conducting a class in calculus. But the "chaotic" school environment included two false fire alarms during the class period. Opportunity to learn depends on school environment as well as course offerings or teacher qualifications.

25. Harris and Herrington (2006) also argue in favor of the "input" perspective, based on their review of research suggesting that achievement gaps narrowed prior to the 1990s because of improved educational resources and more rigorous academic content. For detailed descriptions of different strategies that high schools have successfully used to address achievement gaps, see Ferguson et al. (2010).

Mislevy (1996) notes a caveat about OTL surveys, in that the information may accurately characterize groups but is not necessarily reliable for any given individual student.

SELECTED READINGS

Educational Testing Service (ETS). (2009a). *Guidelines for fairness review of assessments*. Princeton, NJ: Author.

Laitusis, C. C., & Cook, L. (2007). *Large-scale assessment and accommodations: What works?* Arlington, VA: Council for Exceptional Children.

National Research Council (NRC). (2004b). *Keeping score for all: The effects of inclusion and accommodation policies on large-scale educational assessment*. J. A. Koenig & L. F. Bachman (Eds.). Washington, DC: National Academies Press.

Stobart, G. (2005). Fairness in multicultural assessment systems. *Assessment in Education: Principles, Policy & Practice, 12*(3), 275–87.

Thompson, S. J., Johnstone, C. J., & Thurlow, M. L. (2002). *Universal design applied to large-scale assessments* (Synthesis Report 44). Minneapolis: University of Minnesota, National Center on Educational Outcomes.

Wolf, M. K., Kao, J., Herman, J., Bachman, L. F., Bailey, A. L., Bachman, P. L., Farnsworth, T., & Chang, S. M. (2008, January). *Issues in assessing English language learners: English language proficiency measures and accommodation uses: Literature review*. Center for the Study of Evaluation Report 731. (First of a series; see also reports 732, 737, 738, 765, & 766 on the subject of accommodations for ELL.)

Zieky, M. J. (2003). *A DIF primer*. Retrieved August 10, 2008, from the Educational Testing Service website: http://www.ets.org/Media/Tests/PRAXIS/pdf/DIF_primer.pdf.

Chapter Eight

The Meanings and
Uses of Scores

Interpretation [of test scores] presents the problem of establishing proce-
dures suitable for describing, recording, and comparing the performances
of individuals in specific test situations.

—John C. Flanagan, 1951 (p. 695)

Validity and reliability focus on the extent to which a test's informational product is credible, dependable, and helpful for a particular purpose. It might seem, then, that the significance of test scores is discovered only after the fact, by reverse-engineering the product.

Yet embedding and construing meaning in the score-product begins much earlier, with "establishing procedures suitable for describing, recording, and comparing" examinees' performance. In this chapter, we will trace such procedures and the assumptions on which they rely.

Quantifying responses as *raw scores*; converting raw scores into *scaled scores*; comparing an examinee's performance to that of other examinees or to prescribed criteria; establishing norms and setting performance standards; connecting scores across test forms or different tests; detecting incorrect scores; reporting scores to examinees and test users; integrating scores with other kinds of information—all these operations are steps in an ongoing process of interpretation. They are nested inside one another, so that the meanings and uses of scores are contingent upon multiple layers of assumptions.

INTERPRETING EVIDENCE TO PRODUCE
SCORES FOR DIFFERENT PURPOSES

To begin with, the immediate outcome of giving an educational test is not a score. It is a set of responses from each examinee, including any blanks, that will be used as evidence of proficiency in some domain. What follows, as Kane, Mislevy, and others emphasize, is a process of inference and interpretation in light of the claims that one wants to make.

Calculating Raw Scores and (Sometimes)
Turning Them Into Scaled Scores

From the perspective of inference and interpretation, then, the first assumption is that this evidence can be translated into numbers—that examinees' performance can be described and recorded quantitatively. Each response is either marked correct/incorrect or else assigned points on a scale indicating degree of correctness or level of quality (thereby also assuming that levels of quality can be represented as units of equal value). The very existence of scoring rules implies different possible interpretations of examinees' responses.*

Next in the interpretive process is calculating an overall score, which involves assumptions about the relative value of each response as evidence. The simplest and most common approach is to add up the number of correct responses and any other points awarded to arrive at a raw score, which can be expressed as a number correct, percentage correct, or total number of points.

If statisticians are using IRT, then they may use the estimated θ level of proficiency as the raw score. This estimate is not a sum of points but a comparison of the examinee's pattern of responses to those that characterize each θ level.

Apart from these approaches, other methods of calculating a raw score involve judgmental decisions aimed at particular goals. To discourage guessing on multiple-choice items, one could subtract a fraction of a point for an incorrect answer. One could also differentially weight items so that some are worth more points.

The most common scenario here would be a test that combines selected- and constructed-response items, meaning that the former probably

---

*As Stevens (1946) emphasized, "The fact that numerals can be assigned under different rules leads to different scales and different kinds of measurement" (p. 677). For example, one could score the same essay by applying a six-point scale for overall quality, or a four-point scale for each of several different traits, or a binary yes/no checklist of features, and so on. Even a multiple-choice item can be scored in different ways. See chapters 10 and 11 in volume 2 for more about scoring rules and procedures.

outnumber the latter. Depending on priorities, weighting the constructed-response tasks more heavily could help emphasize skills not captured in the selected-response items. Alternatively, weighting the selected-response tasks more heavily would make the test scores more reliable. If correlations with criterion measures (such as future grades) are important, one can investigate how different weighting strategies would affect these correlations. (For more about ways of calculating raw scores, see Kolen, 2006, pp. 156–63.)

A test or test section composed of constructed-response tasks often uses a raw score for reporting the final score. If the test or section contains tasks that measure similar skills, are scored on the same scale, and have equal weight (such as two half-hour essays scored on a 0–6 scale), the final score can be an average rather than the sum of points awarded by raters. This approach makes the reported score more understandable because it echoes the task scale (e.g., 0–6).

However, reporting raw scores for constructed-response tests assumes that different versions of the tasks have similar difficulty and ability to discriminate within the intended examinee population. To support such an assumption, the program has to pretest the tasks and calculate the mean, distribution, and *SD* of scores for each task.

Teachers often score classroom tests in terms of number or percent correct. Thus, the view that John C. Flanagan (1906–1996) took in his 1951 *Educational Measurement* chapter reflected a classroom orientation: "A raw score is a very fundamental piece of information, and should not be relinquished in favor of some other type of score without good reason" (p. 705). Additional useful information would be the specific tasks that students were or were not able to do.

In contrast, from the perspective of larger-scale, multiple-choice testing, William H. Angoff (1919–1993) stated in his parallel 1971 chapter that a raw score "has no inherent meaning and cannot be interpreted without some kind of supporting data" (p. 512).

This apparent contradiction refers to a problem that testing programs encounter. Raw scores on a test form suggest how difficult that version was for that group of examinees but not how the examinees would have performed on another version of the test. Nor, by themselves, do raw scores indicate how well an examinee has met any prescribed standards for performance.

For these reasons, raw scores are often associated with performance categories or else converted to scaled scores. A scaled score is an alternate numeric system with, again, units assumed to be equal in value. ("Derived" or "converted" is more accurate, since even raw scores are a type of scale, but "scaled" is commonly used.)

Transforming raw scores to scaled scores is a way of translating test evidence into more usable information. Scaling permits testing programs to report scores with the same meaning across different test administrations. It also makes possible various mathematical operations and quantitative comparisons. Like inches, degrees Celsius, or pounds, scaled scores can offer a system of measurement units whose meaning is constant, widely recognized, and easy to recall (Angoff, 1971).[1]

Even at a superficial level, a derived/scaled score serves as a language for describing and communicating information about performance; consider, for example, the familiarity of ACT or SAT scores. Types of meaning that can be incorporated into a scale-language include comparisons among examinees and the overall precision of the measurement. A scale efficiently encodes such information, but decoding it requires understanding its context.*

Adding Context by Means of Other Measurements

One way of putting a test's scale in context is to provide another interpretation of performance. In addition to reporting a score on a scale intended to have a stable meaning, testing programs may also provide a measurement whose meaning is conditional. Usually it is in terms of *percentile ranks* that indicate the percentage of current or recent examinees scoring below a particular scaled score. (For example, if an examinee's scaled score is at the 65th percentile, then 65 percent of examinees received a lower scaled score.) Programs often include the raw scores as well (Petersen, Kolen, & Hoover, 1989).

Some testing programs report not only overall scores but also subscores measuring related but distinguishable constructs, such as mathematical computation (adding, dividing, etc.) versus more abstract mathematical problem solving. This approach is especially popular in testing for instructional or diagnostic purposes, even though producing subscores may require lengthening a test because each subscore—based on fewer items—is less reliable than the total score.

Subscores may not be useful unless they can be shown to be sufficiently reliable and valid in themselves; provide more accurate measurement of the construct than does the test as a whole; and are not highly correlated with one another and with the overall score (Haberman, 2005; Monaghan, 2006). On the other hand, sometimes subscores can provide valuable information about

---

*With regard to precision, Livingston (2004) explains that the units in the scale should be small enough so that each additional correct answer is reflected in the examinee's score, but not so small that differences in scores are misinterpreted as more meaningful than is actually the case.

effects of instruction or group differences, as in differential performance on selected-response and constructed-response test sections (S. A. Livingston, personal communication, June 7, 2010). Giving the raw scores for specified groups of items is another possibility.

Conversely, multipart tests that span clearly different constructs, such as mathematics and writing, may report separate scores for each test and an aggregated *composite score*. (Examples are composite scores for the ACT and the Medical College Admission Test, the MCAT®.) Just like items within a single test, the separate tests may be weighted differentially in their contribution to the composite score, especially if the tests' scores are not all equally reliable (Kolen, 2006).

Choosing Norm-Referenced or Criterion-Referenced Score Interpretations

Score interpretations fall into two major categories: *norm-referenced* scores that describe an examinee's performance relative to that of other examinees, and *criterion-referenced* scores that describe an examinee's performance relative to absolute standards or criteria. Usually the former type of score is expressed primarily as a numeric scale and the latter primarily in words, with labels for the performance categories. For any given test, it is possible to use either a relative or an absolute score interpretation, or both.[2]

A secondary consideration is whether there is a need to obtain measurement information that is as fine-grained as possible or else simply enough to classify the examinees in groups, such as pass versus fail. In general—not always—norm-referenced scores favor the former and criterion-referenced scores the latter.

Norm- and criterion-referenced interpretations both have historical resonance. The former dominated in the first half of the twentieth century, when psychometrics emphasized quantifying differences among individuals. Although E. L. Thorndike strongly advocated using performance standards for instructional purposes, as exemplified in his 1910 handwriting scale, the term "criterion-referenced" was not introduced until 1963 and the approach became common only with the rise of minimum-competency and standards-based testing (Biggs, 2001; Koretz & Hamilton, 2006).[3]

With both types of interpretations available, the principle of "form follows function" applies to designing the test's informational product. Norm-referenced interpretations tend to be more useful for contextual, relativistic educational decisions. Criterion-referenced interpretations tend to be more useful for decisions that involve fixed, explicit expectations and standards.

Selection processes involve differentiating among individual examinees. Thus admissions-testing programs such as the ACT, SAT, LSAT, and MCAT use norm-referenced score scales that rank examinees in the same way over many successive test administrations and that provide fine-grained information about performance.

In the context of instruction, norm-referenced percentiles and *stanines* show the distribution of performance within a defined group of students on a particular test form. Stanines are useful for showing very large differences but not nuanced ones; they are a kind of norm-referenced interpretation that uses coarse-grained classification.*

Age equivalents, grade equivalents, or developmental scales (used to screen young children for possible physical or mental delays) provide a statistic based on performance relative to groups with known characteristics, such as age.

Long-established K–12 tests draw on these kinds of score interpretations to compare students' performance to norms based on recent national samples. Such tests include the ITBS, introduced in 1935 by Lindquist and colleagues at the University of Iowa, and the Stanford Achievement Test Series (now the Stanford 10), introduced in 1922 by Terman and colleagues at Stanford University.

In the case of scales based on grade equivalents, students who obtain the average score on a grade-level test taken at the beginning of the school year are considered to be at exactly that grade level, for example, 3.0 for third grade. Each additional 0.1 (3.1, 3.2, etc.) is an extrapolation of projected average scores for each successive month of the school year (Popham, 2000).

However, this approach assumes that student progress can be measured in terms of the length of time an average student takes to acquire a particular level of proficiency—a problematic assumption if very different new skills are introduced at the beginning of the grade. Moreover, one cannot claim that a student is at a higher or lower grade level unless the student actually takes the test intended for the other grade level. Thus some experts recommend percentiles instead (Popham, 2000; Angoff, 1971).

Not all educational decisions require direct comparisons among examinees. Criterion-referenced score interpretations compare a student's current achievement with prescribed instructional goals, curricular standards, or some other type of explicit criteria. Examples include scores for some place-

---

*A stanine scale converts raw or scaled scores to a nine-part scale (1–9) with unequal percentages assigned to each ninth. The top and bottom 4 percent of results become, respectively, scores 9 and 1; then percentage per score point increases symmetrically from either end of the scale to form a bell curve whose peak is 20 percent at the middle score of 5.

ment tests, minimum competency tests, high school diploma tests, AP tests, and many accountability tests as well as licensing or certification tests.[4]

These kinds of criterion-referenced score interpretations tend to focus on classifying examinees rather than on providing nuanced measurement information. However, tests intended to diagnose a student's strengths and weaknesses in terms of certain instructional goals would need additional levels of specific and fine-grained information, such as subscores, analyses of performance in particular areas, or even task-by-task performance.

Some familiar tests in the legal field illustrate how score "form" follows score "function." The sixty-point scale and auxiliary percentile rankings of the LSAT are norm referenced and fine grained to help law schools compare and select applicants. In contrast, states score bar exams by dividing all scores into two categories: pass or fail. Here, the purpose is to protect the public by ensuring that new lawyers have a certain level of knowledge. In each case, the score interpretation reflects the intended use.

Sometimes, as the *Standards* notes, the two kinds of score interpretations intermingle. For example, a norm-referenced scale might become the basis for criterion-referenced performance expectations (such as specific reading skills an average fourth-grade student should attain). Also, it is possible to set norm-referenced cut scores by stipulating a number or percentage of examinees who will qualify for each category, such as "advanced" or "pass."*

ESTABLISHING NORMS AND PERFORMANCE STANDARDS

Norm- and criterion-referenced interpretations call for different types of validity evidence, insofar as the former requires explaining how the norms were established and the latter how the criteria were set. A program that uses both kinds of score interpretations for reporting scores would need both kinds of validity evidence. Any use of classification categories would call for providing indices of dependability or classification consistency.

Not only should testing programs explain in their technical literature how the norms and/or performance standards were determined, but also they should post an accessible version of this information on their official websites.

---

*In educational settings, percentage-based classifications are used more often for cumulative performance, such as academic honors. Many colleges set fixed percentages of graduates who will be awarded degrees *summa, magna,* or *cum laude,* so that the GPA "cut scores" may vary from year to year.

Establishing Norms by Using Reference Groups

Since norm-referenced scores reflect comparisons of an examinee's performance with that of other examinees, the meaning of such scores depends on how "the other examinees" are defined. Testing programs often establish a representative sample or reference group of examinees for this purpose. Defining an appropriate reference group or groups is crucial to the validity of norm-referenced scores.

Essential principles for norm/reference groups first mentioned in the 1955 *Technical Recommendations* still apply: a "technically sound, representative, scientific sample of sufficient size" is required (AERA et al., 1999, p. 51). The testing program should report complete descriptive information about the reference group and procedures used to establish it, including dates.

Some testing programs rely on "user norms"—that is, designating as the reference group all the examinees who take the test within a given time period (Kolen, 2006). For example, when calculating examinees' percentile rankings, admissions testing programs use the population of examinees over the past three years or less because this comparison is relevant to selection. Individual institutions can focus on their own recently accepted students.

In contrast, for tests such as ITBS, Stanford 10, and NAEP, a selected sample of the overall examinee population serves as the reference group. Specifications for reference groups can include geographic ones, such as national or local; demographic subgroups, such as gender, ethnicity, or linguistic background; and age or grade. All of these can be used to provide a context for an individual student's performance. Some norms are intended only for group comparisons; in NAEP, percentile ranks show the average scores for schools and states, not for individual students (Kolen, 2006). (The NAEP program offers an online tool for different views of data according to a wide range of reporting variables, thereby putting scores into different contexts.)[5]

Sampling designs are essentially survey designs, and statistical techniques for selecting participants and weighting the results must be carefully considered. An approach used to sample a large range of test content without lengthening individual tests is *matrix sampling,* in which each student takes some subset of the total collection of test items. This method works well for making group-level comparisons, such as NAEP scores, but not for comparing individual performance to that of a reference group. Thus, state tests may use a combination of matrix sampling and shared items to establish both group and individual norms (Koretz, 2008).[6]

Inevitably, norm-referenced scores are theory laden, insofar as they reflect choices of sample groups for comparison and establish expectations about how students at a particular age or grade level will or should perform. They also reflect assumptions about the existence of quantifiable individual differences. However, if one grants these assumptions, these scores can be evaluated in terms of statistical and methodological soundness. They are also relatively neutral (with the emphasis on "relatively"), when left as unlabeled quantitative data.

The Nature and Purpose of Performance Standards

In contrast, most criterion-referenced scores are explicitly value-laden interpretations because they embody judgments about the quality of an examinee's performance. The purpose is often to make the test results actionable in a particular way—to certify performance, as in high school graduation exams; to describe performance in terms of expectations (as in NAEP descriptions of proficiency levels); or to motivate efforts, as in accountability tests reflecting curricular goals (Green, 1996).

In technical terms, performance standards are classifications, often defined by cut scores at which performances are separated into higher and lower categories (e.g., pass/fail; below basic/basic/proficient/advanced, etc.).* The categories may have numbers, as in AP scores, but usually they are expressed as written labels or descriptions of what each category signifies. The labels' meanings are specific to a particular test, even if similar wording is used in other testing programs.[7]

Because performance standards imply action, to set them is "to establish a policy, and policies are evaluated in terms of their appropriateness, reasonableness, and consistency, rather than in terms of accuracy" (Kane, 1998, p. 129). Thus, the people who set performance standards should state the anticipated benefits and possible negative consequences. Doing so helps in evaluating the reasonableness and efficacy of the standards as policy (Zieky, Perie, & Livingston, 2004).

How these policies are established also demands scrutiny. Methods of setting performance standards have been described as either "test centered" or "examinee centered," but hybrid approaches are also used (see Hambleton & Pitoniak, 2006, for a comprehensive survey). Test-centered methods focus on reviewing test items to determine at what levels cut scores should be set. Examinee-centered methods usually involve classifying actual samples of examinees' performance into the categories that will be used for scores, such as pass/fail, good/excellent, etc. In the standard-setting protocols described below, a given procedure usually can be repeated to set multiple performance levels, such as below basic/basic/proficient/advanced.

---

*Performance standards are distinct from content standards, although the two are related. Content standards specify skills and knowledge that are the goals of instruction; performance standards establish the criteria for evaluating performances of these skills and knowledge.

Test-Centered Methods for Setting Performance Standards

Kane (1998) views test-centered methods as generally more applicable to selected-response or short-answer tests, whereas examinee-centered methods are more suitable to constructed-response tests, especially those requiring evaluations of complex performances, such as an essay. It is logical that test-centered methods would be more appropriate when a test contains or else tightly constrains all possible responses (as in multiple-choice tests) than when a test permits divergent responses, with less predictable characteristics.

The first protocol proposed for test-centered standard setting, the 1954 "Nedelsky Method," introduced the idea of having a panel of subject-matter experts predict how a minimally competent examinee (on the borderline between passing and failing) would perform on each multiple-choice item, then aggregating those data to calculate a minimally qualifying test score. A more flexible and influential process was suggested by Angoff (1971): that the panel "estimate the proportion of minimally acceptable persons who would answer each item correctly," with the sum of these estimates representing the minimally acceptable score (p. 515).*

These early approaches raised certain issues later addressed in "modified Angoff" and other methods. For example, newer methods usually include a comparison of judges' estimates of item difficulty with data from actual examinees, a comparison that might lead judges to revise their expectations for minimum levels of performance. Moreover, the judges may conduct multiple rounds of ratings, rank items in clusters, and/or engage in discussions aimed at reaching consensus. For tests containing items scored along a scale, judges estimate a particular score level for each item rather than probability of correct answer (Hambleton & Pitoniak, 2006).

One recently developed standard-setting protocol is the "bookmark" method, introduced by Lewis, Mitzel, and Green at a 1996 symposium and thereafter increasingly popular. It not only permits the use of IRT data on item difficulty; it begins with these data. All of the test's items are organized or "mapped" from lowest to highest difficulty along the test's θ scale of proficiency.

Bookmarking is done in a literal sense. An "ordered item booklet" presents one test item per page, sequenced from lowest to highest difficulty. The judges place bookmarks between items to indicate that the minimally qualified examinee for a particular performance level would be likely to succeed on items before the bookmark, but unlikely to succeed on items after it. ("Likely" is often defined as 67 percent probability but can be set at a lower

---

*Note that these methods reflect then-current CTT practices by assuming that all examinees take the same nonadaptive test, composed of multiple-choice items and scored by number of correct answers.

or higher probability.) Several rounds of bookmarking and discussion follow. As a reality check, the judges also consider norm-referenced information, that is, they look at estimates of the percentage of examinees who would qualify for each proposed performance level (Karantonis & Sireci, 2006).[8]

Examinee-Centered Methods for Setting Performance Standards

Some examinee-centered methods use external evidence or another criterion measure to help validate the proposed performance standards. For the "borderline group" method proposed by Livingston and Zieky (1982), the judges first use external information to identify a group of examinees whose proficiency appears to be at the dividing line between two performance levels. The midpoint of this group's scores on the test becomes the cut score, because it represents what a "not quite adequate and yet not really inadequate" examinee for that performance category would receive (pp. 34–35).

The "contrasting groups" method, also introduced by Livingston and Zieky in 1982, starts by identifying examinees whose test scores are near each proposed cut score. Then these examinees are classified as qualified or unqualified according to an external criterion or evaluation. The cut score is set at the level where half or more of the examinees earning that score are in the qualified group. A variant procedure suggested by Cohen, Kane, and Crooks (1999) uses correspondences between test and criterion scores obtained by a cross section of examinees at all levels.

Another approach is "latent class analysis," in which students' patterns of responses are analyzed to uncover qualitative categories (see Brown, 2007, for an example). Such analysis seeks to reveal underlying categories of performance, or classes to which examinees belong, that may not lie upon a single quantitative continuum.

Last, examinee-centered methods can focus directly on samples of the examinees' work. The judges classify sample responses (such as essays, solutions of math problems, even entire portfolios) according to proposed scoring rubrics and performance categories. In the process, the judges may modify those rubrics and performance categories, as well as focus on borderline samples and methods for categorizing them. The judges often choose some of the sample responses in each performance category as exemplars for later use in the operational scoring process (Hambleton & Pitoniak, 2006).

Issues Raised by Performance Standards

Because performance standards incorporate so many layers of interpretation, they raise a host of questions. These include why a particular standard-setting method is chosen, who sets the standards, what evidence supports the standards, what safeguards are needed to protect examinees, and what supplementary information is needed.

First, clear guidance in choosing an optimal standard-setting method is not easy to find. Despite the growth in comparative studies, such research often proves inconclusive and difficult to generalize (Hambleton & Pitoniak, 2006). A program would at least need to be able to give reasons why the chosen method is appropriate for the type of construct being measured, the test format, and the intended use of scores.

Second, the perspectives and agendas of standard-setters shape the standards. Usually the focus is on the qualifications of the panel members or judges: their expertise about the subject matter, their ability to form realistic expectations about student performance, and their representation of demographic diversity and the range of expert opinion. However, simply documenting judges' resumes and official protocols may not tell the whole story, especially since standard-setting is as sociopolitical as it is scholarly (or more so). McGinty (2005) suggests investigating judges' cognitive processes, too: how well judges understand the procedures and how certain preconceptions, pressures, and even emotional factors may affect judges' decisions.[9]

Taking a larger view of "who sets the standards," Haertel (2002) points out that not only panels of judges but also policy makers, technical experts, and multiple audiences (including teachers, the public, and the examinees themselves) are all actors in this enterprise. Failing to integrate the various stakeholders' knowledge and concerns can result in performance standards that are unclear, misleading, unrealistic, or counterproductive. He urges that, instead of leaving the standard-setting procedures to the panel of judges, the process be structured to permit broader participation.[10]

Third, performance standards imply particular types of reliability and validity evidence. Apart from investigating the reliability of examinee classifications, one can also investigate the reliability of the standard-setting process itself, by repeating it with more than one set of judges and/or items to see if similar performance standards emerge each time (Zieky et al., 2004). Validity evidence could include criterion measures that show correlations with the score categorizations.

Fourth, performance standards call for certain safeguards for examinees. Because performance standards are an aspect of assessment that clearly serves to reinforce social values and shape identity, the wording of labels and descriptions is significant, and the "least stigmatizing labels, consistent with accurate representation, should always be assigned" (AERA et al., 1999, p. 89). The concept of learning progressions thus has an additional attraction, if the levels or categories can be empirical rather than aspirational—less emotionally charged than the usual performance labels.*

---

*Depending on the purpose and scope of a test, it may be helpful if the labels and descriptions refer more to qualities of the student's performance than to inferences about the student's abilities.

Rules are also needed for areas of potential ambiguity, such as whether or not the standards are "compensatory" (i.e., weak performance in one area can be offset by strong performance in another); and how borderline performance (just above or just below a cut score) is to be handled (Zieky et al., 2004). As a safeguard, before making final pass/fail determinations, some testing programs that include constructed-response tasks require a complete rescoring for any examinee whose total score is just above or below the cut score. [11]

Last, performance standards are score interpretations that add meaning but subtract precision. The labels attach value judgments and qualitative descriptions to examinees' test results. However, the classifications are usually very broad and imprecise—only two to six different levels of performance— whereas norm-referenced numerical scores offer more measurement information. Thus, it may be helpful to include auxiliary norm-referenced scales, percentiles, or raw scores (Koretz, 2008).

CONNECTING SCORES ACROSS TESTS AND DEALING WITH QUESTIONABLE SCORES

Although less obviously an act of interpretation than is setting performance standards, connecting scores across tests is also a way of embedding meaning. Programs that use multiple versions or forms of a test—such as the ACT, GMAT, GRE, or MCAT—translate scores into the same language. Other kinds of translations may permit comparisons between results from different tests of the same or similar construct, so that the scores are, in a sense, speaking a common language.

Psychometricians began early in the 1900s to work on methods of connecting scores across tests. Such transformations may involve *equating* (making scores on alternate versions of the same test interchangeable); aligning scales (putting scores from two different tests on the same scale); or predicting (using performance on one test to predict performance on another test) (Holland & Dorans, 2006).

Equating Scores to Make Test Forms Interchangeable

Equating is a common kind of transformation in large-scale testing programs that rely on interchangeable test forms as a security strategy. Its requirements are rigorous, since the purpose is to make scores equivalent in meaning. By definition, equating is "putting two or more essentially parallel tests on a common scale" (AERA et al., 1999, p. 175). Testing programs build alternate test forms to meet as closely as possible the same parallel specifications—for domain coverage, item format, overall difficulty, and reliability—and each form is administered under the same timing and other standardized conditions. Familiar examples are the test forms constructed for successive administrations of the ACT or SAT.

Indeed, as Holland and Dorans (2006) note, it was the rise of college admissions testing in the 1940s that made equating of test forms an urgent practical necessity. No matter how much care is taken in building each new test form, its average difficulty and its score distribution for a new group of examinees may not match those of previous test forms taken by previous groups of examinees. To put it another way, identical raw scores across parallel test forms do not necessarily have the same meaning, because each new test form may be somewhat more or less difficult than its predecessors.

The two major methods of equating in CTT (called "linear" and "equipercentile"), which had already been devised by the 1940s, start with the raw scores of one "reference" test form. For each successive new test form that follows, the raw scores are adjusted up or down to match the difficulty and distribution of the raw scores on the reference form. Then the adjusted raw scores are converted to the scale on which the program reports examinees' scores. Thus, in effect, group performance on each new test form is translated backward, into a comparison with the group performance on the reference test form. (For an example of translating the raw scores from one test administration into scaled scores, see LSAC, 2007, p. 38.)[12]

To collect the data needed for equating test forms, a testing program needs some kind of overlap in administering at least two test forms. A single group of examinees may take both forms; the two forms may be randomly assigned or "spiraled" among examinees at the same test administration; or two groups may take a shared "anchor" test or set of items in addition to their own tests (Holland & Dorans, 2006; for a complete discussion of equating strategies, see Livingston, 2004). However, over time one must monitor the anchor items, including those previously calibrated via IRT, because they may not necessarily retain their original level of difficulty.

Whatever the equating procedures used, testing programs should provide rationales and documentation, including the limitations of the process, such as estimates of error from population sampling. A validity argument would need to demonstrate that, for the intended examinee population, scores from alternate test forms are indeed interchangeable.

Other Purposes for Connecting Scores

In addition to equating scores from two forms of the same tests, other purposes include connecting scores between old tests and new tests after changes occur in a testing program; between two tests, one of which is intended to predict performance on the other test; between different tests intended to measure the same or similar construct; and between tests intended for different grade levels. As a general rule, the connections become more tenuous as the strict requirements of equating are left further behind, and claims about score comparability should diminish as the tests themselves have less in common.

On occasion, a testing program may need to address changes in test content, format, or conditions of administration (especially a transition from paper-and-pencil to computer format). Scores from the past versions may or may not be interchangeable with those of the revised version. A testing program may also need to address changes in the examinee population and establish a more current reference population as the basis for the score scale. For example, the SAT score scale was adjusted or "recentered" to restore the scale's original meaning: as reflecting a normal distribution of scores with the mean at the midpoint of the scale. Such changes and their implications must be clearly communicated to the public (Dorans, 2002 and 2008).[13]

Another scenario involves two tests measuring the same construct, with the first test designed to predict performance on a second, higher-stakes test. Examples include the PLAN® test, for predicting ACT scores, and the PSAT/NMSQT®, for SAT scores. Historical comparisons of performance on the first and second tests make it possible to project an examinee's likely score range on the second test, but clearly scores on the first and second tests are not interchangeable (Holland & Dorans, 2006). Hence this scenario is a matter of connecting the scores in only one direction, rather than *linking* scores so that the relationship works both ways.

Using a common scale to link different tests covering similar skills and knowledge is not always feasible. For example, a National Research Council report (NRC, 1999b) concluded that creating one scale to link various state and commercial K–12 tests with NAEP could not be justified because of disparities in test content, format, difficulty, purpose, and examinee population. There was debate about whether then-current state tests and NAEP tests were sufficiently comparable to support the attempt made by Bandiera de Mello et al. (2009) to map state proficiency standards onto NAEP proficiency standards.

However, it may be possible to relate scores from two tests measuring similar constructs in a similar examinee population, if many examinees have taken both tests. Such "concordance tables" connect ACT and SAT scores (Dorans, 2008).

Last is an approach called *vertical scaling,* used primarily in K–12 for "growth models." This term describes testing programs intended to trace student progress longitudinally from one grade level to the next. Vertical scaling is a way to connect test forms of increasing difficulty to a common scale for a proficiency, such as math skills, that is designated as unidimensional. (If math skills were seen as including more than one distinct construct or dimension, then additional sets of vertical scales would be needed.)

The purpose is to report scores on the same scale as the student moves from one grade to the next, so that it is easy to see whether or not the student is making overall progress. In IRT, this relationship is expressed graphically as vertical alignment of the test characteristic curves for each grade level along a θ scale (Patz, 2007).

However, the score represents proficiency only with respect to a particular grade level. A third grader who gets the same score as a fourth grader has not reached the fourth grader's level of skills. Vertically scaled scores are not interchangeable across grade levels because they represent performance on tests at different levels of difficulty. (This issue is the same one that applies to grade-level scales.)

For this reason, even a high score on the third-grade math test does not indicate how well the same student would perform on the fourth-grade math test. If, the next year, the student were to get a similar score on the fourth-grade test, it would suggest that the student is doing as well in fourth-grade math as he/she did the previous year in third-grade math. A lower score on the fourth-grade test could suggest that the student is doing less well than in the previous year.

Vertical scaling permits comparisons only between adjacent grade levels and only when the content standards at adjacent grade levels overlap—when there is grade-to-grade instructional continuity, as may occur in reading and mathematics but often does not occur in other subject areas, such as science or social studies. Also, the difference between two test scores—the presumed amount of change or growth—contains about 40 percent more error than either score by itself.

Further, vertical scaling requires data-collection methods that support grade-to-grade links. The overlap can be created in different ways: students in adjacent grades can take a subset of common items or take the tests for both grade levels; or else students can take a separate scaling test with items from all grade levels (Patz, 2007). That students have to take out-of-level items is one criticism of vertical scaling, as well as concerns about the basic assumption that similar scores in different grade levels can have similar meanings (Schafer, 2006).

Scores from vertically scaled tests can be left as norm-referenced interpretations or cut scores can be established for performance standards. The latter, however, can raise concerns about how the performance levels from one year to the next are actually related and the extent to which errors in classifications could affect comparisons from one year to the next.[14]

Setting aside this additional consideration, there is a fundamental principle for all types of score connections: the more overlap in test characteristics and groups of examinees, the stronger the basis for comparing scores. If connecting scores is a priority, then tests and data-collection methods must be designed accordingly.

Maintaining the Quality of Test Scores

A key assumption in the interpretive process is that the test scores are accurately calculated and reported—but that assumption requires constant scrutiny. Especially in large-scale programs, producing test scores involves complex logistical operations. Like any product, scores need quality-control procedures.

Literature about administering and scoring tests suggests how much oversight and rigor are needed to maintain the integrity of the process. Allalouf (2007) provides a detailed anatomy of how scores are computed and reported, with an emphasis on possible mistakes that could occur and the ways to avoid, detect, or handle any such errors. Cohen and Wollack (2006) particularly emphasize the importance of test security to the validity of scores.

In their view, of even greater concern than invalid scores caused by cases of individual cheating (on the part of examinees, teachers, or other test administrators) are collaborative securing breaches that undermine scores and testing programs on a wider scale. Today, the same technological developments that have improved assessment are a double-edged sword because they increase ways in which test security can be compromised. Human observation and prevention as well as electronic countermeasures can help. Less obvious, but equally important, are statistical and data analysis (including erasures on paper-and-pencil answer sheets) to detect anomalies and questionable patterns or trends.[15]

Sometimes a score is questioned by an examinee who believes that the test contains an error or that his/her answers were scored incorrectly. Test makers must establish and publicize procedures for examinees to make inquiries and request reviews or rescores; if a "material error" is found in the test or scores, a corrected score report must be issued to all score users (AERA et al., 1999, pp. 89–90, 66).

On the other hand, it may be the test maker who raises questions. Addressing any mistakes in a test is an obvious necessity; challenging the validity of an examinee's score as fraud or cheating is a more delicate matter. The *Standards* makes an implicit analogy to legal due process in its guidelines for dealing with disputed scores (AERA et al., 1999, pp. 89–90). Documents such as *Procedures for Investigating Testing Irregularities and Questioned Scores* (ACT, 2005) and *Why and How ETS Questions Test Scores* (ETS, 2004) illustrate the types of information that test makers communicate to examinees and test users about score challenges and investigations.

A grayer area is the extent to which test preparation may undermine the meaning of scores. Since most educational tests measure acquired skills and knowledge, separating legitimate learning and test familiarization from coaching that provides an unfair advantage is not always easy. Indeed, Crocker (2003) argues that because test taking is so much a part of education and employment, it is "a legitimate educational skill which teachers have the obligation to impart to their students" (p. 10).

She also suggests five criteria for appropriate activities: "validity, academic ethics, fairness, educational value, and transferability" (2006, p. 126). In other words, do test scores maintain their meaning; are the familiarization activities ethical; are some examinees differentially advantaged or disadvantaged; what is the value of the time spent; and are the acquired skills and knowledge useful beyond the test?

Test makers strive to make their tests less coachable, but the *Standards* advises documenting how much improvement may come from practice or coaching. Research on effects of coaching should also include nontest evidence about whether score improvements represent actual progress in learning, as opposed to short-term memorization or use of test-specific strategies.

In keeping with the laws of nature, examinees will always seek ways to adapt in order to gain competitive advantage. The goal is to make worthwhile learning the best advantage.

REPORTING TEST SCORES

To understand such a complex product as test scores, consumers need a user's manual. Each testing program should "describe in simple language what the test covers, what scores mean, the precision of scores, common misinterpretations of scores, and how scores will be used" (AERA et al., 1999, p. 65). Often this information is divided into a score report containing the examinee's personal test results and a generic interpretive guide. Testing programs create paper and online documents whose focus and level of detail vary according to the intended audience: examinees, parents, teachers, administrators, admissions officers, or policy makers—although too little is known about how audiences actually perceive and use these messages (Moss, 1998).

Desirable Features in Score Reports

Taking a closer look, Goodman and Hambleton (2004) reviewed research about and examples of K–12 score reports and interpretive materials from governmental and commercial testing entities. They advise that K–12 testing programs be sure to describe the skills and knowledge assessed, the meaning of performance levels, and which skills and knowledge "the student does or does not yet possess," as well as report "the results of other comparison groups"—in other words, supplement criterion-referenced score interpretations with norm-referenced ones (p. 196).

General characteristics of effective score reports are: clarity, concision, readability, definitions of essential terms, jargon-free explanations, and essential data presented in multiple ways (numbers, graphs, and narrative text). Other helpful features are sample test questions, directions for obtaining further information, and suggestions for students to improve future performance (Goodman & Hambleton, 2004).

Certainly scores that are to any extent norm-referenced require considering the relevant examinee population and overall distribution of scores or proficiency levels. Percentile and stanine tables display this information in a numeric format; bar graphs and pie charts show it visually. (For examples, see Pearson Education, Inc., 2009.)

Unfortunately, a key finding of Goodman and Hambleton's study was that, despite the requirements of the *Standards,* too often score reports say little or nothing at all about measurement error—that is, about the fundamental imprecision inherent in scores. But given the interdependence of reliability and error, it is necessary to quantify measurement error in order to understand the extent to which scores are consistent and precise—and in order to be transparent about test information.

Thus, the interpretive material should at least indicate that the score represents a specified possible range of scores. More detailed information should explain what the reliability coefficient and the standard error of measurement actually mean. If the test scores are reported as performance levels, then the probability of classification error at each level should be indicated. If the test scores are on a continuous scale, the *SEM* can be depicted graphically with score bands or score ranges; if needed, the program can provide a table of *CSEM*s for different score levels.

An interesting exercise is to pick a testing program, such as a state program, and see how information about error in its technical literature is (or is not) presented in the examinee's score report. For example, a technical manual for the Pennsylvania System of School Assessment explains that reliability data for scores considers only error from content sampling, not occasion. It also gives data on classification consistency for each test's performance levels (Data Recognition Corporation, 2009, pp. 245, 252–55).

In the examinee's score report, the score scale is shown as a horizontal line divided by cut scores marking the four proficiency levels. An arrow points to the location of the examinee's score on the scale. Below is a sentence stating a range of scores within which the student's score "would likely remain" if the student "were to test again." Although not stated, "likely" refers to a 68 percent probability score band, and if the score range crosses a cut score, one can infer that a different classification is possible. However, the concept of classification consistency is not mentioned and the idea of retesting suggests a different occasion rather than a different set of items (Data Recognition Corporation, 2009, pp. 225–28).

Including both visual representations and verbal descriptions of error is helpful (for an example of interpretive material explaining score bands, see LSAC, 2010). But what if programs were to go beyond their existing types of materials and supplement them with score reports that depict error and other aspects of the testing procedure in more interactive ways?

A program could post online score reports that have mouse-over functions with explanatory notes for parts of the report. The score-report display could also have clickable links making it the portal to information: about the meaning of scores, how scores should be used, sample items from the test, materials for improving one's skills in the areas that were tested, other ways to demonstrate proficiency in the domain, and so on.

The purpose of this interactive score report would be twofold—to further assessment literacy and, more important, to further the student's development. With links working away from and back to the score report, it might be easier to see how the test, curriculum, instruction, other coursework, and learning goals are interrelated. Proposals from PARCC (2010, pp. 67–71) and SBAC (2010, pp. 60–70) do envision interactive score reports, but only in the sense that audiences can summon different views of data. The potential exists for a more ambitious approach in which score reports become an educational tool in themselves.

Caveats About Inferring Trends From Scores

In some cases, a student's scores from multiple tests may be used to infer patterns and trends in performance and academic growth. But again, note that each of a student's scores contains measurement error, so that the difference between two scores thus contains even more error than does either score by itself. Moreover, inferences about trends become harder to support as the tests and the examinee populations diverge. The best-case scenario for observing growth would require the same individual or group to participate over time in the same, vertically scaled testing program.

Often scores are used in attempts to identify group trends, but any such attempts must take into account the actual composition of the examinee population. For example, average scores on college admissions tests or state tests may decline as the population widens to include historically lower-scoring examinee groups (e.g., students whose English is limited). Statements about changes in student proficiency at a particular grade level need to take into account the fact that a given grade level is composed of different people each year. Tracing a cohort of students longitudinally over time may be more illuminating, especially for determining causes behind performance (Koretz, 2008).

Further, some apparent group trends may be purely statistical artifacts. Score fluctuations within the standard error of measurement may be caused by random error. Unrepresentative or small samples can be misleading. Group averages may obscure important differences among individuals within the group (Koretz, 2008).

A particular concern is whether patterns of overall score increases in a testing program represent actual progress, "score inflation," or even exclusion of certain examinees. In some cases, rising test scores were later shown to be invalid because of selective sampling, incorrect data aggregation, and other technical flaws (Mason, 2007). Koretz (2008, 2009) suggests that such increases can also result from narrowing the curriculum to focus on mastering anticipated test content, as well as using predictable types of questions in tests (for an account of how this process unfolded in the New York State school system, see Medina, 2010). Sometimes an "audit test" can be used to identify whether or not score inflation is occurring—for example, by comparing state trends to NAEP trends, to the extent that the tests overlap.

That trends depend on context is illustrated in a report by Stedman (2009) on the NAEP long-term trend assessment, which in theory has remained relatively unchanged since the early 1970s (what is now the main NAEP assessment branched off later). However, changes in test content and a shift from percent-correct to scaled scores and achievement levels departed from the original intent. Moreover, politicians have framed the NAEP trends in terms of their agendas; for example, stability indicated either stagnation or resilience. Thus, to understand student performance, one must look at the actual tasks and at accompanying surveys about school and extracurricular experience.

Last, another way of investigating trends, of a sort, is to use *value-added models* to try to measure the effectiveness of teachers or schools by identifying their contribution to student growth, as tracked in a vertically scaled sequence of tests or some other sequence of tests. Both the data and their interpretations depend on the particular tests, statistical methods, and sampling techniques employed.

The fundamental concerns are that researchers cannot assign randomized groups of students to teachers or schools in order to discern effects; scores may be lower if they have no consequences for students; and data collected over one year are less reliable than data collected over multiple years. Possible negative consequences include disincentives for teachers and schools to collaborate and innovate.[16]

For these and other reasons, even experts who see potential in value-added models have strong caveats and agree only about using it in low-stakes situations (Kolen, 2006; Koretz & Hamilton, 2006; Braun, 2005; NRC & NAE, 2010).[17]

In the end, the real meaning of scores and score trends includes and goes beyond technical issues mentioned in score reports and users' guides. It can depend upon such matters as individual examinees' characteristics; changes in the composition of the examinee population; the ways in which test scores are connected; the values embedded in content and performance standards; the effects of testing on administrators, teachers, and students; and the larger, surrounding educational and social conditions. These issues, and others, are extensions of the journalistic questions originally raised in the prologue, and they all are relevant to thinking about "What do the test scores really mean?"

USING TEST SCORES

As if anticipating the idea of systemic validity, Lindquist cautioned in the first edition of *Educational Measurement* that testing must "exercise a desirable influence upon the aims, habits, attitudes, and achievements of students, teachers, counselors, and school administrators" (1951, p. 120).

Setting aside current-day debates about consequences and validity, today's official guidelines ask for evidence about whether using test scores as part of system-wide assessment, individual or institutional accountability, selection processes, placement, and so on, exercises a desirable influence. Three key principles are: (1) each proposed score use has a burden of proof; (2) potential misinterpretations, misuses, or negative outcomes should be addressed and, if possible, averted; and (3) important educational decisions should be based on information beyond a single test score.

Justifying Proposed Uses; Preventing Misuses and Negative Outcomes

These two obligations are flip sides of the validity coin. On the one hand, testing entities must make a case for each proposed interpretation and use of test scores in decision-making processes, including expected outcomes and benefits. On the other hand, testing entities must also make efforts to prevent possible misinterpretations of scores and take into account findings that may suggest indirect, unanticipated outcomes (AERA et al., 1999, pp. 23, 114, 117).

Fulfilling these obligations for each proposed use is especially urgent because tests are susceptible to "technology push," in which the existence of a technology or procedure spurs a search for additional ways to use the technology (Baker, 2001). Yet a test designed for one purpose (e.g., college admissions) cannot be assumed suitable for another (e.g., measuring how well high school students are meeting state performance standards) without separate validation and any necessary changes. For each use, a test should not only measure the specified proficiencies but also reflect learning based on appropriate instruction and lead to "educationally beneficial outcomes" (NRC, 1999a).

Testing programs may define "educationally beneficial outcomes" in different ways, but as a starting point, Popham (2000) suggests that most uses of educational assessments should directly affect classroom instruction in a positive way. These considerations intersect with broader policy issues: for example, using test scores in decisions about grade-to-grade promotion also involves the efficacy of retention as a policy. Furthermore, "consequences" can be construed in many ways, including cost/benefit analysis of time and resources devoted to assessment.

Some of the strategies that Lane and Stone (2002) outline for collecting "consequential evidence" within the framework of validity claims are illustrated in an article by Darling-Hammond and Rustique-Forrester (2005). They draw on studies, surveys, statistics, and other sources of information to examine how the actual consequences of statewide K–12 testing programs compare with the intended outcome of improving instruction. The positive and negative effects of state assessments vary, depending on test content and format, on the ways in which teachers are involved in the assessment processes, and on the ways in which scores are used to make decisions about student promotion, graduation, teacher pay, and school sanctions.

If nothing else, accountability testing illustrates the complexity of investigating consequences. Gathering evidence about effects takes time, as does making any subsequent changes, and other concurrent events may be exerting their own influence on outcomes. Then, effects of the same test may vary for different examinees, as with high school exit exams that affect graduation rates differentially by group (Reardon, Attebury, Arshan, & Kurlaender, 2009). In fact, addressing one type of negative consequence can lead to another, as when concerns about such impact lead to changing the exit exams so much that they no longer serve their original purpose (see Warren & Grodsky, 2009).[18]

Moreover, researchers may differ in their findings about the same questions. For example, Anderson (2009) compared longitudinal data on teaching practices, allocation of instructional time, and curricular emphasis on language arts and mathematics and concluded that NCLB testing did not cause significant changes. In contrast, McMurrer (2007) found much greater impact on instruction and curricula.

Only from multiple such studies can a preponderance of evidence emerge— and that evidence may be puzzling. Dee and Jacob (2010) later concluded that even though NCLB led to increased instructional time for reading skills and not for mathematics skills, it was only in mathematics that any significant achievement gains occurred.

Another category of tests, admissions tests, differs in its purpose from classroom or system-wide assessment. The intended use of scores from admissions tests is to help predict applicants' future performance, and the primary evidentiary support is the scores' predictive validity with respect to future performance (usually first-year college grades). Using high school grades and test scores together can improve predictive validity for college admissions; for graduate school admissions, test scores can actually be more predictive than past grades (Zwick, 2006). However, because each institution has its own approach to weighting test scores, the consequences of score use may differ widely, and research about consequences is often institution specific.[19]

According to the National Association for College Admission Counseling (NACAC, 2008), misuses of these test scores include employing them as the sole criteria for awarding scholarships; as indicators of quality and financial viability for colleges and universities; or for state accountability purposes (unless the tests are modified and separately validated). Other misuses are as part of hiring processes or as "evidence of the educational quality of a school, state, or district" (Zwick, 2006, p. 673).

Yet even using scores as intended in the admissions process can be controversial, primarily because of group differences in average scores. Thus, some schools may turn to formal models for using scores in selection processes. Models may take into account group membership (e.g., proportional selection) or seek a compromise between benefits to individuals and to society— though use of such models may also raise legal issues (Camilli, 2006). The problem is that selection models inevitably embody particular definitions of fairness, and even making these values explicit does not lead to obvious answers (Messick, 1998).

Another important strategy is to use multiple sources of information to evaluate applicants, just as applicants themselves are advised to do when they evaluate prospective institutions. This "strategy" is, in fact, an important principle for score use.

A Holistic Approach to Using Test Scores in Educational Decisions

Every test score contains measurement error and represents a set of assumptions and interpretations that, even if well supported, suggest the possibility of alternatives. Such concerns help spur this directive in the *Standards*:

> In educational settings, a decision or characterization that will have major impact on a student should not be made on the basis of a single test score. Other relevant information should be taken into account if it will enhance the overall validity of the decision. (AERA et al., 1999, p. 146)

The wording is significant, implying that decision-making procedures require evidence and validation, just as assessment procedures do. From a generalizability perspective, one could say that decisions are more dependable when one expands the universe of relevant observations beyond a single test score.

Such an approach is not revolutionary. Teachers have long used many types of information (from students' homework, projects, work in class, etc.) to make instructional decisions and assign grades. Admissions officers may consider not only applicants' test scores but also grades, difficulty of courses taken, personal essays, extracurricular activities, recommendations, portfolios, demographic data, videos, assessments of noncognitive skills associated with success in college, and so on.[20]

Teachers and admissions officers may weigh and synthesize quantitative data via formulae or indexes, but the ideal is to take a holistic approach that also incorporates qualitative information. (Perhaps the worst aspect of ranking schools by admissions test scores is the incentive for schools to make less holistic decisions.)

Yet to emerge is any clear definition of a holistic approach in accountability assessment, whether it is the student, the teacher, or the school that is being held accountable. In the past the term "multiple measures" has been used to describe using different assessments of the same construct for different educational purposes as a way to increase reliability and validity, or else broadening the range of constructs that are assessed (Baker, 2003). Even the ways in which multiple assessment results are combined can differ, depending on whether the method is compensatory, complementary, conjunctive, or confirmatory (see Chester, 2005).[21]

For institutional accountability, the NEA and other educators' and civil rights organizations support a concept of multiple measures that includes such metrics as attendance rates, in-grade retention rates, and graduation rates (Walker & Jehlen, 2007). But even calculating something as seemingly obvious as graduation rates is difficult—and to find solutions for the educational problems that such data may reveal, still more information is needed. Heritage and Yeagley (2005) discuss the use of demographic data, surveys of perceptions and attitudes, and detailed descriptions of school processes. They also call for data tools permitting storage, access, and analysis of the various types of information, as well as for systematic procedures in defining questions, making inquiries, taking action, and evaluating results. Other experts recommend adopting an external school inspectorate of the type employed in some European countries and placing more emphasis on postgraduation outcomes.

All of these efforts, though, require identifying, weighing, selecting, and integrating the best sources of information—and professional measurement standards have had "little theoretical or practical advice to offer about how to combine . . . disparate pieces of information to reach a well-warranted conclusion" (Moss, 2004, p. 247). Proposals such as a virtual "student data backpack " (a file of longitudinal information for each student) as well as the convenience of e-portfolios suggest future possibilities (Raymond, 2008).

The current challenge, then, is to find sound and affordable ways to obtain, synthesize, and use information, including but not limited to test scores—while

Table 8.1. Considerations for Interpreting and Using Test Scores

How are scores calculated and reported?	**Raw scores:** Number or percent correct, or total number of points; points may be weighted or may be averaged across certain tasks. **Scaled scores:** Information is encoded to give scores the same meanings over time. The number of different possible scores or levels should indicate the degree of precision in the scores. **Subscores:** More fine-grained than the total score but less reliable. **Composite:** An overview combining different constructs.
Does the primary score interpretation compare an examinee's performance to that of other examinees or to performance standards? Does the interpretation suit the intended use of the scores?	**Norm-referenced (relative):** Intended to compare and differentiate performances among examinees. Useful for contextual decision making, such as selecting applicants or gauging the status of students within a defined population. **Criterion-referenced (absolute):** Intended to compare examinees' performances to prescribed criteria. Often expressed as verbal labels or descriptions; usually more overtly value laden and less precise than norm-referenced interpretations. **Cut scores:** Represent decisions about pass/fail or mastery levels.
How are any norms or performance standards established? Where is this information available?	**Norms:** Need representative, scientifically valid samples. **Performance standards:** Need to document, explain, and make a case for the value judgments made in setting standards. Are the expectations realistic and labels nonstigmatizing?
How are scores connected across test forms or different tests?	**Equating:** Need test forms with same specs or IRT-calibrated items. **Vertical scaling:** Need continuity in grade-to-grade curricular content. **Any connection:** Need some overlap in items and/or examinees.
What are the quality-control procedures for producing the scores? What kinds of problems could affect the accuracy of scores?	**Scoring:** Protocols for computing scores and detecting any errors (statistical analyses, etc.), procedural checklists. **Test security:** Supervision by humans and via technology. **Score challenges:** Correct any actual errors; due process for examinees. **Test preparation:** Real learning vs. test-taking strategies.
What guidance does the score report offer for understanding and using scores? What additional information or other perspectives are important?	**Score reports:** Should present clear, audience-appropriate information about intended meanings and uses of scores, explain and quantify measurement error, give normative as well as criterion interpretations; may include examples of tasks on test and suggest next steps for student. **Additional context:** Consider ways in which norms and performance standards were set, the composition of examinee population, statistical artifacts, possible score inflation, comparisons with "audit" tests.
What are the intended and unintended outcomes of using the test scores?	**Evidence:** Study actual consequences of using test scores in order to substantiate claims and improve policies on test use; warn against misuses; analyze costs vs. benefits.
In addition to a test score, what other information is needed for a decision?	**Holistic approach:** Identify other relevant sources, such as scores from other tests, work samples, observations, demographic data, surveys, etc.—and find practical ways to integrate the various sources.

continuing to insist on high standards for the quality of those test scores. These goals are actually congruent, for the following reason.

Critics of using tests in high-stakes decisions often cite "Campbell's law," which states that the more heavily policy decisions rely on a particular type of quantitative data, the more susceptible to corruption are both the data and the social process measured by the data. Donald T. Campbell (1916–1996) argued for using qualitative as well as quantitative information and including divergent viewpoints about the meaning of data. He used data from tests as an example: "When test scores become the goal of the teaching process, they both lose their value as indicators of educational status and distort the educational process in undesirable ways" (1976, p. 51). The same statement can be just as true if grades are the goal.[22]

Thus, the paradox is that too exclusive a focus on test scores can undermine their accuracy and meaning. A monoculture is more vulnerable to disease and pests than a rich biodiversity would be.

When a single score is not the arbiter; when a system of checks and balances governs important educational conclusions and decisions; and when assessment is understood as inquiry rather than as solution—then test scores may be more powerful in the sense of being more valid. And the decisions may be wiser.

Chapter VIII: Key Points

- Test scores interpret the samples of evidence elicited by the test. They translate the examinees' responses into quantitative data that are used to compare an examinee's performance to that of other examinees and/or to prescribed standards.
- Score scales provide a language for a particular testing program, such that the encoded meanings are stable over different forms of the test and groups of examinees. Scales convey information about relative standings of examinees and the precision of the test.
- The meaning of scores depends on how the norms were established or the performance standards were set. The latter explicitly embody value judgments and policy choices.
- As a "product" used in reaching conclusions or making decisions, scores should be designed according to the principle of "form follows function." Maintaining scores' integrity requires quality-control procedures for mechanical aspects of accuracy, for security, and so on.
- The extent to which scores from different tests or test forms can be connected depends on how much the tests or forms overlap: in construct, content, format, examinee population, and so on.
- Score reports should convey the meanings, limitations, and proper uses of scores, but further contextual information is needed for inferring trends or causes of performance.
- Validity principles should guide the use of test scores. Test makers and/or users should support proposed score uses with sound rationales and evidence; verify intended outcomes; and recognize and address negative outcomes. Important educational decisions should be holistic, incorporating all relevant information rather than relying on a single test score.

NOTES

1. Sometimes scales have an intrinsic meaning, as in the case of Binet's original mental-age scale (S. A. Livingston, personal communication, June 7, 2010). The topic of measurement scales and the mathematical-statistical operations that they permit (including the question of whether inferences about the measured attributes are scale-specific or scale-free) is an important one, but beyond the scope of the current discussion. For more, see Stevens (1946), Michell (1986), and Luce and Suppes (2002).

2. However, Green (1996) suggests that score interpretation may affect test design, because differentiating performance is the main concern in a norm-referenced score, and covering the content is the main concern in a criterion-referenced score. Thus, for example, using a norm-referenced score might call for including more items that differentiate among high-performing examinees.

3. Although establishing the scale did involve ranking of samples, students' work was to be compared with exemplars illustrating levels of proficiency. E. L. Thorndike (1918) considered "relative" evaluation of educational products useful, but only as a first stage before developing good scales, such as those that astronomers use in rating the magnitude of stars.

4. See also Atkinson and Geiser (2009) for an argument that college admissions tests should be based on curricular standards with criterion-referenced scores indicating levels of mastery.

5. See the website of the National Center for Education Statistics. The "Select Criteria" page, http://nces.ed.gov/nationsreportcard/nde/criteria.asp, offers a menu of categories for tabulating data by grade, year, subject, geographic jurisdiction, and demographic variable.

6. For more about matrix sampling, see Childs and Jaciw (2003). They point out that covering a larger sample of the domain by giving different items to students increases reliability for group-level results.

7. Zieky, Perie, & Livingston (2004) suggest that policy makers draft descriptions of these categories before setting the cut scores. Hambleton and Pitoniak (2006) reproduce the steps for writing performance descriptors originally suggested by Mills and Jaeger in 1998 (p. 453). Perie (2008) offers a more extended guide, which emphasizes that performance-level descriptors convey academic expectations for students.

8. Karantonis and Sireci (2006) note that compared to variants of the Angoff method, the bookmarking method may result in setting lower performance standards and may be problematic for item sets, such as a group of reading items based on a passage. Also, the designated level of probability for correct response affects the order of the items in the booklet and hence the placement of bookmarks.

9. For a case study, see Giraud and Impara (2005). The teachers setting the standards for a school district knew that funds for remediation were limited and that large numbers of failing students would embarrass the district—but that small numbers would seem too lenient. These considerations are not construct-relevant ones.

10. For more about standard-setting procedures, see Plake (2008). She cautions that input from stakeholders other than subject-matter experts should be considered but that nonexperts should not be judges in the standard-setting panel.

11. See, for example, New York State Board of Law Examiners (2008). Any scores on the Bar Exam from 10 points below to 9 points above the passing score trigger an automatic regrading of the entire exam.

Another approach, suitable for computer-administered adaptive tests, involves adding replications to the test rather than to the rating process. Borsboom et al. (2008) suggest giving extra items to examinees who are near a cut score, thereby enhancing fairness and the reliability of examinee classifications.

12. In linear equating, scores on the new form are adjusted to be "the same number of standard deviations above or below the mean of the group" as in the reference form; in equipercentile equating, scores on the new form are adjusted so that their percentile ranks match the percentile ranks on the reference form (Livingston, 2004, pp. 14, 17). Livingston points out that linear equating is problematic because it is so dependent on groups and can lead to having scores on the new form that are beyond the scale range on the reference form. He also emphasizes that any equating is done with respect to a broadly construed, hypothetical target group of examinees. The difficulty of a test form cannot be adjusted for each individual examinee or for all possible subgroups.

13. The recentering did not change examinees' rank order with respect to the particular test form that an examinee took, but it did affect rank ordering on test forms taken after the scale was recentered. Thus, scores from before and after recentering would not be interchangeable (Dorans, 2002).

14. For more detail, see the Winter 2009 issue of *Educational Measurement: Issues and Practice*, which focuses on various aspects of growth models, including vertical scaling and the impact of cut scores. See also Mitzel, 2005, for the pros and cons of different possible approaches to setting vertically aligned performance standards.

15. Test publishers have long been able to analyze patterns of erasures on paper-and-pencil answer sheets. The problem is to make sure that the government agencies responsible for testing programs actually conduct such audits and investigate any anomalies (Dewan, 2010).

16. Compare value-added models with investigating the efficacy of a medicine in clinical trials. These trials require a sufficiently large sample of randomly assigned patients and a control group to determine whether the medicine alone is benefiting the patients.

17. For an accessible explanation of value-added models, see Braun (2005). He emphasizes the difficulty of statistically disentangling the different factors contributing to student progress or lack thereof—and that many factors are beyond the control of teachers or schools. He suggests that the most appropriate uses are to identify teachers and schools that may need support.

Barton (2009) further points out that adequate grade-level achievement or change over the course of a year may be insufficiently defined. On what basis do we set a standard "for how much knowledge should be increased in a year in a particular subject"? (p. 2).

The 2010 NRC-NAE report, reflecting the views of a group of well-known scholars of educational measurement who convened for a workshop, concluded:

> Most of the participants were quite positive about the potential utility of value-added models for low-stakes purposes, but much more cautious about their use for high-stakes decisions. Most agreed that value-added indicators might be tried out in high-stakes contexts, as long as the value-added information is one of multiple indicators used for decision making and the program is pilot-tested first, implemented with sufficient communication and training, includes well-developed evaluation plans, and provides an option to discontinue the program if it appears to be doing a disservice to educators or students. (pp. 66–67)

18. For an anecdotal account of how state tests affected instruction and learning differently depending on the district and grade level, see Traub (2002). Lower-performing students seemed to benefit more.

19. Correlations between scores on admissions tests and freshman-year grades are likely to seem lower than is actually the case, not just because grades are subjective and vary across disciplines, but also because studies measure only students who were admitted and do not show how well the test scores predicted lower levels of performance for rejected applicants (NRC, 1999a).

Some attempts have been made to study the power of admissions tests to predict graduation rates. For example, Salins (2008) argues that higher admissions-test scores were associated with higher graduation rates across campuses in the State University of New York system.

20. An example of a noncognitive measure is Oregon State University's "Insight Resume," which asks applicants to answer six questions about their personal experience (with leadership, knowledge/creativity, dealing with adversity, etc.). See http://oregonstate.edu/admissions/2004req/resume.html. See also Sternberg (2010), who describes the use of tasks and rubrics to assess college applicants' performances and products for evidence of analytical, creative, and practical skills, as well as "wisdom." Sternberg bases this strategy on his theories about intelligence and on qualities associated with success in school and beyond.

21. For a discussion of multiple measures with regard to high school exit exams, see Olson (2001). "Multiple measures" is defined differently in different states and can mean anything from offering opportunities to retake the exam to allowing students to submit alternative types of evidence.

22. (Donald T. Campbell also helped introduce multitrait analysis, in Campbell & Fiske, 1959.) Campbell (1976) formulated what is now called "Campbell's law of social sciences" in a paper about "Assessing the Impact of Planned Social Change." In discussing the use of statistical data such as census, voting, and cost-of-living numbers, he warned: "The more any quantitative social indicator is used for social decision-making, the more subject it will be to corruption pressures and the more apt it will be to distort and corrupt the social processes it is intended to monitor" (p. 49).

With regard to grades as alternate indicators, consider the example of parents in Fairfax, Virginia, who organized to overturn tougher grading standards instituted to fight grade inflation in schools. Part of the reason for the parents' activism was the perception that college admissions officers were focusing more on grades and less on test scores (Fitzpatrick, 2009).

SELECTED READINGS

Betebenner, D. W., & Linn, R. L. (2009, December). *Growth in student achievement: Issues in measurement, longitudinal data analysis, and accountability.* Princeton, NJ: Educational Testing Service.

Cizek, C. J. (Ed.). (2001). *Setting performance standards: Contents, methods, and perspectives.* Mahwah, NJ: Lawrence Erlbaum Associates

Heritage, M., & Yeagley, R. (2005, June). Data use and school improvement: Challenges and prospects. *Yearbook of the National Society for the Study of Education, 104*(2), 320–39.

Koretz, D. (2008). *Measuring up: What educational testing really tells us.* Cambridge, MA: Harvard University Press.

Medina, J. (2010, October 11). Warning signs long ignored on New York's school tests. *New York Times.*

Mertler, C. A. (2007). *Interpreting standardized test scores: Strategies for data-driven instructional decision making.* Thousand Oaks, CA: Sage Publications, Inc.

National Research Council (NRC) & National Academy on Education (NAE). (2010). *Getting value out of value-added: Report of a workshop.* H. Braun, N. Chudowsky, & J. Koenig (Eds.). Committee on Value-Added Methodology. Washington, DC: National Academies Press.

Popham, J. W. (2000). *Modern educational measurement: Practical guidelines for educational leaders* (3rd ed.). Boston: Allyn and Bacon.

Glossary

Absolute decisions. In generalizability theory, these are criterion-referenced score interpretations that categorize an examinee's performance according to preestablished standards, usually determined by cut scores. Examples include pass/fail or proficiency levels (e.g., advanced/adequate/basic/below basic). The opposite is "relative decisions."

Accommodation(s). A change or changes to a standardized test's format, content, timing, or administration procedures, as appropriate, to make the test accessible to examinees who have a particular type of physical or learning disability or who are English Language Learners. Strictly speaking, accommodations are only those changes that do not alter the construct being assessed or the meaning of the scores—as opposed to modified or alternate assessments, which do change the construct and score meaning.

Accountability assessment. Usually refers to testing and other types of measurement intended to evaluate the effectiveness of curricula and instruction within and across educational institutions; sometimes refers to testing for student accountability, as in high school exit exams. The results may be associated with rewards and/or sanctions.

Alignment study or analysis. Usually, a study in which evaluators make judgments about how well the tasks in a test represent the academic standards or proficiency domain that the test is supposed to cover. Alignment studies may also be conducted to compare the content of different tests.

Alternate assessment. Usually refers to a substitute assessment created for students whose disability or lack of proficiency in English prevent them from being able to take the same test as other students, even with accommodations or modifications. Scores do not have the same meaning as those from the original standardized test. (Around the 1980s, "alternative assessment" meant any approach other than a multiple-choice test, such as portfolios or essay exams, but in recent times this usage is less common.)

Analysis of variance (ANOVA). Statistical methods used in testing to calculate the amount of variance that each facet of a measurement procedure (e.g., the tasks, raters, occasions, examinee-task interactions, etc.) contributes to the observed score.

Assessment. Formal tests and other procedures for observing and evaluating a person's knowledge, skills, cognitive abilities, attitudes, or other characteristics.

Bias. In qualitative terms, cultural bias refers to test content that may advantage or disadvantage certain demographic and ethnic groups. In terms of statistics, item bias can refer to a particular test item's being relatively more difficult for one demographic subgroup of examinees than it is for others (although further investigation is needed to determine whether or not the item is actually unfair). Test bias refers to differential meanings of the same test score for different subgroups.

Bloom's taxonomy; the revised taxonomy. The hierarchical classification of educational objectives set forth in Bloom et al.'s 1956 work on the cognitive domain. In 2001, Anderson and Krathwohl published a revised, more process-oriented version of the cognitive taxonomy.

Classical test theory. A body of mathematical theory and techniques pertaining to measurement. In psychometrics, classical test theory assumes that if a person could take parallel versions of the same test an infinite number of times (with no memory of the previous occasions), the mean score would be a "true" score free of measurement error. Any observed or actual test score X equals the true score T combined with some positive or negative measurement error E, that is, $X = T + E$. CTT assumes that errors of measurement are random, unpredictable, and independent of each other or of any systematic influences on scores.

Coefficient alpha. Also known as Cronbach's α (Greek letter alpha). A method of computing test-score reliability in terms of a single test form's internal consistency. In contrast to other methods of calculating test-score reliability, this one can be used with tests containing polytomous items (i.e., items scored on a scale, not just items with correct/incorrect answers).

Coefficient of equivalence. A reliability coefficient that addresses error from content sampling but not from time sampling. It answers the question, "How consistent are examinees' scores across different, but equivalent, samplings of a particular domain?"

Coefficient of stability. A reliability coefficient that addresses error from time sampling but not from content sampling. It answers the question,

"How consistent are examinees' scores for the same test across different occasions?"

Cognitive task analysis. Derived from methods of analyzing workplace tasks, CTA deconstructs an intellectual task by investigating the cognitive strategies and processes that experts (or novices) use to accomplish it. This approach may be used to identify learning objectives and to design assessment tasks.

Composite score. An overall score combining the scores from tests of different constructs (as is done, for example, with ACT scores). Each individual test score may be weighted equally, or they may be differently weighted, especially if they have different reliabilities.

Concurrent validity, concurrent evidence. Evidence concerning how well test scores correspond with scores from a criterion measure that is contemporary with the test. For example, a validity study for a state-mandated math test might investigate how well students' scores correlate with grades in math courses that the students are taking concurrently.

Condition. See "facets."

Conditional standard error of measurement (CSEM). See "standard error of measurement."

Construct. A mental characteristic or attribute (e.g., proficiency in some academic subject) that a test is designed to measure; the construct is the theoretical explanation for how examinees perform on a test.

Construct-irrelevant variance. A threat to validity that can occur when a test measures too much. That is, the test actually measures other constructs or factors in addition to, or instead of, the intended construct.

Construct underrepresentation. A threat to validity that can occur when a test measures too little. That is, the tasks in the test omit important aspects of the intended construct and thus fail to measure it adequately.

Construct validity. The extent to which performance on a test can be explained by a person's possessing the mental attribute or characteristic that the test is intended to measure.

Constructed-response. Any type of test task requiring the examinee to supply or generate an answer (whether numbers, sentences, essay, drawing, speech, etc.) rather than to select an answer.

Content domain. A specified body of demonstrable and observable knowledge, skills, or other behaviors; usually subsidiary to a theoretical construct that cannot be directly observed. The tasks in a test should comprise a representative sampling from the content domain.

Content standards. Statements about or descriptions of what students at a particular grade level should know, understand, or be able to do in some subject area (e.g., math, reading, history).

Content-related evidence (aka **content validity, content relevance**). Evidence that the content domain has been defined appropriately for the stated test purpose and that the test as a whole is sufficiently representative of this domain. Now considered subsidiary to construct validity.

Convergent evidence. A type of construct-validity evidence provided by finding correspondences between students' performance on a test and on other measures of the same construct—preferably measures that are different in kind, such as a portfolio or grades. See also "discriminant evidence."

Correlation. A quantitative relationship between two or more different variables. Correlations can be negative (inverse), nonexistent, or positive. Positive correlations indicate systematic similarity and negative correlations indicate systematic dissimilarity.

Correlation coefficient. There are different types of correlation coefficients, but often it is a number indicating the linear relationship between two different variables (e.g., test scores and grades, or scores on parallel test forms). The correlation coefficient shows the extent to which the two variables are changing along with each other, in terms of both direction (positive or negative) and amount. The scale for correlation coefficients goes upward from -1 (completely negative or inverse correspondence) to 0 (no correspondence) to +1 (completely positive or perfect correspondence). Although a correlation coefficient shows how two variables move together or covary, it does not explain what causes the relationship.

Craniometry. Measurement of the bones of the skull. Nineteenth-century craniometrists used measurements of the skull interior (cranial capacity) to estimate total brain volume (size) and assumed that the estimated brain size corresponded directly with amount of intelligence.

Criterion, criterion measures, criterion-related validity evidence. The criterion measure for a test is, to the extent possible, a real-life performance of the proficiencies or attributes that this test is intended to measure. It can also be an outcome (e.g., future course grades or employment success). Validity arguments often include evidence that performance on the test and on a relevant criterion measure are positively correlated; if not, the validity of the test scores may be undermined.

Criterion-referenced scores. Score interpretations that compare an examinee's performance on a test to a prescribed set of proficiency levels, expectations, or standards (rather than to the performance of other examinees). Also see "absolute decisions." The opposite is "norm-referenced scores."

Cronbach's α, coefficient alpha. See "reliability coefficient."

Cut score. A prescribed score point or level at which a distinction is made between the performance categories for a particular test (e.g., pass/fail or advanced/adequate/limited).

Diagnostic assessment. Assessment intended to identify specific strengths, weaknesses, or other relevant factors in cognitive or affective attributes. The purpose is usually to help make decisions about appropriate instruction or remediation, if needed.

Dichotomous scoring. Scoring an answer to a test question in a binary manner (correct vs. incorrect).

Differential item functioning (DIF). In large-scale testing, analyses are conducted to determine whether or not each test item functions in the same way across ethnic, gender, or other identified subgroups. That is, the item's difficulty and discrimination should be similar for all examinees with the same overall test scores or θ level. If not, then further investigation is needed to find out whether or not the item is measuring the same construct for all examinees regardless of subgroup membership.

Differential test functioning (DTF). For a given test, DTF refers not simply to the phenomenon of different average scores across subgroups but to scores' having different meanings according to subgroup membership. In other words, a particular test score may have different meanings depending on the subgroup to which the examinee belongs.

Difficulty (of an item). In CTT, item difficulty is defined by the percentage of examinees who answer it correctly; in IRT, item difficulty is defined in terms of its assigned level along the trait continuum.

Dimensionality (of a test). As defined by Tate (2002), the "minimum number of examinee abilities measured by the test items" (p. 181). Techniques such as factor analysis are used to identify test dimensions. Usually, tests that report a single score are intended to be unidimensional.

Discriminant evidence. A type of construct-validity evidence provided by finding low correspondence (dissimilarity) between scores on a test intended to assess a particular construct and scores on measures of other constructs. For example, scores on measures of verbal skills versus math skills should exhibit lower correspondence than scores across various measures of verbal skills. See also "convergent evidence."

Discrimination, discriminating. The extent to which a test question accurately differentiates (discriminates) between examinees at different levels of proficiency. Usually proficiency is defined by the examinee's overall score on the test.

Distribution. The overall pattern for a set of data points or observations. In testing, distribution often refers to how a group's scores for a test are spread across the score scale. Of particular interest is how the scores are dispersed or vary from their mean. See "normal distribution."

Domain. See "content domain."

Equating. The process of making scores from two or more versions (forms) of the same test interchangeable, often facilitated by including a shared set of items on each form. As the most rigorous type of score linking, equating requires that the forms be built to the same specifications for content, format, difficulty, score reliability, and so on.

Error bands. See "score bands."

Error of measurement, measurement error. The random inconsistency or unreliability that is likely to characterize any particular measurement or observation of a phenomenon—such as an examinee's test score. It is represented as E in classical test theory. See "true score" for more about error.

Essay test. A test requiring examinees to produce written responses, which may be brief or lengthy texts.

Facets. In generalizability theory, facets are factors that constitute sources of variance in a measurement procedure (e.g., tasks, raters, occasions). A facet is a certain category of interchangeable observations or replications, such as test forms, with regard to the object of measurement. Each replication or observation (such as one test form) is called a "condition" of the facet.

Factor analysis. A statistical method for investigating the underlying structure of relationships or dimensions among different variables. Finding positive correlations between and among variables helps support the case that the variables may be related in a meaningful way or even interdependent—and vice versa for negative correlations.

Fairness. The technical definitions of (and requirements for) fairness are "lack of bias" and "equitable treatment in the testing process" but not "opportunity to learn" or "equality of outcomes of testing" (AERA et al., 1999, pp. 74–76).

Flag, flagging. A notation in a score report indicating that the examinee took the test under nonstandard conditions (e.g., an oral version of a reading comprehension test) that may have affected measurement of the intended construct and hence the score's meaning. The flagged score may not be comparable to scores obtained under the standard conditions.

Focal group. A category of examinees (usually defined by gender or ethnicity) whose performance on a test question is compared to that of a reference group in order to investigate whether the question may advantage or disadvantage those examinees. See "differential item functioning."

Form. See "test form."

Formative assessment. Practices of gathering and using information about student learning that are intended to help teachers adapt instruction appropriately and/or to guide students in their own efforts.

g. See "Spearman's *g*."

Generalizability coefficient. In generalizability theory, a version of a reliability coefficient. It is used for score interpretations involving relative decisions (that is, norm-referenced scores).

Generalizability theory. A body of theory and methods that builds on classical test theory and analysis of variance techniques but goes beyond them conceptually. GT loosens the strict CTT requirement for replications (such as parallel test forms) and posits instead faceted "universes" of acceptably interchangeable observations about the object of measurement (usually a person). Moreover, GT offers methods for analyzing how the facets or factors affecting a score (e.g., raters, items, occasions) contribute to score variance, and how increasing the number of "conditions" (that is, of replications or interchangeable observations) for a particular facet would reduce error. GT is thus especially helpful for designing measurement procedures to optimize reliability as much as is feasible.

Index of dependability. In generalizability theory, an index of dependability indicates the reliability of absolute decisions—that is, score interpretations that involve classifications or performance standards, such as pass/fail.

Instrument. A formal procedure, such as a test or questionnaire, used to collect observations for the purposes of measurement.

Intelligence quotient (IQ). A way of calculating a score on an intelligence test, with 100 representing the average score for the examinee's age level.

Internal consistency. An estimate of test-score reliability based on a single test form administered on a single occasion. The methods for calculating internal consistency essentially divide up items into different possible pairings and compare performance between these pairings. Calculations may use K-R formulae, the Spearman-Pearson split-half approach, coefficient alpha, or other methods.

Interrater reliability. A type of reliability relevant when different raters independently evaluate the same responses. Expressed as a percentage or as a coefficient, this statistic usually indicates the extent to which raters' scores for any given response tend to agree (which may be defined solely as the same score or may include adjacent scores as well).

Item. A question or task on a test.

Item analysis. Statistical procedures conducted to evaluate the performance of an item, especially its difficulty and discrimination.

Item characteristic curves. In item response theory, these are curves on an *x-y* graph that relate the difficulty of an item to the probability that examinees at any specified trait level (i.e., proficiency or θ level) will choose the correct answer. These graphs also show, for each incorrect answer, the θ levels of the examinees who chose it.

Item parameters. In item response theory, these are the statistical characteristics established via calibration for a given test item; they are intended to be invariant across test forms and examinee populations. Each item has a difficulty parameter associated with a particular trait level; items may also have discrimination and pseudoguessing parameters.

Item response theory. A psychometric framework based on the assumption that an underlying construct, such as proficiency in an academic subject, can be represented as a quantitative continuum of levels. This approach then assumes that an examinee with a given amount of this construct is likely to perform in particular ways.

Thus, if the construct is an ability or proficiency, examinees who are more proficient are more likely to be able to respond successfully to difficult tasks. IRT offers methods for establishing the difficulty level of each task in the test. Then, one can estimate an examinee's level of proficiency by considering the difficulty levels of the tasks that the examinee can and cannot perform successfully.

Latent trait. An underlying psychological characteristic or attribute; a construct. Item response theory was originally called "latent trait theory."

Learning progressions. A view of learning as growth in levels of sophistication and expertise within a particular discipline. The emphasis is on continuity—how learning builds over time upon a framework of conceptual understanding of "big ideas"—rather than on discrete, grade-level objectives. Learning progressions are intended to be empirically validated models rather than aspirational goals.

Linking. Usually, the process of transforming a score on one test to a score on another test that measures the same or similar knowledge and skills.

Matrix sampling. A method of sampling used to maximize the range of different items administered and to obtain information about groups, not individuals. Rather than giving identical test forms to many different students, the test makers give each student some subset of the pool of test items.

Measurement invariance. This criterion is fulfilled when a test "measures the same attribute in the same way in different subpopulations," even if the average group score differs across groups (Borsboom et al., 2008, p. 76).

Modification, modified assessment. A version of a standardized assessment altered to meet the needs of a student with a disability or limited English proficiency, such that the changes result in a test score whose meaning is different. In contrast, an "accommodation" is an alteration that produces scores comparable with those from standard administrations of the test.

Multiple-choice. A form of selected-response test question, in which the examinee selects one answer choice from among those provided with the question.

Norm-referenced scores. Score interpretations that compare an examinee's performance on a test to that of the other examinees. Also called "relative decisions." The opposite is "criterion-referenced scores."

Normal distribution. Also known as a "bell curve." In biology and other disciplines, the distribution of a given characteristic across a large population is likely to follow a pattern of symmetrical distribution around the mean, with the preponderance of data points relatively close to the mean. In CTT, test forms are constructed to try to distribute the overall pattern of examinees' scores in this manner, although the actual scores do not necessarily conform to a normal distribution. (See Figure G.1.)

Objective test or item. Test or item for which all the possible responses are predesignated as correct or incorrect. The response can thus be scored "objectively," without judgment or evaluation. All selected-response items would fall into this category; so too would constructed-response items for which there is only one correct answer (such as a math problem whose answer is a number). See also "subjective test."

Observed score. The actual score that an examinee obtains on a test; the X in $X = T + E$. See "true score" for more about the relationship between the observed score, true score, and error.

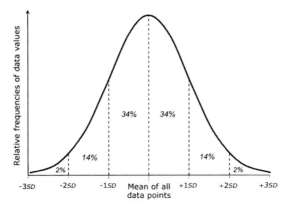

Figure G.1. Normal distribution and standard deviations. The graph shows a "bell curve" of normally distributed data points. In this distribution, 68 percent of all the data points lie within ±1 *SD* of the mean; 95 percent lie within ±2 *SD*; and 99.7 percent lie within ±3 *SD*.

Observer effect. Refers to the idea that the act of observation is not neutral but causes some kind of effect or change in the thing or person being observed.

p value. In classical test theory, a statistic for a given selected-response test question indicating the percentage of examinees who chose the correct answer. Sometimes appears as $P+$.

Percentile rank. A comparison of a given score to the overall distribution of scores for a particular test. Usually (not always) refers to the percentage of scores that are below the given score.

Performance assessment. Originally derived from vocational testing, the complete term "performance and product assessment" usually refers to examinees' demonstrating proficiency by engaging in a process or creating some kind of product. A performance assessment might, for example, require examinees to speak in a particular language, carry out a laboratory protocol, or explain how to solve a math problem.

Performance standards. The criteria to which criterion-referenced score interpretations refer. Performance standards are a way of classifying levels of performance. They are expressed as labels (e.g., pass vs. fail; advanced vs. adequate vs. basic vs. below basic) or descriptions for each level or category of performance.

Polytomous scoring. Scoring the answer to a test question on a scale rather than as simply correct/incorrect. For example, a selected-response item that permits partial credit or an essay that is scored on a 0–6 scale is scored polytomously.

Predictive evidence (aka *predictive validity*). Evidence of correspondence between test scores and the scores for a criterion measure that occurs later in time than the test does. A typical example is a comparison between scores on college admissions tests and subsequent first-year college grades, traditionally expressed as a correlation coefficient. Now considered subsidiary to construct validity.

Pretesting. Experimental tryouts of test questions on examinees. These tryouts may be conducted separately or as part of regular test administrations, but typically the scores on these questions do not count toward examinees' official scores. The purpose is to gather statistical and sometimes qualitative information about the questions, which test developers then use to approve, revise, or reject items.

Psychometrics. A discipline concerned with investigating and systematically measuring mental attributes. It includes both educational and psychological assessment.

Random error. Uncorrelated, unrelated types of measurement errors that affect the reliability of test scores, such as examinee fatigue, mood, or guesswork; inconsistent judgments by different raters; particular sample of the content domain; or other fluctuating phenomena.

Rater (aka *reader, marker, scorer, evaluator*). In formal assessment procedures, a person who evaluates and scores students' work according to a prescribed protocol, often using written scoring guidelines.

Raw score. A sum of the correct answers or points awarded on a test. Sometimes certain test questions, such as essays, are weighted more heavily; sometimes a penalty for incorrect answers is included (e.g., minus ¼ point for each incorrect answer). In large-scale programs, test-form equating is used to transform raw scores into scaled scores.

Reference group, reference population, or norm group. A sample group of examinees intended to represent the entire population of examinees who take a particular test (or, sometimes, a defined subset of the entire population). Norm-referenced scores often compare individual or group performance on the test to that of a reference group.

Relative decisions. In generalizability theory, these are contextual, norm-referenced score interpretations that use a continuous score scale to rank or place each examinee's performance in relation to that of other examinees. The opposite is "absolute decisions."

Reliability. The consistency of a test's scores across a specific kind of replication of the measurement procedures. As a concept in classical test theory, it is the ratio of the variance of true scores to the variance of observed scores. See "error of measurement."

Reliability coefficient. A correlation coefficient showing how a group's test scores vary systematically between two replications of the measurement. Depending on the type of replication, it can reflect consistency with respect to occasion or to content sampling (or both), and using different methods can result in different kinds of replications (for example, split-half versus Cronbach's alpha). Thus, it can differ for the same test depending on the examinee population and method used to calculate it.

Rubric. See "scoring guide."

Scale, score scale. A particular system of numerical units, usually assumed to be equal in value, in which a test's scores are reported. Scaled scores are derived from "raw scores."

Score bands, error bands. A way of illustrating the standard error of measurement (*SEM*) for a given score on a test. Score bands show a range of points above and below the observed or actual score in order to estimate a range, within specified probabilities, that may include the true score. (See note 8, chapter 6, and Harvill, 1991, for why these probabilities are somewhat tentative. The *SEM* reflects prediction of observed scores from a given true score, i.e., a normal distribution of observed scores around their mean. The

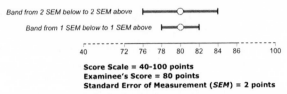

Figure G.2. Score bands showing error in a test score. Tentatively, there is a 68 percent probability that the lower band includes the examinee's true score, and a 95 percent probability that the upper band includes the examinee's true score.

score band treats the observed score as if it were the true score, which is not necessarily the case.)

Score bands help emphasize that score fluctuations for the same student or small differences in scores among students may be caused by random error rather than by different levels of proficiency. Often a lack of overlap between two students' score bands is taken to indicate that the students really do have different levels of proficiency, but again, as Harvill (1991, p. 186) cautions, one cannot be certain.

In the example shown in Figure G.2, there is 68 percent confidence or probability that the smaller band, extending from 1 *SEM* below the observed score to 1 *SEM* above the observed score (from about 78 to 82), includes the examinee's true score.

There is a 95 percent probability that the larger band, which extends from 2 *SEM* below the observed score to 2 *SEM* above (from about 76 to 84), includes the examinee's true score. Again, though, these probabilities are tentative because of the assumption, not necessarily correct, that the observed score is likely to be close to the true score.

Scoring guide. The prescribed, standardized scoring criteria that raters use for evaluating a student-produced response or portfolio of student work (e.g., essay, speech, math calculation, science experiment, etc.). Also called a "rubric."

Selected-response question. Any multiple-choice, true-false, matching, or other type of test question for which the examinee selects one or more answers from those provided on the test.

Spearman's g. In 1904, Charles Spearman proposed that correlations among various sensory-discrimination tests, school grades, teacher ratings, and interviews indicated a general factor or *g*, possibly a unitary construct underlying all mental abilities.

Speeded, speededness. A test is undesirably "speeded" if it is not intended to measure how quickly the examinee can work, yet its time limits prevent a significant number of examinees from being able to complete or at least consider all the questions.

Standard deviation (SD). A way of indicating the spread or distribution of data points, such as scores, below and above the mean—that is, the extent to which the data points vary from the mean. Technically, it is the square root of the variance in the distribution. The *SD* for a test is expressed in terms of units in the test's score scale. The more closely scores cluster around the mean, the smaller the *SD*, and vice versa. See "normal distribution" for an illustration of standard deviation in this kind of distribution.

Standard error of measurement (SEM). An estimate of the amount of error likely to be present in an examinee's test score. Technically, it is the standard deviation of the distribution of error scores for a particular test and particular population. The *SEM* is expressed as a number of units or points on the test's score scale and is presented as a plus or minus range around the examinee's score. (See "score bands.") Sometimes testing programs calculate conditional *SEM*s (*CSEM*s) associated with particular levels in the test's score scale, rather than using one *SEM* for all scores.

Standardized test. An assessment procedure in which the conditions are held as uniform as possible across every administration: nature of test content, level of difficulty, types and number of questions, mode of presentation, timing, scoring criteria, and so on. A test can be standardized (or even nonstandardized) regardless of whether it uses selected- or constructed-response tasks. The goal is to produce test scores that have the same meaning across different examinees, versions of the test, and testing occasions.

Standards, the. Refers to the **Standards for Educational and Psychological Testing**. Periodically revised and expanded since the 1950s, this document contains guidelines representing the professional consensus of the American Educational Research Association, the American Psychological Association, and the National Council on Measurement in Education.

Standards-based assessment. Assessment that measures achievement/proficiency in terms of specified academic content standards (i.e., statements about what students should learn and be able to do) and is scored in terms of prescribed performance standards (i.e., criterion-referenced proficiency levels).

Stanine scale. A scale that converts raw or scaled scores to a nine-part scale (1–9) with unequal percentages assigned to each ninth. The top and bottom 4 percent of results become, respectively, scores 9 and 1; then percentage per score point increases symmetrically from either end of the scale to form a bell curve whose peak is 20 percent at the middle score of 5.

Stereotype threat. A theory introduced by Steele and Aronson (1995), which posits that commonly held beliefs about the intellectual abilities of a group can affect how well a member of that group performs on a test whose stated purpose is to measure those abilities. For example, a female student taking a math test could be adversely affected by believing or fearing that women are less skilled at math than men are. Moreover, the theory suggests that reminding an examinee about his/her membership in a negatively stereotyped group can exacerbate any adverse effects. Thus, for example, a female examinee might be disadvantaged by having to indicate her gender right before taking a math test or by having to take a math test with far more males than females present.

Subjective test or item. Test or item whose responses cannot automatically be marked as correct or incorrect but must be evaluated for degree of quality. The opposite of "objective test."

Subscore. A score for a section or group of items within a test. Because subscores are based on fewer items than is the total test score, subscores are usually less reliable.

Summative assessment. Retrospective assessment intended to provide information about student achievement, usually after completion of a curricular unit, course, semester, or year.

Systematic error. Refers to consistent error; for example, any test content that routinely advantages or disadvantages certain groups of examinees. The true score necessarily includes (one might say, conceals) any systematic error because, unlike random error, systematic error is not reduced by replications.

Systemic validity. A concept proposed by Frederiksen and Collins (1990), who saw educational systems as dynamic, evolving entities. "Systemic validity" means the extent to which using a particular test can "induce in the educational system curricular and instructional changes that foster the development of the cognitive skills that the test is designed to measure" (p. 5). This concept puts test consequences in the foreground by emphasizing effects on curricula, instruction, and learning.

Test characteristic curves. In item response theory, curves that depict test performance on an *x-y* graph. These curves show the relationship between the expected observed scores and any estimated θ level of the proficiency/trait.

Test form. A version of a test constructed to resemble all other versions as closely as possible, by conforming to the same specifications for content and for statistical characteristics. Equating methods are used to make scores from parallel test forms interchangeable.

Test specifications or blueprints. Plans that specify the content, format, and statistical characteristics of items to be included in each test form. The specifications include the proportion of items representing each topic and the desired statistical characteristics of the overall test form.

Theta, or θ. In item response theory, refers to the quantitative continuum or scale for the mental attribute that a test is intended to measure, such as proficiency in reading skills. For score reporting, an examinee's estimated θ level is translated into a scaled score or performance category.

True score. In classical test theory, a hypothetical concept that refers to a score free from random error. It is specific to an examinee taking a particular test. The true score is the average score that would be expected if the examinee were to retake parallel forms of the test an infinite number of times, with no memory of the previous tests and no change from instruction, growth, or other factors. The true score is represented as T in the equation $X = T + E$, which indicates that any observed or actual score X is a combination of the true score and some amount of error E.

Universal design. UD for learning or assessment is intended to promote accessibility for all students, not just those with disabilities or limited English proficiency. The principle is to minimize any irrelevant, unnecessary barriers in a test that may be created by language, visual format, physical requirements, or other variables extraneous to the targeted construct.

Universe score. In generalizability theory, the true score associated with a specified universe or collection of interchangeable observations (different test forms, different raters, different occasions, etc.). A universe score is less restrictive than a true score because the replications do not have to be parallel.

Validation. As defined in the *Standards*, the process of "developing a scientifically sound validity argument to support the intended interpretation of test scores and their relevance to the proposed use" (AERA et al., 1999, p. 9).

Validity. As defined in the *Standards*, "the degree to which all the accumulated evidence supports the intended interpretation of test scores for the proposed purpose" (AERA et al., 1999, p. 11). Validity involves the justification for intended score meanings and uses, not simply for a test by itself.

Validity argument. Akin to a legal argument; a comprehensive presentation of the reasoning and evidence relevant to the stated claims about what a particular test's scores mean and how they should be used.

Validity coefficient. A term sometimes used to refer to the correlation coefficient relating test scores to scores (or other data) from a criterion measure.

Validity study. A research investigation focused on an aspect of the validity argument, such as a test's correlations with external criteria or a test's relationships with other measures of the same construct.

Value-added models (of assessment). Testing programs designed (often using vertical scaling) to investigate the effects of teachers and/or schools on students' progress.

Variable. A variable is a trait, attribute, or characteristic (such as temperature, location, test scores, gender, age, etc.) that can differ across things or people. In measurement, a variable is some kind of quantitative value, such as test scores, that can vary across different entities.

Variance. Refers to how widely the data points in a given distribution—such as a group's test scores—are spread about their mean. Technically, it would be the average squared difference between the data points and their mean.

Vertical scaling. A method of linking test scores in order to measure student growth from one year to the next. Performance on tests of increasing difficulty is aligned vertically along the same proficiency scale.

References

Abedi, J., & Lord, C. (2001). The language factor in mathematics tests. *Applied Measurement in Education, 14*(3), 219–34.

Achieve, Inc. (2009). *The American diploma project network* and *Research and methodology.* Retrieved February 20, 2009, from http://www.achieve.org/node/604 and http://www.achieve.org/Research.

ACT, Inc. (2005). *Procedures for investigating testing irregularities and questioned scores.* Retrieved October 7, 2008, from http://www.act.org/aap/pdf/Testing Irregularity.pdf.

ACT, Inc. (2007). *The ACT technical manual.* Retrieved August 5, 2008, from http://www.act.org/aap/pdf/ACT_Technical_Manual.pdf.

ACT, Inc. (2008). *Fairness report for the ACT tests, 2006–2007.* Retrieved August 5, 2008, from http://www.act.org/research/researchers/pdf/aap_fairness.pdf.

Adams, J. (2000). *Testing accommodations for students with disabilities. TBI Challenge! 4*(1). Retrieved January 25, 2008, from the Brain Injury Association of America website: http://www.biausa.org/publications/testingaccomodations.htm.

Airasian, P. W., & Abrams, L. M. (2002). What role will assessment play in school in the future? In R. W. Lissitz & W. D. Schafer (Eds.), *Assessment in educational reform: Both means and end* (pp. 50–65). Boston: Allyn & Bacon.

Allalouf, A. (2007). Quality control procedures in the scoring, equating, and reporting of test scores. *Educational Measurement: Issues and Practice, 26*(1), 36–43.

Altermatt, E. R., & Kim, M. E. (2004, September). Getting girls de-stereotyped for SAT exams. *Education Digest, 70*(1), 43–47.

American Educational Research Association (AERA), American Psychological Association (APA), & National Council on Measurement in Education (NCME). (1985). *Standards for educational and psychological testing.* Washington, DC: American Psychological Association.

American Educational Research Association (AERA), American Psychological Association (APA), & National Council on Measurement in Education (NCME).

(1999). *Standards for educational and psychological testing.* Washington, DC: American Educational Research Association.

American Educational Research Association (AERA) & National Council on Measurements Used in Education (NCMUE). (1955, January). *Technical recommendations for achievement tests.* Washington, DC: National Education Association.

American Federation of Teachers (AFT). (2008a). *Characteristics of strong, standards-based assessment systems.* Retrieved February 26, 2008, from http://www.aft.org/topics/sbr/character-assess.htm.

American Federation of Teachers (AFT). (2008b). *Sizing up state standards.* Retrieved May 31, 2008, from http://www.aft.org/pubs-reports/downloads/teachers/standards2008.pdf.

American Federation of Teachers (AFT), National Council on Measurement in Education (NCME), & National Education Association (NEA). (1990). *Standards for teacher competence in the educational assessment of students.* Retrieved February 25, 2008, from the Buros Institute of Mental Measurements website: http://www.unl.edu/buros/bimm/html/article3.html.

American Psychological Association (APA). (1954). *Technical recommendations for psychological tests and diagnostic techniques.* Washington, DC: Author.

American Psychological Association (APA), American Educational Research Association (AERA), & National Council on Measurement in Education (NCME). (1966). *Standards for educational and psychological tests and manuals.* Washington, DC: American Psychological Association.

American Psychological Association (APA), American Educational Research Association (AERA), & National Council on Measurement in Education (NCME). (1974). *Standards for educational and psychological tests.* Washington, DC: American Psychological Association.

Anderson, L. W. (2009). Upper elementary grades bear the brunt of accountability. *Phi Delta Kappan, 90*(6), 413–18.

Anderson, L. W., & Krathwohl, D. R. (Eds.). (2001). *A taxonomy for learning, teaching, and assessing: A revision of Bloom's taxonomy of educational objectives.* New York: Longman.

Anderson, R. D., & DeMars, C. (2002). Differential item functioning: Investigating item bias. *Assessment Update, 14*(3), 12, 16.

Angoff, W. H. (1971). Scales, norms, and equivalent scores. In R. L. Thorndike (Ed.), *Educational Measurement* (2nd ed., pp. 508–600). Washington, DC: American Council on Education.

Angoff, W. H. (1988). Validity: An evolving concept. In H. Wainer & H. I. Braun (Eds.), *Test validity* (pp. 19–32). Hillsdale, NJ: Lawrence Erlbaum Associates.

Aronson, J. (2004). The threat of stereotype. *Educational Leadership, 62*(3), 14–19.

Associated Press. (2008, April 22). Teacher suspended for refusing to give state test.

Association of American Colleges and Universities. (2007, September 5). *AAC&U takes assessment to the next level with launch of new initiative, VALUE—Valid Assessment of Learning in Undergraduate Education.* Retrieved February 27, 2008, from http://www.aacu.org/press_room/press_releases/2007/value.cfm.

Association of Test Publishers. (1997–2004). *Frequently asked questions.* Retrieved March 11, 2008, from http://www.testpublishers.org/faq.htm.

Atkinson, R. C., & Geiser, S. (2009, April). *Reflections on a century of college admissions tests*. Center for Studies in Higher Education, University of California at Berkeley, Research & Occasional Paper Series: CSHE.4.09. Retrieved April 22, 2009, from http://cshe.berkeley.edu/publications/docs/ROPS-AtkinsonGeiser-Tests-04-15-09.pdf.

Ayers, L. P. (1918). History and present status of educational measurements. In G. M. Whipple (Ed.), *The seventeenth yearbook of the National Society for the Study of Education: The measurement of educational products* (Part 2, pp. 9–15). Bloomington, IL: Public School Publishing Company. Available at the Internet Archive website: http://www.archive.org/stream/measurementofedu00whiprich.

Baker, E. L. (2001). Testing and assessment: A progress report. *Educational Assessment, 7*(1), 1–12.

Baker, E. L. (2003, September). *Multiple measures: Toward tiered systems*. Center for the Study of Evaluation Report 607. Retrieved February 16, 2008, from the National Center for Research on Student Evaluations, Standards, and Testing website: http://www.cse.ucla.edu/products/Reports/R607.pdf.

Baker, E. L. (2007). The end(s) of testing. *Educational Researcher 26*, 309–17.

Baker, E. L. (2009, January 23). *Assessments for the 21st century: Mapping the path to a new generation of assessments*. Presentation to the National Association of State Boards of Education. Retrieved November 11, 2009, from http://www.cse.ucla.edu.

Baker, E. L., Abedi, J., Linn, R. L., & Niemi, D. (1996). Dimensionality and generalizability of domain-independent performance assessments. *Journal of Educational Research, 89*(4), 197–205.

Baldwin, D. G. (in press). Fundamental challenges in developing and scoring constructed-response assessments. In N. Elliot & L. Perelman (Eds.), *Writing assessment in the 21st century: Essays in honor of Edward M. White*. Cresskill, NJ: Hampton Press.

Bandiera de Mello, V., Blankenship, C., & McLaughlin, D. H. (2009). *Mapping state proficiency standards onto NAEP scales: 2005–2007* (NCES 2010-456). Washington, DC: National Center for Education Statistics, Institute of Education Sciences, U.S. Department of Education.

Barton, P. E. (2009, August 13). *Comment on proposed regulations for education stimulus funds*. Retrieved November 30, 2009, from the Albert Shanker Institute website: http://www.albertshanker.org/Barton-1.pdf.

Barton, P. E., & Coley, R. J. (2009). *Parsing the achievement gap II*. Princeton, NJ: Educational Testing Service.

Beaton, A., Tougas, F., Rinfret, N., Huard, N., & Delisle, M. N. (2007). Strength in numbers? Women and mathematics. *European Journal of Psychology of Education— EJPE, 22*(3), 291–306.

Berlak, H. (1992a). The need for a new science of assessment. In A. R. Tom (Series Ed.) & H. Berlak, F. M. Newmann, E. Adams, D. A. Archbald, T. Burgess, J. Raven, & T. A. Romberg, SUNY Series, *Teacher preparation and development: Toward a new science of educational testing and assessment* (pp. 1–21). Albany: State University of New York Press.

Berlak, H. (1992b). Toward the development of a new science of educational testing and assessment. In A. R. Tom (Series Ed.) & H. Berlak, F. M. Newmann, E. Adams, D. A. Archbald, T. Burgess, J. Raven, & T. A. Romberg, SUNY Series, *Teacher preparation and development: Toward a new science of educational testing and assessment* (pp. 181–206). Albany: State University of New York Press.

Berlak, H. (2000). Cultural politics, the science of assessment and democratic renewal of public education. In A. Filer (Ed.), *Educational assessment and testing: Social practice and social product* (pp. 189–206). London: Routledge Falmer.

Berliner, David C. (2009). *Poverty and potential: Out-of-school factors and school success.* Boulder, CO, and Tempe, AZ: Education and the Public Interest Center & Education Policy Research Unit. Retrieved June 1, 2010, from http://epicpolicy .org/publication/poverty-and-potential.

Bertenthal, M., Pellegrino, J., Huff, K., & Wilbur, M. (2009, June 22). *The future of Advanced Placement.* Presentation delivered at the CCSSO Conference on Assessment, Los Angeles, CA. Retrieved February 22, 2010, from http://www.ccsso.org/ content/PDFs/NCSA09_120_MarciaWilbur.pdf.

Betebenner, D. W., & Linn, R. L. (2009, December). *Growth in student achievement: Issues in measurement, longitudinal data analysis, and accountability.* Paper presented at the Exploratory Seminar, Princeton, NJ. Retrieved May 10, 2010, from the K-12 Center for Assessment and Performance Management website: http: //www .k12center.org/publications.html.

Biggs, J. (2001). Assessment of student learning: Where did we go wrong? *Assessment Update, 13*(6), 6–11.

Bird, A. (2008). Thomas Kuhn. In E. N. Zalta (Ed.), *The Stanford encyclopedia of philosophy* (Spring 2008 ed.). Retrieved May 7, 2008, from http://plato.stanford .edu/archives/spr2008/entries/thomas-kuhn/.

Black, P., & Wiliam, D. (1998). Inside the black box: Raising standards through classroom assessment. *Phi Delta Kappan, 80*(2), 139–48.

Bloom, B. S. (1968). *Toward a theory of testing which includes measurement-evaluation-assessment* (Report No. 9). Los Angeles: Center for the Evaluation of Instructional Programs (ERIC No. ED036878).

Bloom, B. S., Englehart, M. D., Furst, E. J., Hill, W. H., & Krathwohl, D. R. (1956). *Taxonomy of educational objectives: The classification of educational goals. Handbook 1: Cognitive domain.* New York: David McKay Company, Inc.

Bock, R. D. (1997). A brief history of item response theory. *Educational Measurement Issues and Practice, 16*(4), 21–33.

Bolt, S. E., & Thurlow, M. L. (2004). Five of the most frequently allowed testing accommodations in state policy: Synthesis of research. *Remedial and Special Education, 25*(3), 141–52.

Borsboom, D. (2005). *Measuring the mind: Conceptual issues in contemporary psychometrics.* Cambridge: Cambridge University Press.

Borsboom, D., Mellenbergh, G. J., & van Heerden, J. (2004). The concept of validity. *Psychological Review, 111*(4), 1061–71.

Borsboom, D., Romeijn, J., & Wicherts, J. (2008). Measurement invariance versus selection invariance: Is fair selection possible? *Psychological Methods, 13*(2), 75–98.

Boyd, R. (2002). Scientific realism. In E. N. Zalta (Ed.), *The Stanford encyclopedia of philosophy* (Summer 2002 ed.). Retrieved May 12, 2008, from http://plato.stanford.edu/archives/sum2002/entries/scientific-realism/.

Bracey, G. W. (1995). *Final exam: A study of the perpetual scrutiny of American education.* Alexandria, VA: Technos Press of the Agency for Instructional Technology.

Braun, H. I. (2005). *Using student progress to evaluate teachers: A primer on value-added models.* Princeton, NJ: Educational Testing Service.

Brennan, R. L. (2000). (Mis) Conceptions about generalizability theory. *Educational Measurement: Issues and Practice, 19*(1), 5–10.

Brennan, R. L. (2001a). An essay on the history and future of reliability from the perspective of replications. *Journal of Educational Measurement, 38*(4), 295–317.

Brennan, R. L. (2001b). *Generalizability theory.* New York: Springer-Verlag.

Brennan, R. L. (2001c). Some problems, pitfalls, and paradoxes in educational measurement. *Educational Measurement: Issues and Practice, 20*(4), 6–18.

Brennan, R. L. (2004, June). *Revolutions and evolutions in current educational testing.* The Iowa Academy of Education Occasional Research Paper No. 7. Retrieved April 22, 2009, from http://www.education.uiowa.edu/iae/iae-z-op-brennan-1-7.pdf.

Brennan, R. L. (2006). Editor's preface. In R. L. Brennan (Ed.), *Educational measurement* (4th ed., pp. xv–xvii). Westport, CT: American Council on Education and Praeger Publishers.

Brewster, M. (2004, July 24). Henry Chauncey: The aptitude tester. *Business Week.*

Brigham, C. C. (1923). *A study of American intelligence.* Princeton, NJ: Princeton University Press. Retrieved July 9, 2010, from the Internet Archive website: http://www.archive.org/stream/studyofamericani00briguoft/studyofamericani00brig uoft_djvu.txt.

Brinley, J. M. E. (2009, May 14). Et tu, College Board? *Washington Post.*

Broadfoot, P. (2000). Preface. In A. Filer (Ed.), *Educational assessment and testing: Social practice and social product* (pp. ix–xii). London: Routledge Falmer.

Broer, M., Lee, Y. W., Rizavi, S., & Powers, D. (2005). *Ensuring the fairness of GRE writing prompts: Assessing differential difficulty.* ETS Research Report RR-05-11. Princeton, NJ: Educational Testing Service.

Brown, J. (1992). *The definition of a profession: The authority of metaphor in the history of intelligence testing, 1890–1930.* Princeton, NJ: Princeton University Press.

Brown, R. S. (2007). Using latent class analysis to set performance standards. *Educational Assessment, 12*(3&4), 283–301.

Buckendahl, C. W., & Hunt, R. (2005). Whose rules? The relation between the "rules" and "law" of testing. In R. P. Phelps (Ed.), *Defending standardized testing* (pp. 147–58). Mahwah, NJ: Lawrence Erlbaum Associates.

Bushaw, W. J., & McNee, J. A. (2009). Americans speak out: Are policy makers listening? *Phi Delta Kappan, 91*(1), 9–23.

Camara, W. J., & Lane, S. (2006). A historical perspective and current views on the *Standards for Educational and Psychological Testing. Educational Measurement: Issues and Practice, 25*(3), 35–41.

Camilli, G. (2006). Test fairness. In R. L Brennan (Ed.), *Educational Measurement* (4th ed., pp. 221–56). Westport, CT: American Council on Education and Praeger Publishers.

Campbell, C., & Collins, V. L. (2007). Identifying essential topics in general and special education introductory assessment textbooks. *Educational Measurement: Issues and Practice, 26*(1), 9–18.

Campbell, D. T. (1976, December). *Assessing the impact of planned social change.* (Western Michigan University Occasional Paper Series, No. 8; paper originally delivered at Dartmouth College, Hanover, NH). Retrieved May 23, 2008, from the Western Michigan University website: http://www.wmich.edu/evalctr/pubs/ops/ops08.pdf.

Campbell, D. T., & Fiske, D. W. (1959). Convergent and discriminant evidence by the multitrait-multimethod matrix. *Psychological Bulletin, 56*(2), 81–105.

Cattell, J. McK. (1890). Mental tests and measurements. *Mind, 15*, 373–81. Retrieved February 1, 2008, from Classics in the History of Psychology website: http://psychclassics.yorku.ca/Cattell/mental.htm.

Cavanaugh, S. (2008, July 16). Testing officials again tackle accommodations and exclusions for special student populations. *Education Week, 27*(41).

Chapelle, C. A., Enright, M. K., & Jamieson, J. (2010). Does an argument-based approach to validity make a difference? *Educational Measurement: Issues and Practice, 29*(1), 3–13.

Chapman, P. D. (1988). *Schools as sorters: Lewis M. Terman, applied psychology, and the intelligence testing movement, 1890–1930.* New York: New York University Press.

Cherry, R. D., & Meyer, P. R. (2009). Reliability issues in holistic assessment. In B. Huot & P. O'Neill (Eds.), *Assessing writing: A critical sourcebook*, pp. 29–56. Boston: Bedford/St. Martin's. (Reprinted from *Validating holistic scoring for writing assessment: Theoretical and empirical foundations*, pp. 109–141, M. M. Williamson & B. Huot, Eds., 1993, Cresskill, NJ: Hampton Press.)

Chester, M. D. (2005). Making valid and consistent inferences about school effectiveness from multiple measures. *Educational Measurement: Issues and Practice, 24*(4), 40–52.

Childs, R. A., & Jaciw, A. P. (2003). Matrix sampling of items in large-scale assessments. *Practical Assessment, Research & Evaluation, 8*(16).

Cizek, C. J. (Ed.). (2001). *Setting performance standards: Contents, methods, and perspectives.* Mahwah, NJ: Lawrence Erlbaum Associates.

Clark, R. E., and Estes, F. (1996). Cognitive task analysis. *International Journal of Educational Research, 25*(5), 403–17.

Clarke, M. M., Madaus, G. F., Horn, C. L., & Ramos, M. A. (2000). Retrospectives on educational testing and assessment in the 20th century. *Journal of Curriculum Studies, 32*(2), 159–81.

Cohen, A. S., Kane, M. T., & Crooks, T. J. (1999). A generalized examinee-centered method for setting standards on achievement tests. *Applied Measurement in Education, 12*(4). 343–66.

Cohen, A. S., & Wollack, J. A. (2006). Test administration, security, scoring, and reporting. In R. L. Brennan (Ed.), *Educational Measurement* (4th ed., pp. 355–86). Westport, CT: American Council on Education and Praeger Publishers.

Cole, N. S., & Moss, P. A. (1989). Bias in test use. In R. L. Linn, (Ed.), *Educational measurement* (3rd ed., pp. 201–19). New York: American Council on Education and Macmillan Publishing Company.

Cole, N. S., & Zieky, M. J. (2001). The new faces of fairness. *Journal of Educational Measurement, 38*(4), 369–82.

Common Core State Standards Initiative (CCSSI). (2010a). *The Common Core state standards for English language arts and literacy in history/social studies, science, and technical subjects.* Retrieved June 19, 2010, from http://www.corestandards .org/assets/CCSSI_ELA%20Standards.pdf.

Common Core State Standards Initiative (CCSSI). (2010b). *The Common Core state standards for mathematics.* Retrieved June 19, 2010, from http://www.corestandards .org/assets/CCSSI_Math%20Standards.pdf.

Cook, W. W. (1951). The functions of measurement in the facilitation of learning. In E. F. Lindquist (Ed.), *Educational measurement* (1st ed., pp. 3–46). Washington, DC: American Council on Education.

Corcoran, T., Mosher, F. A., & Rogat, A. (2009, May). *Learning progressions in science: An evidence-based approach to reform.* Philadelphia, PA: Consortium for Policy Research in Education.

Council of Chief State School Officers. (2008). *Models of alignment analyses.* Retrieved May 26, 2008, from http://www.ccsso.org/Projects/Alignment_Analysis/ models/.

Council of Chief State School Officers & Association of Test Publishers. (2010). *Operational best practices for statewide large-scale assessment programs.* Washington, DC: Author.

Craf, J. R. (1943, March). From school to army. *Stanford Business School Bulletin.* Retrieved October 27, 2007, from http://www.gsb.stanford.edu/news/history/time-line/military.html.

Crocker, L. (2003). Teaching for the test: Validity, fairness, and moral action. *Educational Measurement: Issues and Practice, 22*(3), 5–11.

Crocker, L. (2006). Preparing examinees for test taking: Guidelines for test developers and test users. In S. M. Downing & T. M. Haladyna (Eds.), *Handbook of test development* (pp. 115–28). Mahwah, NJ: Lawrence Erlbaum Associates.

Cronbach, L. J. (1996). Coefficient alpha and the internal structure of tests. In A. W. Ward, H. W. Ward, & M. Murray-Ward (Eds.), *Educational measurement: Origins, theories, and explications* (Vol. 1, pp. 257–69). Lanham, MD: University Press of America, Inc. (Original article published in 1951)

Cronbach, L. J. (1957). The two disciplines of scientific psychology. *American Psychologist, 12*, 671–84.

Cronbach, L. J. (1971). Test validation. In R. L. Thorndike, (Ed.), *Educational measurement* (2nd ed., pp. 443–507). Washington, DC: American Council on Education.

Cronbach, L. J. (1988). Five perspectives on validity argument. In H. Wainer & H. I. Braun (Eds.), *Test validity* (pp. 3–17). Hillsdale, NJ: Lawrence Erlbaum Associates.

Cronbach, L. J., Gleser, G. C., Nanda, H., & Rajaratnam, N. (1972). *The dependability of behavioral measurements: Theory of generalizability for scores and profiles.* New York: John Wiley and Sons.

Cronbach, L. J., & Meehl, P. E. (1955). Construct validity in psychological tests. *Psychological Bulletin, 52,* 281–302.

Cronbach, L. J., Rajaratnam, N., & Gleser, G. C. (1996). Theory of generalizability: A liberalization of reliability theory. In A. W. Ward, H. W. Ward, & M. Murray-Ward (Eds.), *Educational measurement: Origins, theories, and explications* (Vol. 1, pp. 271–86). Lanham, MD: University Press of America, Inc. (Original article published in 1963)

Cureton, E. E. (1951). Validity. In E. F. Lindquist (Ed.), *Educational measurement* (1st ed., pp. 621–94). Washington, DC: American Council on Education.

Daniel, M. H. (1999). Behind the scenes: Using new measurement methods on the DAS and KAIT. In S. E. Embretson & S. L. Hershberger (Eds.), *The new rules of measurement: What every psychologist and educator should know* (pp. 37–63). Mahwah, NJ: Lawrence Erlbaum Associates.

Darling-Hammond, L. (2006). *Standards, assessment, and educational policy: In pursuit of genuine accountability.* Eighth annual William H. Angoff Memorial Lecture, presented at Educational Testing Service, Princeton, NJ, on October 30, 2002. Retrieved on February 18, 2008, from the Educational Testing Service website: http://www.ets.org/Media/Research/pdf/PICANG8.pdf.

Darling-Hammond, L. (2010). *Performance counts: Assessment systems that support high-quality learning.* Washington, DC: Council of Chief State School Officers.

Darling-Hammond, L., & Rustique-Forrester, E. (2005, June). The consequences of student testing for teaching and teacher quality. *Yearbook of the National Society for the Study of Education, 104*(2), 289–319.

Data Recognition Corporation. (2009). *Technical report for the 2009 Pennsylvania System of State Assessment.* Retrieved June 22, 2010, from http://www.portal .state.pa.us/portal/server.pt/community/technical_analysis/7447.

Deary, I. J., Lawn, M., & Bartholomew, D. J. (2008). A conversation between Charles Spearman, Godfrey Thomson, and Edward L. Thorndike: The International Examinations inquiry meetings 1931–1938. *History of Psychology, 11*(2), 122–42.

Dee, T. S., & Jacob, B. (2010). *The impact of No Child Left Behind on students, teachers, and schools.* Retrieved September 28, 2010, from http://www.brookings.edu/~/ media/Files/Programs/ES/BPEA/2010_fall_bpea_papers/2010fall_deejacob.pdf.

Delandshere, G. (2001). Implicit theories, unexamined assumptions and the status quo of educational assessment. *Assessment in Education: Principles, Policy, and Practice, 8*(2), 113–33.

DeMars, C. E. (2000). Test stakes and item format interactions. *Applied Measurement in Education, 13*(1), 55–77.

Dewan, S. (2010, February 13). Experts say schools need to screen for cheating. *New York Times.*

Dorans, N. J. (2002). *The recentering of SAT® scales and its effects on score distributions and score interpretations.* CB Research Report No. 2002–11, Educational Testing Service RR-02-04. New York: The College Board.

Dorans, N. J. (2008). *The practice of comparing scores from different tests.* Retrieved September 8, 2008, from the Educational Testing Service website: http://www.ets .org/Media/Research/pdf/RD_Connections6.pdf.

Downing, S. M., & Haladyna, T. M. (Eds.). (2006). *Handbook of test development.* Mahwah, NJ: Lawrence Erlbaum Associates.

Duckworth, A. L., & Seligman, M. E. P. (2005). Self-discipline outdoes IQ in predicting academic performance of adolescents. *Psychological Science, 16*(12), 939–44.

Durán, R. P., Brown, C., & McCall, M. (2002). Assessment of English-language learners in the Oregon Statewide Assessment System: National and state perspectives. In G. Tindal & T. M. Haladyna (Eds.), *Large-scale assessment programs for all students: Validity, technical adequacy, and implementation* (pp. 371–94). Mahwah, NJ: Lawrence Erlbaum Associates.

Dweck, C. S. (2007). The perils and promises of praise. *Educational Leadership, 65*(2), 34–39.

Ebel, R. L. (1996). Must all tests be valid? In A. W. Ward, H. W. Ward, & M. Murray-Ward (Eds.), *Educational measurement: Origins, theories, and explications* (Vol. 1, pp. 209–223). Lanham, MD: University Press of America, Inc. (Original published in 1961)

Editorial Projects in Education. (2007). *EPE research center: No Child Left Behind.* Retrieved October 28, 2007, from http://www.edweek.org/rc/issues/no-child-left-behind/.

Education Sciences Reform Act of 2002, Pub. L. No. 107–279. Retrieved from the U.S. Department of Education website: http://www.ed.gov/policy/rschstat/leg/ PL107-279.pdf.

Educational Testing Service (ETS). (2002). *Standards for quality and fairness.* Princeton, NJ: Author. Retrieved March 1, 2008, from http://www.ets.org/Media/ About_ETS/pdf/standards.pdf.

Educational Testing Service (ETS). (2004). *Why and how ETS questions test scores.* Retrieved September 25, 2008, from http://www.ets.org/Media/Tests/PRAXIS/ pdf/whyandhow.pdf.

Educational Testing Service (ETS). (2009a). *Guidelines for fairness review of assessments.* Princeton, NJ: Author. Retrieved January 5, 2010, from http://www.ets.org/ Media/About_ETS/pdf/overview.pdf.

Educational Testing Service (ETS). (2009b). *Guidelines for the assessment of English Language Learners.* Princeton, NJ: Author. Retrieved May 14, 2010, from http:// www.ets.org/Media/About_ETS/pdf/ELL_Guidelines.pdf.

Educational Testing Service (ETS). (2009c). *International principles for fairness review of assessments.* Princeton, NJ: Author. Retrieved June 11 2010, from http://www .ets.org/Media/About_ETS/pdf/frintl.pdf.

Elliot, N. (2005). *On a scale: A social history of writing assessment in America.* New York: Peter Lang Publishing, Inc.

Elliott, R. (1987). *Litigating intelligence: IQ tests, special education, and social science in the courtroom.* Dover, MA: Auburn House Publishing Company.

Elliott, S., Chudowsky, N., Plake, B. S., & McDonnell, L. (2006). Using the *Standards* to evaluate the redesign of the U.S. naturalization tests: Lessons for the measurement community. *Educational Measurement: Issues and Practice, 25*(3), 22–26.

Elman, B. A. (1991). Political, social, and cultural reproduction via civil service examinations in late imperial China. *The Journal of Asian Studies, 50*(1), 7–28.

Embretson, S. E. (1998). A cognitive design system approach to generating valid tests: Application to abstract reasoning. *Psychological Methods, 3*(3), 380–96.

Embretson, S. E. (1999). Issues in the measurement of cognitive abilities. In S. E. Embretson & S. L. Hershberger (Eds.), *The new rules of measurement: What every psychologist and educator should know* (pp. 1–15). Mahwah, NJ: Lawrence Erlbaum Associates.

Embretson, S. E. (2007). Construct validity: A universal validity system or just another test evaluation procedure? *Educational Researcher, 36*(8), 449–55.

Embretson, S. E., & Reise, S. P. (2000). *Item response theory for psychologists.* Mahwah, NJ: Lawrence Erlbaum Associates.

ERIC Clearinghouse on Tests, Measurement, and Evaluation. (1985). *Legal issues in testing* (ERIC identifier ED289884). Retrieved October 28, 2007, from ERIC Digests website: http://www.ericdigests.org/pre-927/legal.htm.

Feldt, L. S., & Brennan, R. L. (1989). Reliability. In R. L. Linn (Ed.), *Educational measurement* (3rd ed., pp. 105–46). New York: American Council on Education and Macmillan Publishing Company.

Ferguson, R. F., Hackman, S., Hanna, R., & Ballantine, A. (2010). *How high schools become exemplary: Ways that leadership raises achievement and narrows gaps by improving instruction in 15 public schools.* Retrieved September 28, 2010, from http://www.agi.harvard.edu.

Ferrara, S. (2006). Toward a psychology of large-scale educational achievement testing: Some features and capabilities. *Educational Measurement: Issues and Practice, 25*(4), 2–5.

Ferrara, S. & De Mauro, G. (2006). Standardized assessment of individual achievement in K–12. In R. L. Brennan (Ed.), *Educational measurement* (4th ed., pp. 579–621). Westport, CT: American Council on Education and Praeger Publishers.

Filer, A. (Ed.). (2000). *Educational assessment and testing: Social practice and social product.* London: Routledge Falmer.

Fitzpatrick, L. (2009, January 28). Virginia parents fight for easier grading standards. *Time.* Retrieved January 28, 2009, from http://www.time.com/time/nation/article/0,8599,1874266,00.html.

Flanagan, J. C. (1951). Units, scores, and norms. In E. F. Lindquist (Ed.), *Educational measurement* (1st ed., pp. 695–763). Washington, DC: American Council on Education.

Fox, J. D. (2003). From products to process: An ecological approach to bias detection. *International Journal of Testing, 3*(1), 21–47.

Frederiksen, J. R., & Collins, A. (1990). *A systems approach to educational testing.* Technical Report 2, Center for Technology in Education, New York (ERIC Document Reproduction Service No. ED325484).

Frisbie, D. A. (2005). Measurement 101: Some fundamentals revisited. *Educational Measurement: Issues and Practice, 24*(3), 21–28.

Fullinwider, R. K., & Lichtenberg, J. (2004). *Leveling the playing field: Justice, politics, and college admissions.* Lanham, MD: Rowman & Littlefield Publishers, Inc.

Garcia, S. M., & Tor, A. (2009). The N-effect: More competitors, less competition. *Psychological Science, 20*(7), 871–77.

Gardner, H. (1983). *Frames of mind: The theory of multiple intelligences.* New York: Basic Books.

Garrison, M. J. (2004). Measure, mismeasure, or not measurement at all? Psychometrics as political theory. *Scholar-Practitioner Quarterly, 2*(4), 61–76.

Gersten, R. (2009, October 21). No success like failure? *Education Week.*

Giordano, G. (2005). *How testing came to dominate American schools: The history of educational assessment.* New York: Peter Lang Publishing, Inc.

Gipps, C. (1994). Developments in educational assessment: What makes a good test? *Assessment in Education: Principles, Policy & Practice, 1*(3), 283–92.

Giraud, G., & Impara, J. C. (2005). Making the cut: The cut score setting process in a public school district. *Applied Measurement in Education, 18*(3), 289–312.

Glenn, D. (2010, May 9). Carol Dweck's attitude: It's not about how smart you are. *The Chronicle of Higher Education.*

Goertz, M. E., Oláh, L. N., & Riggan, M. (2010). *From testing to teaching: The use of interim assessments in classroom teaching.* Philadelphia, PA: Consortium for Policy Research in Education.

Goodman, D. P., & Hambleton, R. K. (2004). Student test score reports and interpretive guides: Review of current practices and suggestions for future research. *Applied Measurement in Education, 17*(2), 145–220.

Gorin, J. S. (2006). Test design with cognition in mind. *Educational Measurement: Issues and Practice, 25*(4), 21–35.

Gould, S. J. (1981). *The mismeasure of man.* New York: W.W. Norton & Company.

Green, B. F. (1996). *Setting performance standards: Content, goals, and individual differences.* Second annual William H. Angoff Memorial Lecture, Princeton, NJ. Retrieved September 17, 2008, from the Educational Testing Service website: http://www.ets.org/Media/Research/pdf/PICANG2.pdf.

Greenberg, M. (n.d.). *The GI Bill of Rights.* Retrieved October 27, 2007, from the U.S. Department of State Bureau of International Information website: http://usinfo .state.gov/products/pubs/historians/chapter07.htm.

Gronlund, N. E. (2006). *Assessment of student achievement* (8th ed.). Boston, MA: Pearson Education, Inc.

Gulliksen, H. O. (1950). *Theory of mental tests.* New York: John Wiley & Sons, Inc.

Guskey, T. (2007). Multiple sources of evidence: An analysis of stakeholders' perceptions of various indicators of student learning. *Educational Measurement: Issues and Practice, 26*(1), 19–27.

Gutting, G. (2003). Michel Foucault. In E. N. Zalta (Ed.), *The Stanford Encyclopedia of Philosophy* (Fall 2003 ed.). Retrieved January 29, 2008, from http://plato .stanford.edu/archives/fall2003/entries/foucault.

Haberman, S. (2005). *When can subscores have value?* ETS Research Report RR-05-08. Princeton, NJ: Educational Testing Service.

Haertel, E. H. (2002). Standard setting as a participatory process: Implications for validation of standards-based accountability programs. *Educational Measurement: Issues and Practice, 21*(1), 16–22.

Haertel, E. H. (2006). Reliability. In Brennan, R. L. (Ed.), *Educational measurement* (4th ed., pp. 65–110). Westport, CT: American Council on Education and Praeger Publishers.

Haertel, E. H., & Herman, J. L. (2005). A historical perspective on validity arguments for accountability testing. *Yearbook of the National Society for the Study of Education, 104*(2), 1–34.

Haladyna, T. M. (1999). *Developing and validating multiple-choice test items* (2nd ed.). Mahwah, NJ: Lawrence Erlbaum Associates.

Haladyna, T. M. (2006). Roles and importance of validity studies in test development. In S. M. Downing & T. M. Haladyna (Eds.), *Handbook of test development* (pp. 739–55). Mahwah, NJ: Lawrence Erlbaum Associates.

Hambleton, R. K. (1989). Principles and selected applications of item response theory. In R. L. Linn (Ed.), *Educational measurement* (3rd ed., pp. 147–200). New York: American Council on Education and Macmillan Publishing Company.

Hambleton, R. K., & Jones, R. W. (1993). Comparison of classical test theory and item response theory and their applications to test development. *Instructional topics in educational measurement series,* module 16. Retrieved June 10, 2008, from the National Council on Measurement in Education website: http://www.ncme.org/pubs/items/24.pdf.

Hambleton, R. K., & Pitoniak, M. J. (2006). Setting performance standards. In R. L. Brennan (Ed.), *Educational measurement* (4th ed., pp. 443–70). Westport, CT: American Council on Education and Praeger Publishers.

Hamilton, L. S., Stecher, B. M., Marsh, J. A., McCombs, J. S., Robyn, A., Russell, J. L., Naftel, S., & Barney, H. (2007). *Standards-based accountability under No Child Left Behind: Experiences of teachers and administrators in three states.* Retrieved June 3, 2008, from the Rand Corporation website: http://www.rand.org/pubs/monographs/2007/RAND_MG589.pdf.

Hanson, F. A. (2000). How tests create what they are intended to measure. In A. Filer (Ed.), *Educational assessment and testing: Social practice and social product* (pp. 67–81). London: Routledge Falmer.

Harris, D. N., & Herrington, C. D. (2006). Accountability, standards, and the growing achievement gap: Lessons from the past half-century. *American Journal of Education, 112*(2), 209–38.

Harris, W. G. (2006). The challenges of meeting the *Standards*: A perspective from the test publishing community. *Educational Measurement: Issues and Practice, 25*(3), 42–45.

Harvill, L. M. (1991). Standard error of measurement. *Instructional topics in educational measurement series,* module 9. Retrieved June 10, 2008, from the National Council on Measurement in Education website: http://www.ncme.org/pubs/items/16.pdf.

Hatfield, G. (2007). *Psychology old and new.* Retrieved March 27, 2008, from the University of Pennsylvania website: http://www.cis.upenn.edu/~hatfield/.

Heaney, K. J., & Pullin, D. C. (1998). Accommodations and flags: Admissions testing and the rights of individuals with disabilities. *Educational Assessment, 5*(2), 71–93.

Heckman, J. J., Humphries, J. E., & Mader, N. S. (June 2010). *The GED* [Abstract]. NBER Working Paper No. 16064. Retrieved June 8, 2010, from the National Bureau of Economic Research website: http://www.nber.org/papers/w16064.

Herbart, J. F. (1877). Probability and necessity of applying mathematics in psychology (H. Haanel, Trans). *Journal of Speculative Philosophy, 11,* 251–64. (Reprinted from undated original.) Retrieved June 15, 2008, from http://psychclassics.yorku. ca/Herbart/mathpsych.htm.

Heritage, M. (2008). *Learning progressions: Supporting instruction and formative assessment.* Washington, DC: Council of Chief State School Officers.

Heritage, M., & Yeagley, R. (2005, June). Data use and school improvement: Challenges and prospects. *Yearbook of the National Society for the Study of Education, 104*(2), 320–39.

Hillocks, G. (2002). *The testing trap: How state writing assessments control learning.* New York: Teachers College Press.

Hogan, T. P., Benjamin, A., & Brezinski, K. L. (2000/2003). Reliability methods: A note on the frequency of use of various types. In B. Thompson (Ed.), *Score reliability: Contemporary thinking on reliability issues* (pp. 59–68). Thousand Oaks, CA: Sage Publications, Inc. (Reprinted from *Educational and Psychological Measurement, 60,* 523–531.)

Holland, P. W., & Dorans, N. J. (2006). Linking and equating. In R. L. Brennan (Ed.), *Educational measurement* (4th ed., pp. 187–220). Westport, CT: American Council on Education and Praeger Publishers.

Hollander, P. (1982). Legal context of educational testing. In A. K. Wigdor & W. Garner (Eds.), *Ability testing: Uses, consequences, and controversies* (Vol. 2, pp. 195–232). Washington, DC: National Academies Press.

Hollenbeck, K. (2002). Determining when test alterations are valid accommodations or modifications for large-scale assessments. In G. Tindal & T. M. Haladyna (Eds.), *Large-scale assessment programs for all students: Validity, technical adequacy, and implementation* (pp. 395–425). Mahwah, NJ: Lawrence Erlbaum Associates.

Howell, J. S., Kurlaender, M., & Grodsky, E. (2009, April). *Postsecondary Preparation and remediation: Examining the effect of the Early Assessment Program at California State University.* Retrieved May 12, 2010, from the Association for Institutional Research website at http://www.airweb.org/images/Kurlaender%20 Final%20Report.pdf.

Huot, B. A. (2002). *(Re)Articulating writing assessment for teaching and learning.* Logan: Utah State University Press.

Institute of Education Sciences. (2008a). *Children 3 to 21 years old served in federally supported programs for the disabled, by type of disability: Selected years, 1976–77 through 2003–04.* Retrieved August 20, 2008, from the National Center for Education Statistics website: http://nces.ed.gov/fastfacts/display.asp?id=64.

Institute of Education Sciences. (2008b). *National Assessment of Educational Progress: Frequently asked questions.* Retrieved February 25, 2008, from the National Center for Education Statistics website at http://nces.ed.gov/nationsreportcard/faq .asp.

International Business Machines. (n.d.). *Archives: IBM 805 test scoring machine.* Retrieved October 27, 2007, from http://www03.ibm.com/ibm/history/exhibits/specialprod1/specialprod1_9.html.

International Test Commission (ITC). (2000, April 21). *ITC guidelines on adapting tests.* Retrieved March 10, 2008, from http://www.intestcom.org/guidelines/test+adaptation.php.

International Test Commission (ITC). (2001). International guidelines for test use. *International Journal of Testing, 1*(2), 93–114.

International Test Commission (ITC). (2005). *International guidelines on computer-based and Internet-delivered testing.* Retrieved March 10, 2008, from http://www.intestcom.org/guidelines/index.html.

International Test Commission (ITC). (2008). *International guidelines for test use.* Retrieved March 10, 2008, from http://www.intestcom.org/guidelines/guidelines+for+test+use.php.

Jensen, A. R. (1969). How much can we boost IQ and scholastic achievement? *Harvard Educational Review, 39*, 1–123.

Johnsen, T. B. (2005, September 2). *On the history of measurement: Was Galileo also the inventor of Classical Test Theory?* Retrieved June 12, 2008, from the University of Bergen website: http://www.galton.uib.no/downloads/History%20of%20measurement.pdf.

Johnson, R. L., Penny, J., & Gordon, B. (2000). The relation between score resolution methods and interrater reliability: An empirical study of an analytic scoring rubric. *Applied Measurement in Education, 13*(2), 121–38.

Joint Committee on Educational Standards. (2003). *The student evaluation standards.* Thousand Oaks, CA: Corwin Press.

Joint Committee on Testing Practices. (2004). *Code of fair testing practices in education.* Retrieved March 10, 2008, from the American Psychological Association website: http://www.apa.org/science/fairtestcode.html.

Joint Organizational Statement on the "No Child Left Behind" Act. (2004, October 21). Retrieved February 20, 2008, from the National Education Association website: http://www.nea.org/esea/nclbjointstatement.html.

Kane, M. T. (1992). An argument-based approach to validity. *Psychological Bulletin, 112*(3), 527–35.

Kane, M. T. (1996). The precision of measurements. *Applied Measurement in Education, 9*(4), 355–79.

Kane, M. T. (1998). Choosing between examinee-centered and test-centered standard-setting methods. *Educational Assessment, 5*(3), 129–45.

Kane, M. T. (2004). Certification testing as an illustration of argument-based validation. *Measurement, 2*(3), 135–70.

Kane, M. T. (2006). Validation. In R. L. Brennan (Ed.), *Educational measurement* (4th ed., pp. 17–64). Westport, CT: American Council on Education and Praeger Publishers.

Kane, M. T. (2010). *Errors of measurement, theory, and public policy.* Twelfth annual William H. Angoff Memorial Lecture, presented at Educational Testing Service, Princeton, NJ, on November 19, 2008. Retrieved March 30, 2010, from the Educational Testing Service website: http://www.ets.org/Media/Research/pdf/PICANG12.pdf.

Karantonis, A., & Sireci, S. G. (2006). The bookmark standard-setting method: A literature review. *Educational Measurement: Issues and Practice, 25*(1), 4–12.

Kelly, F. J. (1916). The Kansas silent reading tests. *Journal of Educational Psychology, 7*(5), 63–80.

Kishiyama, M. M., Boyce, W. T., Jimenez, A. M., Perry, L. M., & Knight, R. T. (2009). Socioeconomic disparities affect prefrontal function in children. *Journal of Cognitive Neuroscience, 21*(6), 1106–15.

Klein, S., Liu, O. U., & Sconing, J. (2009, September 2009). *Test validity study (TVS) report.* Retrieved November 12, 2009, from the Voluntary System of Accountability Program website: http://www.voluntarysystem.org/docs/reports/TVSReport_Final.pdf.

Kleinfield, N. R. (2002, June 5). The Elderly Man and the Sea? Test sanitizes literary texts. *New York Times.*

Kober, N. (2002, October). *Test talk for leaders: What tests can and cannot tell us.* Retrieved February 20, 2008, from the Center on Education Policy website: http://www.cep-dc.org/document/docWindow.cfm?fuseaction=document.viewDocument&documentid=61&documentFormatId=637.

Kobrin, J. L., Sathy, V., & Shaw, E. J. (2007). *Subgroup performance differences on the SAT Reasoning Test™.* CB Research Report No. 2006-5. New York: The College Board.

Kolen, M. J. (2006). Scaling and norming. In R. L. Brennan (Ed.), *Educational Measurement* (4th ed., pp. 155–86). Westport, CT: American Council on Education and Praeger Publishers.

Kopriva, R. (2000). *Ensuring accuracy in testing for English language learners.* Retrieved August 30, 2008, from the Council of Chief State School Officers website: http://www.ccsso.org/publications/index.cfm.

Koretz, D. (2006). Steps toward more effective implementation of the *Standards for Educational and Psychological Testing. Educational Measurement: Issues and Practice, 25*(3), 46–50.

Koretz, D. (2008). *Measuring up: What educational testing really tells us.* Cambridge, MA: Harvard University Press.

Koretz, D. (2009, December). *Some implications of current policy for educational measurement.* Paper presented at the Exploratory Seminar, Princeton, NJ. Retrieved May 10, 2010, from the K–12 Center for Assessment and Performance Management website: http: //www.k12center.org/publications.html.

Koretz, D., & Barton, K. (2004). Assessing students with disabilities: Issues and evidence. *Educational Assessment, 9*(1 & 2), 29–60.

Koretz, D. M., & Hamilton, L. S. (2006). Testing for accountability in K–12. In R. L. Brennan (Ed.), *Educational measurement* (4th ed., pp. 531–78). Westport, CT: American Council on Education and Praeger Publishers.

Lague, D. (2008, January 6). 1977 exam opened escape route into China's elite. *New York Times.*

Laitusis, C. C., & Cook, L. (2007). *Large-scale assessment and accommodations: What works?* Arlington, VA: Council for Exceptional Children.

Lane, S., & Stone, C. A. (2002). Strategies for examining the consequences of assessment and accountability programs. *Educational Measurement: Issues and Practice, 21*(1), 23–29.

Lane, S., & Stone, C. A. (2006). Performance assessment. In R. L. Brennan (Ed.), *Educational measurement* (4th ed., pp. 387–432). Westport, CT: American Council on Education and Praeger Publishers.

Langenfeld, T. E., & Crocker, L. M. (1994). The evolution of validity theory: Public school testing, the courts, and incompatible interpretations. *Educational Assessment, 2*(2), 149–65.

Law School Admission Council (LSAC). (2007). LSAT practice test, Form 8LSN75. Retrieved June 22, 2010, from http://www.lsac.org/pdfs/SamplePTJune.pdf.

Law School Admission Council (LSAC). (2008). *About the LSAT.* Retrieved May 26, 2008, from http://www.lsat.org/LSAT/about-the-lsat.asp.

Law School Admission Council (LSAC). (2010). *LSAT scores as predictors of law school performance.* Retrieved June 22, 2010, from http://www.lsac.org/pdfs/LSAT-Score-Predictors-of-Performance.pdf.

Lawrence, I. M., Rigol, G. W., Van Essen, T., & Jackson, C. A. (2003). *A historical perspective on the content of the SAT®.* College Board Research Report No. 2003-3, ETS RR-03-10. New York: College Entrance Examination Board.

Learning Disabilities Association of America. (2008). *Learning Disabilities Association of America legislative agenda: Education.* Retrieved February 20, 2008, from http://www.ldaamerica.us/legislative/agenda.asp.

Lee, H. C. (2002, December). *The validity of driving simulator to measure on-road performance of older drivers.* Paper presented at the Conference of Australian Institutes of Transport Research, Victoria, Australia. Retrieved April 23, 2008, from the Sidra Solutions website: http://www.sidrasolutions.com/documents/CAITR2002_HoeLeePaper.pdf.

Lee, W. Y., & Kantor. R. (2005). *Dependability of new ESL writing test scores: Evaluating prototype tasks and alternative rating schemes.* ETS Research Report RR-05-14. Princeton, NJ: Educational Testing Service.

Leighton, J. P., & Gierl, M. J. (2007). Defining and evaluating models of cognition used in educational measurement to make inferences about examinees' thinking processes. *Educational Measurement: Issues and Practice, 26*(2), 3–16.

Lemann, N. (1999). *The big test: The secret history of the American meritocracy.* New York: Farrar, Straus and Giroux.

Leslie, M. (2000, July/August). The vexing legacy of Lewis Terman. Retrieved May 15, 2008, from the *Stanford Magazine* website: http://www.stanfordalumni.org/news/magazine/2000/julaug/articles/terman.html.

Lindquist, E. F. (1936). The theory of test construction; The construction of tests. In H. E. Hawkes, E. F. Lindquist, & C. R. Mann (Eds.), *The construction and use of achievement examinations* (pp. 17–106 & 107–60). Cambridge, MA: American Council on Education and Riverside Press.

Lindquist, E. F. (1951). Preliminary considerations in objective test construction. In E. F. Lindquist (Ed.), *Educational measurement* (1st ed., pp. 119–58). Washington, DC: American Council on Education.

Linn, R. L. (1998). Partitioning responsibility for the evaluation of consequences of assessment programs. *Educational Measurement: Issues and Practice, 17*(2), 28–30.

Linn, R. L. (2001). A century of standardized testing: Controversies and pendulum swings. *Educational Assessment, 7*(1), 29–38.

Linn, R. L. (2006). Following the *Standards*: Is it time for another revision? *Educational Measurement: Issues and Practice, 25*(3), 54–56.

Lissitz, R. W., & Samuelsen, K. (2007). A suggested change in terminology and emphasis regarding validity and education. *Educational Researcher, 36*(8), 437–48.

Lissitz, R. W., & Shafer, W. D. (2002). *Assessment in educational reform: Both means and end.* Boston: Allyn and Bacon.

Livingston, S. A. (2004). *Equating test scores (without IRT).* Retrieved September 17, 2008, from the Educational Testing Service website: http://www.ets.org/Media/Research/pdf/LIVINGSTON.pdf.

Livingston, S. A., & Lewis, C. (1993). *Estimating the consistency and accuracy of classifications based on test scores.* ETS Research Report RR-93-48. Princeton, NJ: Educational Testing Service.

Livingston, S. A., & Zieky, M. J. (1982). *Passing scores: A manual for setting standards of performance on educational and occupational tests.* Retrieved October 4, 2008, from the Educational Testing Service website: http://www.ets.org/Media/Research/pdf/passing_scores.pdf.

Loevinger, J. (1957). Objective tests as instruments of psychological theory. *Psychological Reports, 3,* Monograph Supplement 9, 635–94.

Longino, H. (2006). The social dimensions of scientific knowledge. In E. N. Zalta (Ed.), *The Stanford encyclopedia of philosophy* (Fall 2006 ed.). Retrieved May 5, 2008, from http://plato.stanford.edu/archives/fall2006/entries/scientific-knowledge-social.

Lord, F. M. (1980). *Applications of item response theory to practical testing problems.* Hillsdale, NJ: Lawrence Erlbaum Associates.

Lord, F. M., & Novick, M. R., with contributions by Birnbaum, A. (1968). *Statistical theories of mental test scores.* Reading, MA: Addison-Wesley.

Lu, Y., & Sireci, S. G. (2007). Validity issues in test speededness. *Educational Measurement: Issues and Practice, 26*(4), 29–37.

Luce, R. D., & Suppes, P. (2002). Representational measurement theory. In H. Pashler (Series Ed.) & J. Wixted (Vol. Ed.), *Stevens' handbook of experimental psychology,* Vol. 4. *Methodology in experimental psychology* (3rd ed., pp. 1–38). New York: John Wiley & Sons, Inc.

Lunsford, A. A. (1986). The past—and future—of writing assessment. In K. L. Greenberg, H. S. Wiener, & R. A. Donovan, *Writing assessment: Issues and strategies* (pp. 1–12). New York & London: Longman, Inc.

MacArthur, C., & Cavalier, A. (2004). Dictation and speech recognition technology as test accommodations. *Exceptional Children, 71*(1), 43–58.

Madaus, G. F. (1993). A national testing system: Manna from above? An historical/technical perspective. *Educational Assessment, 1*(1), 9–26.

Madaus, G. F. (2001, February). *A brief history of attempts to monitor testing.* Statements from the National Board on Educational Testing and Public Policy, 2(2). Retrieved April 24, 2008, from the Boston College website: http://www.bc.edu/research/nbetpp/publications/v2n2.html.

Madaus, G. F., & Kellaghan, T. (1993). Testing as a mechanism of public policy: A brief history and description. *Measurement & Evaluation in Counseling & Development, 26*(1), 6–10.

Madaus, G. F., & O'Dwyer, L. (1999). A short history of performance assessment: Lessons learned. *Phi Delta Kappan, 80*(9), 688–95.

Madaus, G. F., & Stufflebeam, D. L. (1989). Preface. In G. F. Madaus & D. L. Shufflebeam (Eds.), *Educational evaluation: Classic works of Ralph W. Tyler* (pp. xi–xv). Boston: Kluwer Academic Publishers.

Mangels, J. A., Butterfield, B., Lamb, J., Good, C., & Dweck, C. S. (2006). Why do beliefs about intelligence influence learning success? A social cognitive neuroscience model. *Social Cognitive & Affective Neuroscience. 1*(2): 75–86.

Marcoulides, G. A. (1999). Generalizability theory: Picking up where the Rasch IRT model leaves off? In S. E. Embretson & S. L. Hershberger (Eds.), *The new rules of measurement: What every psychologist and educator should know* (pp. 129–52). Mahwah, NJ: Lawrence Erlbaum Associates.

Mason, E. J. (2007). Measurement issues in high stakes testing: Validity and reliability. *Journal of Applied School Psychology, 23*(2), 27–46.

Mattern, K. D., Patterson, B. F., Shaw, E. J., Kobrin, J. L., & Barbuti, S. M. (2008). *Differential validity and prediction of the SAT®.* CB Research Report No. 2008-4. New York: The College Board.

McCall, W. A. (1922). *How to measure in education.* New York: Macmillan Company.

McConn, M. (1936). The uses and abuses of examinations. In H. E. Hawkes, E. F. Lindquist, & C. R. Mann (Eds.), *The construction and use of achievement examinations* (pp. 443–78). Cambridge, MA: American Council on Education and the Riverside Press.

McGaghie, W. C. (2002, September 4). Assessing readiness for medical education: Evolution of the Medical College Admission Test. *Journal of the American Medical Association, 288*(9), 1085–90.

McGinty, D. (2005). Illuminating the black box of standard setting: An exploratory qualitative study. *Applied Measurement in Education, 18*(3), 269–87.

McGlone, M. S., & Pfiester, R. A. (2007). The generality and consequences of stereotype threat. *Sociology Compass, 1*(1), 174–90.

McGrew, K. S. (2005). The Cattell-Horn-Carroll (CHC) theory of cognitive abilities: Past, present and future. In D. Flanagan & P. Harrison (Eds.), *Contemporary intellectual assessment: Theories, tests, and issues* (2nd ed., pp. 136–202). New York: Guilford Press.

McGrew, K. S. (2009). CHC theory and the human cognitive abilities project. *Intelligence, 37,* 1–10.

McMorris, R. F., Boothroyd, R. A., & Pietrangelo, D. J. (1997). Humor in educational testing: A review and discussion. *Applied Measurement in Education, 10*(3), 269–97.

McMurrer, J. (2007, December). *Choices, changes, and challenges: Curriculum and instruction in the NCLB era* (revised version). Washington, DC: Center on Education Policy.

McNamara, T., & Roever, C. (2006). Psychometric approaches to fairness: Bias and DIF; Fairness reviews and codes of ethics. *Language Learning, 56*(Supplement 2), 81–128 and 129–48.

Mehrens, W. A. (2000). Defending a state graduation test: *GI Forum v. Texas Education Agency.* Measurement perspectives from an external evaluator. *Applied Measurement in Education, 13*(4), 387–401.

Mehrens, W. A. (2002). Consequences of assessment: What is the evidence? In G. Tindal & T. M. Haladyna (Eds.), *Large-scale assessment programs for all students: Validity, technical adequacy, and implementation* (pp. 149–77). Mahwah, NJ: Lawrence Erlbaum Associates.

Mehrens, W. A., & Popham, W. J. (1992). How to evaluate the legal defensibility of high-stakes tests. *Applied Measurement in Education, 5*(3), 265–83.

Melcher, G. (1918). Suggestions for experimental work. In G. M. Whipple (Ed.), *The seventeenth yearbook of the National Society for the Study of Education: The measurement of educational products* (Part 2, pp. 139–51). Bloomington, IL: Public School Publishing Company. Available at the Internet Archive website: http://www.archive.org/stream/measurementofedu00whiprich.

Merriam-Webster (2008). Main entry for "valid." *Merriam-Webster's Online Dictionary.* Retrieved April 17, 2008, from http://www.merriam-webster.com/dictionary/validity.

Mertler, C. A. (2007). *Interpreting standardized test scores: Strategies for data-driven instructional decision making.* Thousand Oaks, CA: Sage Publications, Inc.

Messick, S. (1988). The once and future issues of validity: Assessing the meaning and consequences of measurement. In H. Wainer & H. I. Braun (Eds.), *Test validity* (pp. 33–45). Hillsdale, NJ: Lawrence Erlbaum Associates.

Messick, S. (1989). Validity. In R. L. Linn (Ed.), *Educational measurement* (3rd ed., pp. 13–103). New York: American Council on Education and Macmillan Publishing Company.

Messick, S. (1992). *The interplay of evidence and consequences in the validation of performance assessments.* ETS Research Report RR-92-39. Princeton, NJ: Educational Testing Service.

Messick, S. (1998, November). *Consequences of test interpretation and use: The fusion of validity and values in psychological assessment.* ETS Research Report RR-98-48. Princeton, NJ: Educational Testing Service.

Meyer, C. S., Hagmann-von Arx, P., Lemola, S., & Grob, A. (2010). Correspondence between the general ability to discriminate sensory stimuli and general intelligence. *Journal of Individual Differences, 31*(1), 46–56.

Meyler, A., Keller, T. A., Cherkassky, V. L., Gabrieli, J. D. E., & Just, M. A. (2008). Modifying the brain activation of poor readers during sentence comprehension with extended remedial instruction: A longitudinal study of neuroplasticity. *Neuropsychologia, 46*, 2580–92.

Michell, J. (1986). Measurement scales and statistics: A clash of paradigms. *Psychological Bulletin, 100*(3), 398–407.

Michell, J. (1999). *Measurement in psychology: A critical history of a methodological concept.* Port Chester, NY: Cambridge University Press.

Millsap, R. E. (1997). Invariance in measurement and prediction: Their relationship in the single-factor case. *Psychological Methods, 2*(3), 248–60.

Mislevy, R. J. (1994, October). *Can there be reliability without "reliability"?* ETS Research Memorandum RM-94-18-ONR. Princeton, NJ: Educational Testing Service.

Mislevy, R. J. (1996, May). *Evidence and inference in educational assessment.* Center for the Study of Evaluation Report 414. Retrieved February 10, 2009, from the National Center for Research on Student Evaluations, Standards, and Testing website: http://research.cse.ucla.edu/Reports/TECH414.PDF.

Mislevy, R. J., & Huang, C. W. (2006, May). *Measurement models as narrative structures.* Center for the Study of Evaluation Report 680. Retrieved February 16, 2008, from the National Center for Research on Student Evaluations, Standards, and Testing website: http://www.cse.ucla.edu/products/reports/R680.pdf.

Mislevy, R. J., Steinberg, L. S., & Almond, R. G. (2003). On the structure of educational assessments. *Measurement: Interdisciplinary Research and Perspectives, 1*(1), 3–62.

Mitzel, H. C. (2005, June). *Consistency for state achievement standards under NCLB.* Retrieved June 23, 2010, from the Council of Chief State School Officers website: http://www.ccsso.org/content/pdfs/CAS%20Series%202.Final.pdf.

Monaghan, W. (2006, July). *The facts about subscores.* Retrieved July 8, 2008, from the Educational Testing Service website: http://www.ets.org/Media/Research/pdf/RD_Connections4.pdf.

Monroe, W. S. (1918). Existing tests and standards. In G. M. Whipple (Ed.), *The seventeenth yearbook of the National Society for the Study of Education: The measurement of educational products* (Part 2, pp. 71–104). Bloomington, IL: Public School Publishing Company.

Monroe, W. S., DeVoss, J. C., & Kelly, F. J. (1924). *Educational tests and measurements* (2nd ed.). Cambridge, MA: Riverside Press.

Moss, P. A. (1994). Can there be validity without reliability? *Educational Researcher, 23*(2), 5–12.

Moss, P. A. (1998). The role of consequences in validity theory. *Educational Measurement: Issues and Practice, 17*(2), 6–12.

Moss, P. A. (2004). The meaning and consequences of "reliability." *Journal of Educational and Behavioral Statistics, 29*(2), 245–49.

Moss, P. A., Pullin, D., Gee, J. P., & Haertel, E. H. (2005). The idea of testing: Psychometric and sociocultural perspectives. *Measurement, 3*(2), 63–83.

National Academies. (2007). *Lessons learned about testing.* Retrieved March 16, 2008, from http://www7.nationalacademies.org/bota/Lessons_Learned_Brochure.pdf.

National Academies. (2008). *The Board on Testing and Assessment.* Retrieved March 16, 2008, from http://www7.nationalacademies.org/bota/.

National Association for College Admission Counseling (NACAC). (2008, September). *Report on the use of standardized tests in undergraduate admission.* Retrieved October 21, 2008, from http://www.nacacnet.org/NR/rdonlyres/FE4E1899-653F-4D92-8629-86986D42BF5C/0/TestingComissionReport.pdf.

National Association for the Advancement of Colored People (NAACP). (2007, May 9). *NAACP policy handbook 1976–2006: Resolutions approved by the national board of directors.* Retrieved on February 20, 2006, from http://www.naacp.org/pdfs/resolutions/Policy_Handbook_Draft-5.9.07.pdf.

National Center for Fair and Open Testing (FairTest). (2008, January 25). *"No Child Left Behind" after six years: An escalating track record of failure.* Retrieved November 9, 2010, from http://www.fairtest.org/NCLB-After-Six-Years.

National Center on Response to Intervention. (2010, April). *Essential components of RTI: A closer look at Response to Intervention.* Washington, DC: U.S. Department of Education, Office of Special Education Programs.

National Clearinghouse for English Language Acquisition. (2008). *The growing numbers of Limited English Proficient students.* Retrieved August 25, 2008, from http://www.ncela.gwu.edu/policy/states/reports/statedata/2005LEP/GrowingLEP_0506.pdf.

National Commission on Educational Excellence. (1983). *A nation at risk: The imperative for educational reform.* Retrieved October 23, 2007, from the U.S. Department of Education website: http://www.ed.gov/pubs/NatAtRisk/index.html.

National Commission on Testing and Public Policy. (1990). *From gatekeeper to gateway: Transforming testing in America.* Chestnut Hill, MA: Author.

National Council of La Raza. (2008). *Latino high school reform project: No Child Left Behind.* Retrieved February 20, 2008, from http://www.nclr.org/content/policy/detail/998/.

National Council of Teachers of English. (2004, November). *Framing statements on assessment: Revised report of the Assessment and Testing Study Group of the NCTE Executive Committee.* Retrieved February 26, 2008, from http://www.ncte.org/collections/assessment/resources/118875.htm.

National Council of Teachers of Mathematics. (2008). *Large-scale assessment tool.* Retrieved February 27, 2008, from http://www.nctm.org/resources/content.aspx?id=10796.

National Council on Measurement in Education (NCME). (2010, March). Comments from members: The separation of consequences from validity. *Newsletter, 18*(1), 4–11.

National Education Association (NEA). (2008). *Testing plus: Real accountability with real results.* Retrieved February 25, 2008, from http://www.nea.org/accountability/testplus.html.

National Institute on Student Achievement, Curriculum, and Assessment, Office of Educational Research and Improvement. (1998, June). *The educational system in Japan: Case study findings.* Retrieved January 28, 2008, from the U.S. Department of Education website: http://www.ed.gov/pubs/JapanCaseStudy/index.html.

National Research Council (NRC). (1999a). *Myths and tradeoffs: The role of tests in undergraduate admissions.* A. Beatty, M. R. C. Greenwood, and R. L. Linn (Eds.); Steering Committee for the Workshop on Higher Education Admissions. Washington, DC: National Academies Press.

National Research Council (NRC). (1999b). *Uncommon measures: Equivalence and linkage among educational tests.* Committee on Equivalency and Linkage of Educational Tests, M. J. Feuer, P. W. Holland, B. F. Green, M. W. Bertenthal, and F. C. Hemphill (Eds). Washington, DC: National Academies Press.

National Research Council (NRC). (2001). *Knowing what students know: The science and design of educational assessment.* Committee on the Foundations of Assessment. J. Pellegrino, N. Chudowsky, & R. Glaser (Eds.); Board on Testing and Assessment, Division of Behavioral and Social Sciences and Education. Washington, DC: National Academies Press.

National Research Council (NRC). (2002a). *Achieving high educational standards for all: Conference summary.* T. Ready, C. Edley, & C. E Snow (Eds.). Division of Behavioral and Social Sciences and Education. Washington, DC: National Academies Press.

National Research Council (NRC). (2002b). *Scientific research in education.* Committee on Scientific Principles for Education Research. R. J. Shavelson & L. Towne (Eds.). Division of Behavioral and Social Sciences and Education. Washington, DC: National Academies Press.

National Research Council (NRC). (2004a). *Advancing scientific research in education.* Committee on Research in Education. L. Towne, L. L. Wise, & T. M. Winters (Eds). Division of Behavioral and Social Sciences and Education. Washington, DC: National Academies Press.

National Research Council (NRC). (2004b). *Keeping score for all: The effects of inclusion and accommodation policies on large-scale educational assessment.* J. A. Koenig & L. F. Bachman (Eds). Committee on Participation of English Language Learners and Students with Disabilities in NAEP and Other Large-Scale Assessments. Washington, DC: National Academies Press.

National Research Council (NRC). (2005). *Systems for state science assessments.* M. R. Wilson & M. W. Bertenthal, Eds. Committee on Test Design for K-12 Science Achievement. Washington, DC: National Academies Press.

National Research Council (NRC). (2009, October 5). *Letter report to the U.S. Department of Education on the Race to the Top Fund. Board on Testing and Assessment.* Washington, DC: National Academies Press.

National Research Council (NRC) & National Academy on Education (NAE). (2010). *Getting value out of value-added: Report of a workshop.* H. Braun, N. Chudowsky, & J. Koenig (Eds.). Committee on Value-Added Methodology. Washington, DC: National Academies Press.

National Science Teachers Association. (2001, August). *Position statement: Assessment.* Retrieved February 25, 2008, from http://www.nsta.org/about/positions/assessment.aspx.

New York State Board of Law Examiners. (2008). *The bar examination.* Retrieved June 28, 2008, from http://www.nybarexam.org/barexam.htm.

Newman, D. (2008). *Toward school districts conducting their own rigorous program evaluations.* Palo Alto, CA: Empirical Education, Inc.

Newton, P. E. (2005). The public understanding of measurement inaccuracy. *British Educational Research Journal, 31*(4), 419–42.

Nowakowski, J. R. (1981, November). *Interview with Ralph Tyler* (Western Michigan University, The Evaluation Center, Occasional Paper Series No. 13). Retrieved October 27, 2007, from the Western Michigan University website: http://www.wmich.edu/evalctr/pubs/ops/ops13.html.

Olson, L. (2001, January 10). Test debate: What counts as multiple? *Education Week, 20*(16), 1.

Otterman, S. (2010, June 20). Schools struggle to educate the disabled. *New York Times.*

Oyserman, D., Bybee, T., & Terry, K. (2006). Possible selves and academic outcomes: How and when possible selves impel action. *Journal of Personality and Social Psychology, 91*(1), 188–204.

Parkes, J. (2007). Reliability as argument. *Educational Measurement: Issues and Practice, 4*(26), 2–10.

Parkes, J., & Stevens, J. (2003). Legal issues in school accountability systems. *Applied Measurement in Education, 16*(2), 141–58.

Partnership for Assessment of Readiness for College and Careers (PARCC). (2010, June 23). *Application for the Race to the Top comprehensive assessment systems competition.* Retrieved September 8, 2010, from http://www.fldoe.org/parcc/.

Patz, R. J. (2007, January). *Vertical scaling in standards-based educational assessment and accountability systems.* Retrieved October 4, 2008, from the Council of Chief State School Officers website: http://www.ccsso.org/content/pdfs/Vertical Scaling.pdf.

Pearson Education, Inc. (2009). *ReadyGraphsPlus sample report.* Retrieved June 22, 2010, from http://www.pearsonassessments.com/hai/images/dotcom/stanford10/ ReadyGraphsSampleReports.pdf.

Penfield, R. D., & Lam, T. C. M. (2000). Assessing differential item functioning in performance assessment: Review and recommendations. *Educational Measurement: Issues and Practice, 19*(3), 5–15.

Perie, M. (2008). A guide to understanding and developing performance-level descriptors. *Educational Measurement: Issues and Practice, 27*(4), 15–29.

Peter D. Hart Research Associates, Inc. (2008, January 9). *How should colleges assess and improve student learning? Employers' views on the accountability challenge.* Retrieved February 27, 2008, from the Association of American Colleges and Universities website: www.aacu.org/advocacy/leap/documents/2008_ Business_Leader_Poll.pdf.

Petersen, N. S., Kolen, M. J., & Hoover, H. D. (1989). Scales, norming, and equating. In R. L. Linn (Ed.), *Educational measurement* (3rd ed., pp. 221–62). New York: American Council on Education and MacMillan Publishers.

Pew Research Center for the People and the Press. (2007, June 13). *Mixed grades for a federal education law: No Child Left Behind builds no consensus among the public about either its strong or weak points.* Retrieved February 18, 2008, from http://pewresearch.org/pubs/508/no-child-left-behind.

Phelps, S. (Ed.). (2006). Educational accommodations. *Encyclopedia of everyday law.* Gale Group, Inc., 2003. Retrieved December 7, 2007, from E-Notes website: http://www.enotes.com/everyday-law-encyclopedia/educational-accommodations.

Phillips, S. E. (2002). Legal issues affecting special populations in large-scale testing programs. In G. Tindal & T. M. Haladyna (Eds.), *Large-scale assessment programs for all students: Validity, technical adequacy, and implementation* (pp. 109–48). Mahwah, NJ: Lawrence Erlbaum Associates.

Phillips, S. E., & Camara, W. J. (2006). Legal and ethical issues. In R. L. Brennan (Ed.), *Educational measurement* (4th ed., pp. 733–55). Westport, CT: American Council on Education and Praeger Publishers.

Pitoniak, M. J., & Royer, J. M. (2001). Testing accommodations for examinees with disabilities: A review of psychometric, legal, and social policy issues. *Review of Educational Research, 71*(1), 53–104.

Plake, B. (2008). Standard setters: Stand up and take a stand! *Educational Measurement: Issues and Practice, 27*(1), 3–9.

Plucker, J. A. (Ed.). (2003). *Human intelligence: Historical influences, current controversies, teaching resources.* Retrieved October 26, 2007, from the Indiana University website: http://www.indiana.edu/~intell.

Popham, W. J. (1997). Consequential validity: Right concern—wrong concept. *Educational Measurement: Issues and Practice, 16*(2), 9–13.

Popham, W. J. (2000). *Modern educational measurement: Practical guidelines for educational leaders* (3rd ed.). Boston: Allyn and Bacon.

Popham, W. J. (2003). Seeking redemption for our psychometric sins. *Educational Measurement: Issues and Practice, 22*(1), 45–48.

Popham, W. J. (2007). Instructional insensitivity of tests: Accountability's dire drawback. *Phi Delta Kappan, 89*(2), 146–55.

Porter, T. M. (1996). *Trust in numbers: The pursuit of objectivity in science and public life.* Ewing, NJ: Princeton University Press.

Powers, D. E. (2000, October). *Computing reader agreement for the GRE® Writing Assessment.* ETS Research Memorandum RM-00-8. Princeton, NJ: Educational Testing Service.

President's Commission on Excellence in Special Education. (2002, July 1). *A new era: Revitalizing special education for children and their families.* Retrieved January 20, 2008, from the U.S. Department of Education website: http://www.ed.gov/inits/commissionsboards/whspecialeducation/reports/images/Pres_Rep.pdf.

Pulliam, J. D. (1991). *History of education in America* (5th ed.). New York: Macmillan Publishing Company.

Quinn, L. (2002). *An institutional history of the GED.* Retrieved October 27, 2007, from the University of Wisconsin at Milwaukee website: http://www.uwm.edu/Dept/ETI/reprints/GEDHistory.pdf.

Rae-Dupree, J. (2008, May 4). Can you become a creature of new habits? *New York Times.*

Rawls, John. (1971). *A theory of justice.* Cambridge, MA: Harvard University Press.

Raymond, M. (2008). The student data backpack. In M. Kanstoroom and E. C. Osberg (Eds.), *A byte at the apple: Rethinking education data for the post-NCLB era* (pp. 142–58). Washington, DC: Thomas B. Fordham Institute.

Reardon, S. F., Atteberry, A., Arshan, N., & Kulaender, M. (2009, April). *Effects of the California High School Exit Exam on student persistence, achievement, and graduation.* Stanford University Institute for Research on Education Policy & Practice, Working Paper # 20009-12. Retrieved April 23, 2009, from http://www.stanford.edu/group/irepp/cgi-bin/joomla/index.php.

Rebell, M. A. (2008). Equal opportunity and the courts. *Phi Delta Kappan, 89*(6), 432–39.

Resnick, D. (1982). History of educational testing. In A. K. Wigdor & W. Garner (Eds.), *Ability testing: Uses, consequences, and controversies* (Vol. 2, pp. 173–94). Washington, DC: National Academies Press.

Resnick, L. B. (2006). Making accountability really count. *Educational Measurement: Issues and Practice, 25*(1), 33–37.

Reynolds, C. R., Livingston, R. B., & Willson, V. (2006). *Measurement and assessment in education.* Boston: Allyn and Bacon.

Roediger, H. L., & Karpicke, J. D. (2006). Test-enhanced learning: Taking memory tests improves long-term retention. *Psychological Science, 17*(3), 249–55.

Ryan, K. (2002). Assessment validation in the context of high-stakes assessment. *Educational Measurement: Issues and Practice, 21*(1), 7–15.

Sack, K. (1991, March 14). Appellate panel grants reprieve to law on tests. *New York Times.*

Sackett, P. R., Schmitt, N., Ellingson, J. E., & Kabin, M. B. (2001). High-stakes testing in employment, credentialing, and higher education: Prospects in a post-affirmative-action world. *American Psychologist, 56*(4), 302–18.

Salins, P. D. (2008, November 17). The test passes, colleges fail. *New York Times.*

Schafer, W. D. (2006). Growth scales as an alternative to vertical scales. *Practical Assessment, Research, & Evaluation, 11*(4).

Scholastic, Inc., & Gates Foundation. (2010). *Primary sources: America's teachers on America's schools.* Retrieved May 10, 2010, from the Scholastic website: http://www.scholastic.com/primarysources/download.asp.

Schwartz, W. (1995, December). *Opportunity to Learn standards: Their impact on urban students* (ERIC identifier ED389816). New York: ERIC Clearinghouse on Urban Education.

Schwarz, P. A. (1971). Prediction instruments for educational outcomes. In R. L. Thorndike (Ed.), *Educational measurement* (2nd ed., pp. 303–31). Washington, DC: American Council on Education.

Shaftel, J., Yang, X., Glasnapp, D., & Poggio, J. (2005). Improving assessment validity for students with disabilities in large-scale assessment programs. *Educational Assessment, 10*(4), 357–75.

Shale, D. (1996). Essay reliability: Form and meaning. In E. M. White, W. D. Lutz, & S. Kamusikiri (Eds.), *Assessment of writing: Politics, policies, practices* (pp. 76–96). New York: Modern Language Association.

Shavelson, R. J., Webb, N. M., & Rowley, G. L. (1989). Generalizability theory. *American Psychologist, 44*(6), 922–32.

Sheinker, J., & Erpenbach, W. J. (2007, April). *Alternate assessments for students with significant cognitive disabilities—strategies for states' preparation for and response to peer review.* Retrieved July 7, 2008, from the Council of Chief State School Officers website: http://www.ccsso.org/content/PDFs/AltAssmnts Criteria%2005 1607.pdf.

Shepard, L. A. (1989). Why we need better assessments. *Educational Leadership, 46*(7), 4–9.

Shepard, L. A. (1993). Evaluating test validity. In L. Darling-Hammond (Ed.), *Review of research in education* (Vol. 19, pp. 405–50). Washington, DC: American Educational Research Association.

Shepard, L. A. (2000). The role of assessment in a learning culture. *Educational Researcher, 29*(7), 4–14.

Sireci, S. G., Han, K. T., & Wells, C. (2008). Methods for evaluating the validity of test scores for English Language Learners. *Educational Assessment, 13,* 108–31.

Sireci, S. G., & Parker, P. (2006). Validity on trial: Psychometric and legal conceptualizations of validity. *Educational Measurement: Issues and Practice, 25*(3), 27–34.

Sireci, S. G., Scarpati, S. E., & Li, S. (2005). Test accommodations for students with disabilities: An analysis of the interaction hypothesis. *Review of Educational Research, 75*(4), 457–90.

SMARTER Balanced Assessment Consortium (SBAC). (2010, June 23). *Race to the Top assessment program application for new grants.* Retrieved September 8, 2010, from http://www.k12.wa.us/SMARTER/RTTTApplication.aspx.

Smith, J. L. (2004). Understanding the process of stereotype threat: A review of mediational variables and new performance goal directions. *Educational Psychology Review, 16*(3), 177–206.

Song, W., & Hsu, Y. (2008, March). *Economic and noneconomic outcomes for GED credential recipients.* Paper presented at the annual conference of the American Educational Research Association, New York.

Spearman, C. (1904). "General intelligence" objectively determined and measured. *American Journal of Psychology, 15,* 201–93. Retrieved October 26, 2007, from the Classics in the History of Psychology website: http://psychclassics.yorku.ca/Spearman/.

Stanford University. (1994, February 28). *Ralph Tyler, one of century's foremost educators, dies at 91.* Retrieved October 27, 2007, from the Stanford University News Service website: http://news-service.stanford.edu/pr/94/940228Arc4425.html.

Stedman, L. C. (2009). *The NAEP long-term trend assessment: A review of its transformation, use, and findings.* Washington, DC: National Assessment Governing Board.

Steele, C. M., & Aronson, J. (1995). Stereotype threat and the intellectual test performance of African Americans. *Journal of Personality and Social Psychology, 69*(5), 797–811.

Sternberg, R. J. (1988). *The triarchic mind: A new theory of human intelligence.* New York: Viking Penguin.

Sternberg, R. J. (2010). *College admissions for the 21st century.* Cambridge, MA: Harvard University Press.

Stevens, S. S. (1946). On the theory of scales of measurement. *Science, 103*(2684), 677–80.

St. Pierre, E. A. (2006). Scientifically based research in education: Epistemology and ethics. *Adult Education Quarterly, 56,* 239–66.

Stobart, G. (2005). Fairness in multicultural assessment systems. *Assessment in Education: Principles, Policy & Practice, 12*(3), 275–87.

Strong American Schools. (2008). *Diploma to nowhere.* Washington, DC: Author.

Stutz, T. (2010, May 22). Texas State Board of Education approves new curriculum standards. *Dallas Morning News.*

Suen, H. K., & Yu, L. (2006). Chronic consequences of high-stakes testing? Lessons from the Chinese civil service exam. *Comparative Education Review, 50*(1), 46–65.

Superfine, B. M. (2005, November). The politics of accountability: The rise and fall of Goals 2000. *American Journal of Education, 112,* 10–43.

Tashlik, P. (2010). Changing the national conversation on assessment. *Phi Delta Kappan, 91*(6), 55–59.

Tate, R. (2002). Test dimensionality. In G. Tindal & T. M. Haladyna (Eds.), *Large-scale assessment programs for all students: Validity, technical adequacy, and implementation* (pp. 181–211). Mahwah, NJ: Lawrence Erlbaum Associates.

Taylor, R. L. (2006). *Assessment of exceptional students: Educational and psychological procedures* (7th ed.). Boston: Pearson/Allyn and Bacon.

Terman, L. M. (1916). *The measurement of intelligence* (Chapter 1). Boston: Houghton Mifflin. Retrieved June 14, 2008, from http://psychclassics.yorku.ca/Terman/terman1.htm.

Terman, L. M. (1918, June). The use of intelligence tests in the army. *Psychological Bulletin, 15*(6), 177–87.

Thompson. M. E. (1911). *Psychology and pedagogy of writing.* Baltimore: Warwick & York, Inc.

Thompson, S. J., Johnstone, C. J., & Thurlow, M. L. (2002). *Universal design applied to large-scale assessments* (Synthesis Report 44). Minneapolis: University of Minnesota, National Center on Educational Outcomes. Retrieved March 10, 2008, from the National Center on Educational Outcomes website: http://education.umn.edu/NCEO/OnlinePubs/Synthesis44.html.

Thompson, S., & Thurlow, M. (2002). *Universally designed assessments: Better tests for everyone!* (Policy Directions No. 14). Minneapolis: University of Minnesota, National Center on Educational Outcomes. Retrieved September 1, 2008, from http://education.umn.edu/NCEO/OnlinePubs/Policy14.htm.

Thorndike, E. L. (1910). The contribution of psychology to education. *The Journal of Educational Psychology, 1*, 5–12.

Thorndike, E. L. (1918). The nature, purposes, and general methods of measurements of educational products. In G. M. Whipple (Ed.), *The seventeenth yearbook of the National Society for the Study of Education: The measurement of educational products* (Part 2, pp. 16–24). Bloomington, IL: Public School Publishing Company. Available at the Internet Archive website: http://www.archive.org/stream/measuremento fedu00whiprich.

Thorndike, R. L. (1951). Reliability. In E. F. Lindquist, *Educational measurement* (1st ed., pp. 560–620). Washington, DC: American Council on Education.

Thorndike, R. L. (1971a). Concepts of culture-fairness. *Journal of Educational Measurement, 8*, 63–70.

Thorndike, R. L. (1971b). Educational measurement for the Seventies. In R. L. Thorndike (Ed.), *Educational Measurement* (3rd ed., pp. 3–16). Washington, DC: American Council on Education.

Thorndike, R. M. (1999). IRT and intelligence testing: Past, present, future. In S. E. Embretson & S. L. Hershberger (Eds.), *The new rules of measurement: What every psychologist and educator should know* (pp. 17–35). Mahwah, NJ: Lawrence Erlbaum Associates.

Thornton, S. (2006). Karl Popper. In E. N. Zalta (Ed.), *The Stanford encyclopedia of philosophy* (Winter 2006 ed.). Retrieved January 22, 2008, from http://plato.stanford.edu/archives/win2006/entries/popper.

Threlfall, J., Nelson, N., & Walker, A. (2007, June). *Report to QCA on an investigation of the construct relevance of sources of difficulty in the Key Stage 3 ICT tests.* Retrieved August 17, 2008, from the National Assessment Agency web-site: http://www.naa.org.uk/libraryAssets/media/Leeds_University_research_report.pdf.

Thurber, R. S., Shinn, M. R., & Smolkowski, K. (2002). What is measured in mathematics tests? Construct validity of curriculum-based mathematics measures. *School Psychology Review, 31*(4), 498–513.

Toulmin, S. E. (1958). *The uses of argument.* Cambridge: Cambridge University Press.

Traub, J. (2002, April 7). The test mess. *New York Times.*

Traub, R. E. (1997). Classical test theory in historical perspective. *Educational Measurement: Issues and Practice, 16*(4), 8–14.

Traub, R. E., & Rowley, G. L. (1991). Understanding reliability. *Instructional topics in educational measurement series,* module 8. Retrieved June 10, 2008, from the National Council on Measurement in Education website: http://www.ncme.org/pubs/items/15.pdf.

Triplett, C. F., & Barksdale, M. A. (2005). Third through sixth graders' perceptions of high-stakes testing. *Journal of Literacy Research, 37*(2), 237–60.

Trybus, M. (2007). Understanding scientifically based research: A mandate or decision tool? *Delta Kappa Gamma Bulletin, 73*(4), 5–8.

Tyler, R. W. (1989). Constructing achievement tests. In G. F. Madaus & D. L. Shufflebeam (Eds.), *Educational evaluation: Classic works of Ralph W. Tyler* (pp. 17–91). Boston: Kluwer Academic Publishers. (Original published in 1934)

Tyler, R. W. (1936). Identification and definition of the objectives to be measured. In H. E. Hawkes, E. F. Lindquist, & C. R. Mann (Eds.), *The construction and use of achievement examinations* (pp. 3–16). Cambridge, MA: American Council on Education and the Riverside Press.

Tyler, R. W. (1969). *Basic principles of curriculum and instruction.* Chicago: University of Chicago Press. (Original published in 1949)

UCLA Institute for Democracy, Education, and Access. (2003). *Opportunity to Learn (OTL): Does California's school system measure up?* Retrieved September 8, 2008, from http://justschools.gseis.ucla.edu/solution/pdfs/OTL.pdf.

U.S. Department of Education, Office of Elementary and Secondary Education. (2007, December 21). *Standards and assessments peer review guidance: Information and examples for meeting requirements of the No Child Left Behind Act of 2001.* Retrieved March 17, 2008, from http://www.ed.gov/policy/elsec/guid/saaprguidance.pdf.

U.S. Department of Education. (2009, November 13). *Race to the Top assessment competition: Public and expert input meeting on technology and innovation.* Retrieved January 4, 2010, from http://www.ed.gov/programs/racetothetop-assessment/boston-transcript.pdf.

U.S. Equal Employment Opportunity Commission (EEOC). (2008, June 23). *Employment tests and selection procedures.* Retrieved April 22, 2009, from http://www.eeoc.gov/policy/docs/factemployment_procedures.html.

U.S. Government Accountability Office. (2009, September). *No Child Left Behind Act: Enhancements in the Department of Education's review process could improve state academic assessments.* Report No. GAO-09-11. Retrieved October 7, 2009, from http://www.gao.gov/new.items/d09911.pdf.

Valentine, John A. (1987). *The College Board and the school curriculum: A history of the College Board's influence on the substance and standards of American education, 1900–1980.* New York: College Entrance Examination Board.

von Mayrhauser, R. T. (1992). The mental testing community and validity: A prehistory. *American Psychologist, 47*(2), 244–53.

Walker, M. E. (2007, March). *Is test score reliability necessary?* Retrieved February 28, 2008, from the Educational Testing Service website: http://www.ets.org/Media/Research/pdf/RD_Connections5.pdf.

Walker, T., & Jehlen, A. (2007). "Multiple measures" momentum. *NEA Today, 26*(2), 27.

Waller, N. G., Thompson, J. S., & Wenk, E. (2000). Using IRT to separate measurement bias from true group differences on homogeneous and heterogeneous scales: An illustration with the MMPI. *Psychological Methods, 5*(1), 125–46.

Walser, N. (2007). Response to intervention. *Harvard Education Letter, 23*(1).

Walters, A. M., Lee, S., & Trapani, C. (2004). *Stereotype threat, the test-center environment, and performance on the GRE General Test.* ETS Research Report RR-04-37. Princeton, NJ: Educational Testing Service.

Wang, L., Beckett, G. H., and Brown, L. (2006). Controversies of standardized assessment in school accountability reform: A critical synthesis of multidisciplinary research evidence. *Applied Measurement in Education, 19,* 305–28.

Ward, A. W., Stoker, H. W., & Murray-Ward, M. (1996). *Educational measurement: Origins, theories and explications,* Vol. I: *Basic concepts and theories,* & Vol. II: *Theories and applications.* Lanham, MD: University Press of America, Inc.

Warren, J., & Grodsky, E. (2009). Exit exams harm students who fail them—and don't benefit students who pass them. *Phi Delta Kappan, 90*(9), 645–49.

Webb, N. L. (2006). Identifying content for achievement tests. In S. M. Downing & T. M. Haladyna (Eds.), *Handbook of test development,* pp. 155–80. Mahwah, NJ: Lawrence Erlbaum Associates.

Wendler, C., Feigenbaum, M., & Escandón, M. (2001, December). *Defining group membership: The impact of multiple versus single ethnic/racial categories on testing practices.* The College Board Research Notes RN-13. Retrieved August 25, 2008, from the College Board website: http://professionals.collegeboard.com/research/pdf/rn13_11425.pdf.

Wicherts, J. M., Dolan, C. V., & Hessen, D. J. (2005, November). Stereotype threat and group differences in test performance: A question of measurement invariance. *Journal of Personality and Social Psychology, 89*(5), 696–716.

Wiggins, G. (1989). A true test: Toward more authentic and equitable assessment. *Phi Delta Kappan, 70*(9), 703–13.

Wiliam, D. (2000). The meanings and consequences of educational assessment. *Critical Quarterly, 42*(1), 105–27.

Willis, J. (2008). Building a bridge from neuroscience to the classroom. *Phi Delta Kappan, 89*(6), 424–27.

Winerip, M. (2009, January 30). Still doing the math, but for $100K a year. *New York Times.*

Wines, M. (2007, December 30). One test and 600,000 destinies in South Africa. *New York Times.*

Wise, L. L. (2006). Encouraging and supporting compliance with standards for educational tests. *Educational Measurement: Issues and Practice, 25*(3), 51–53.

Wise, S. L., & DeMars, C. E. (2005). Low examinee effort in low-stakes assessment: Problems and potential solutions. *Educational Assessment, 10*(1), 1–17.

Witte, S. P., Trachsel, M., & Walters, K. (1986). Literacy and the direct assessment of writing: A diachronic perspective. In K. L. Greenberg, H. S. Wiener, & R. A. Donovan (Eds.), *Writing assessment: Issues and strategies* (pp. 13–34). New York & London: Longman, Inc.

Wolf, M. K., Herman, J., Bachman, L. F., Bailey, A. L., & Griffin, N. (2008, July). *Recommendations for assessing English language learners: English language proficiency measures and accommodation uses: Recommendations Report.* Center for the Study of Evaluation Report 737. Retrieved August 30, 2008, from the National Center for Research on Student Evaluations, Standards, and Testing website: http://www.cse.ucla.edu/products/reports/R737.pdf.

Wolf, M. K., Herman, J., Kim, J., Abedi, J., Leon, S., Griffin, N., Bachman, P. L., Chang, S. M., Farnsworth, T., Jung, H., Nollner, J., & Shin, H. W. (2008, August). *Providing validity evidence to improve the assessment of English language learners.* Center for the Study of Evaluation Report 738. Retrieved August 30, 2008, from the National Center for Research on Student Evaluations, Standards, and Testing website: http://www.cse.ucla.edu/products/reports/R738.pdf.

Wolf, M. K., Kao, J., Griffin, N., Herman, J., Bachman, P. L., Chang, S. M., & Farnsworth, T. (2008, January). *Issues in assessing English language learners: English language proficiency measures and accommodation uses: Practice review.* Center for the Study of Evaluation Report 732. Retrieved August 30, 2008, from the National Center for Research on Student Evaluations, Standards, and Testing website: http://www.cse.ucla.edu/products/reports/R732.pdf.

Wolf, M. K., Kao, J., Herman, J., Bachman, L. F., Bailey, A. L., Bachman, P. L., Farnsworth, T., & Chang, S. M. (2008, January). *Issues in assessing English language learners: English language proficiency measures and accommodation uses: Literature review.* Center for the Study of Evaluation Report 731. Retrieved August 30, 2008, from the National Center for Research on Student Evaluations, Standards, and Testing website: http://www.cse.ucla.edu/products/reports/R731.pdf.

Yeager, M. (2007, October). *Understanding NAEP: Inside the nation's report card.* Washington, DC: Education Sector.

Yen, W. M., & Fitzpatrick, A. R. (2006). Item response theory. In R. L. Brennan (Ed.), *Educational Measurement* (4th ed., pp. 111–53). Westport, CT: American Council on Education and Praeger Publishers.

Yin, Y., & Shavelson, R. J. (2004, November). *Application of generalizability theory to concept-map assessment research.* Center for the Study of Evaluation Report 640. Retrieved February 16, 2008, from the National Center for Research on Student Evaluations, Standards, and Testing website: http://www.cse.ucla.edu/products/reports/r640.pdf.

Yoakum, C. S., & Yerkes, R. M. (1920). *Army mental tests.* New York: Henry Holt and Company. Available at the Internet Archive website: http://www.archive.org/stream/armymentaltests013695mbp.

Ysseldyke, J., Thurlow, M., & Shin H. (1995). *Opportunity-to-learn standards* (Policy Directions No. 4). Minneapolis: University of Minnesota, National Center on Educational Outcomes. Retrieved August 30, 2008, from http://education.umn. edu/NCEO/OnlinePubs/Policy4.html.

Ysseldyke, J., Dennison, A., & Nelson, R. (2004, May). *Large-scale assessment and accountability systems: Positive consequences for students with disabilities.* Retrieved February 27, 2008, from the National Center on Educational Outcomes website: http://cehd.umn.edu/nceo/OnlinePubs/Synthesis51.html.

Zabala, D., Minnichi, A, McMurrer, J, & Briggs, L. (2008, August 13). *State high school exit exams: Moving toward end-of-course exams.* Retrieved October 22, 2008, from the Center on Educational Policy website: http://www.cep-dc.org/ index.cfm?fuseaction=document_ext.showDocumentByID&nodeID=1&Docume ntID=244.

Zau, A. C., & Betts, J. R. (2008). *Predicting success, preventing failure: An investigation of the California High School Exit Exam.* Retrieved April 24, 2009, from the Public Policy Institute of California website: http://www.ppic.org/content/pubs/ report/R_608AZR.pdf.

Zenisky, A. L., Hambleton, R. K., & Robin, F. (2004). DIF detection and interpretation in large-scale science assessments: Informing item writing practices. *Educational Assessment, 9*(1 & 2), 61–78.

Zhang, Y., Dorans, N. J., and Matthews-López, J. L. (2005). *Using DIF dissection method to assess effects of item deletion.* CB Research Report No. 2005-10; Educational Testing Service RR-05-23. New York: The College Board.

Zieky, M. J. (1993). Practical questions in the use of DIF statistics. In P. W. Holland and H. Wainer (Eds.), *Differential item functioning.* Hillsdale, NJ: Lawrence Erlbaum Associates.

Zieky, M. J. (2003). *A DIF primer.* Retrieved August 10, 2008, from the Educational Testing Service website: http://www.ets.org/Media/Tests/PRAXIS/pdf/ DIF_primer.pdf.

Zieky, M. J. (2006). Fairness reviews in assessment. In S. M. Downing & T. M. Haladyna (Eds.), *Handbook of test development* (pp. 359–76). Mahwah, NJ: Lawrence Erlbaum Associates.

Zieky, M. J., Perie, M., & Livingston, S. (2004). *A primer on setting cut scores on tests of educational achievement.* Retrieved August 21, 2008, from the Educational Testing Service website: http://www.ets.org/Media/Research/pdf/Cut_Scores_ Primer.pdf.

Zwick, R. (2006). Higher education admissions testing. In R. L. Brennan (Ed.), *Educational measurement* (4th ed., pp. 647–79). Westport, CT: American Council on Education and Praeger Publishers.

Other Resources

(See also the "Selected Reading" at the end of each chapter.)

INTERNET RESOURCES

The following organizations provide information online about educational assessment, including some articles and research studies free of charge. An asterisk indicates a venue offering extensive free resources.

*Achieve, Inc. (http://www.achieve.org)
*ACT, Inc. (http://www.act.org)
*Alliance for Excellent Education (http://www.all4ed.org)
American Association of School Administrators (http://www.aasa.org)
American Educational Research Association (http://www.aera.net)
American Federation of Teachers (http://www.aft.org)
American Institutes for Research (http://www.air.org)
American Psychological Association (http://www.apa.org)
Assessment and Qualifications Alliance (http://www.aqa.org.uk/index.php)
Assessment Reform Group (http://www.assessment-reform-group.org)
Association of American Colleges and Universities (http://www.aacu.org)
Association for Supervision and Curriculum Development (http://www.ascd.org)
Berkeley Assessment and Evaluation Research Center (http://bearcenter.berkeley.edu/index.php)
Board on Testing and Assessment (http://www7.nationalacademies.org/bota)
Buros Institute of Mental Measurements (http://www.unl.edu/buros/bimm/index.html)
Cambridge Assessment (http://www.cambridgeassessment.org.uk/ca)
Center for K–12 Assessment and Performance Management (http://www.k12center.org)

Center for the Study of Testing, Evaluation, and Educational Policy (http://www
.bc.edu/research/csteep/)
*Center on Education Policy (http://www.cep-dc.org)
Classics in the History of Psychology (http://psychclassics.yorku.ca)
*College Board (http://www.collegeboard.com)
College Puzzle Blog, from Stanford University (http://collegepuzzle.stanford.edu)
Collegiate Learning Assessment (http://www.collegiatelearningassessment.org)
Council of Chief State School Officers (http://www.ccsso.org)
CTB/McGraw-Hill (http://www.ctb.com)
Departments of Education for each state: (search by individual state)
Education Next (http://www.hoover.org/publications/ednext)
*Education Resources Information Center (http://www.eric.ed.gov:80)
*Education Sector (http://www.educationsector.org)
Education Week—best single source for news on assessment issues (http://www
.edweek.org/ew/index.html)
*Educational Testing Service (http://www.ets.org)
Evaluation Center at Western Michigan University—includes the Joint Committee on
Standards for Educational Evaluation (http://www.wmich.edu/evalctr)
FairTest: National Center for Fair and Open Testing (http://www.fairtest.org)
International Association for the Evaluation of Educational Achievement (http://
www.iea.nl)
International Language Testing Association (http://www.iltaonline.com)
International Reading Association (http://www.reading.org)
International Test Commission (http://www.intestcom.org)
*National Academies Press (http://www.nap.edu) —The Education section offers all
the National Research Council reports online
*National Alternate Assessment Center (http://www.naacpartners.org)
*National Assessment Governing Board (http://www.nagb.org/flash.htm)
National Assessment of Educational Progress (http://nationsreportcard.gov) or (http://
nces.ed.gov/NATIONSREPORTCARD)
National Association for the Education of Young Children (http://www.naeyc.org)
National Association of Elementary School Principals (http://www.naesp.org)
National Association of Secondary School Principals (http://www.principals.org)
National Association of Special Education Teachers (http://www.naset.org)
National Board on Educational Testing and Public Policy (http://www.bc.edu/
research/nbetpp)
*National Center for Education Statistics (http://nces.ed.gov)
National Center for Learning Disabilities (http://www.ncld.org)
*National Center for Research on Evaluation, Standards, and Student Testing, aka
CRESST (http://www.cse.ucla.edu)
National Center on Education and the Economy (http://www.ncee.org)
National Center on Educational Outcomes (http://www.cehd.umn.edu/nceo)
National Council for Social Studies (http://www.socialstudies.org)
National Council of Teachers of English (http://www.ncte.org)
National Council of Teachers of Mathematics (http://www.nctm.org)

*National Council on Measurement in Education (http://www.ncme.org)—See the newsletters and the ITEMS instructional modules (http://www.ncme.org/pubs/items. cfm)

National Education Association (http://www.nea.org)

National Research Council, Center for Education (http://www7.nationalacademies .org/cfe); see also the National Academies Press

National Science Teachers Association (http://www.nsta.org)

New York Times: Education section (http://www.nytimes.com/pages/education)

Pearson Educational Measurement Group (http://www.pearsonedmeasurement.com)

Practical Assessment, Research, and Evaluation (http://pareonline.net)

*Reducing Stereotype Threat (http://www.reducingstereotypethreat.org)

Teachers of English to Speakers of Other Languages (http://www.tesol.org)

Teachers.tv (http://www.teachers.tv)

*Technology and Assessment Collaborative (http://www.bc.edu/research/intasc/ index.html)—inTACT publishes the *Journal of Technology, Learning, and Assessment* (http://escholarship.bc.edu/jtla)

Thomas B. Fordham Institute (http://www.edexcellence.net/template/index.cfm)

*United States Department of Education (http://www.ed.gov/index.jhtml)—EdPubs site for free documents (http://edpubs.ed.gov/Default.aspx); Individuals with Disabilities Education Act (http://idea.ed.gov)

Washington Post: Education section (also see the education-related blogs) (http:// www.washingtonpost.com/wp-dyn/content/education)

JOURNALS AND MAGAZINES FOR EDUCATORS THAT INCLUDE COVERAGE OF ASSESSMENT ISSUES

American Educator
The Chronicle of Higher Education
Education News
Education Next
Education Week
Educational Leadership
Harvard Educational Review
Inside Higher Education
The Phi Delta Kappan
The School Administrator
Teacher Magazine
Teachers' College Record

JOURNALS THAT FOCUS ON ASSESSMENT

Applied Measurement in Education
Assessment and Evaluation in Higher Education

Assessment in Education: Principles, Policy & Practice
Educational and Psychological Measurement
Educational Assessment
Educational Measurement: Issues and Practice
International Journal of Testing
Journal of Applied Technology in Testing
Journal of Educational Measurement
Journal of Writing Assessment
Language Testing
Measurement
Practical Assessment, Research, and Evaluation

A FEW REFERENCE WORKS
ON ASSESSMENT

(For complete publication information, listed by author, see "References.")
Assessment of Student Achievement (8th ed.). Gronlund (2006).
Educational Measurement. Brennan (2006). The earlier editions are also worth owning: Lindquist (1951), Thorndike (1971), and Linn (1989).
Handbook of Test Development. Downing & Haladyna (2006).
Measurement and Assessment in Education. Reynolds, Livingston, & Willson (2006).
Modern Educational Measurement: Practical Guidelines for Educational Leaders (3rd ed.), Popham (2000).
Standards for Educational and Psychological Testing. AERA et al. (1999).

Acknowledgments

Testwise owes an enormous debt to Thomas F. Koerner, the vice president and editorial director of Rowman & Littlefield, Education Division. He suggested the project, and his advice and encouragement throughout have been invaluable.

The reviewers who offered excellent guidance on improving the manuscript were Douglas G. Baldwin, George W. Elford, Samuel A. Livingston, and Michael J. Zieky. In particular, Dr. Livingston not only gave significant substantive assistance on statistical matters but also suggested a sequence for explaining aspects of classical test theory. Every writer should be fortunate enough to have perceptive feedback of the caliber that these experts so generously contributed, and any errors that remain in the text are entirely my own. Looking further back in time, I am also grateful to the mentors and colleagues at Educational Testing Service who taught me about test design and development.

Without the support of my husband, David B. Searls, this entire enterprise would not have been possible. He helped in countless ways, including his crucial work on the figures, index, and cover image.

Volume 1 of *Testwise* is dedicated to a teacher who exemplifies the ideals of her profession: my mother, Alice Wallerstein.

Index

(Boldface page numbers refer to definitions; italic numbers refer to tables and figures.)

About the Author

Nora Vivian Odendahl is a graduate of Dartmouth College magna cum laude and holds a PhD in English from Princeton University. During her sixteen years as a test developer at Educational Testing Service, she specialized in assessment of writing skills and of reading skills. Dr. Odendahl worked on international, national, and state testing programs, including the GMAT®, GRE®, LSAT®, TExES™, and Praxis Series™.

Much of Dr. Odendahl's work focused on innovations in assessment. Projects to which she contributed included noncognitive measures, computer-based systems for writing instruction, and automated essay scoring. She also created online tutorials for training GMAT and GRE essay readers. As a member of the Cognitively Based Assessments of, for, and as Learning (CBAL) initiative, she designed the prototypes for an online test of writing and critical-thinking skills.